HURLING

THE WARRIOR GAME

Diarmuid O'Flynn

ROTATION PLAN

The Collins Press

PUBLISHED IN 2011 BY
The Collins Press
West Link Park
Doughcloyne
Wilton
Cork

First published in hardback 2008

Photographs © *Irish Examiner*: pages 1, 6, 34, 42, 54 (bottom), 63, 74, 97, 106, 110, 127, 141, 146, 162–3, 193, 204 (bottom), 210–1, 216, 221, 255, 264, 268, 271, 282, 284, 292, 297, 316,
© *Evening Echo:* pages x, 60, 305.
© Sportsfile: pages 14, 29, 30, 50, 54 (top), 79, 82, 90, 114–5, 131, 169, 180 (bottom), 186, 190, 196, 204 (top), 240, 242, 275, 278, 308.
© Sportsfile Connolly Collection: pages 103, 118, 172, 237.
© Kieran Clancy: page 44.
© Pat Nolan: pages 37, 66, 250, 258.
© Pat McGuinness: page 134.
© Patjoe Whelahan: page 151.
© Paddy Shanahan: page 312.

British Library Cataloguing in Publication Data
O'Flynn, Diarmuid.
    Hurling : the warrior game.
    1. Hurling (Game) 2. Hurling players–Ireland.
    I. Title
    796.3'5-dc22

ISBN-13: 9781848891081

Design and Typesetting by designmatters
Printed in Spain by GraphyCems

Cover photographs
Front (clockwise from top): Henry Shefflin is chased by Pat Sheehan of Limerick on the evening the refurbished Gaelic Grounds opened its doors *(Irish Examiner)*; Seánie McMahon stands strong against Waterford's John Mullane on 26 March 2005 (Sportsfile); Galway's Joe Cooney is 'tackled' by Noel Hickey, Kilkenny, in the All-Ireland Senior Hurling Championship semi-final at Croke Park, Dublin, on 13 August 2000 (Sportsfile). *Back*: D.J. Carey is gang-tackled by four Clare defenders, Brian Quinn and Sean McMahon to the fore, in Ennis, County Clare, on 21 March 2004 (Sportsfile).

CONTENTS

ACKNOWLEDGEMENTS

This book results firstly from a suggestion by the publisher and secondly from the generosity, wisdom and eloquence of all those interviewed.

Define the hurling positions? It's a tough ask, but I hope we've come close. If we haven't, mea culpa. The list of interviewees was taken primarily from the top award-winners, position by position, in the all-time All-Star list (including the GPA All-Stars), with a few personal choices thrown in for good measure. Since hurling knowledge is spread across a range of counties, there was an attempt to include All-Star representatives from as many of those counties as possible. A few didn't make the list, however, and to the outstanding hurling people in Westmeath, Carlow, Kerry, etc., sincere apologies. No slight is meant, I hope none is taken.

I would like to thank Brian Lynch and Gillian Hennessy for all their hard work.

Most importantly, I would like to thank the fifty-seven interviewees, all of whom gave freely of their time and their knowledge. Without them, these pages would have been blank.

A BRIEF INTRODUCTION TO HURLING

Hurling is a game similar to hockey, in that it is played with a small ball and a curved wooden stick. It is Europe's oldest field game. When the Celts came to Ireland as the last ice age was receding, they brought with them a unique culture, their own language, music, script and pastimes. One of these pastimes was a game now called hurling. It features in Irish folklore to illustrate the deeds of heroic mystical figures and it is chronicled as a distinct Irish pastime for at least 2,000 years.

The stick or 'hurley' (called *camán* in Irish) is curved outwards at the end, to provide the striking surface. The ball or *sliothar* is similar in size to a hockey ball but has raised ridges.

Hurling is played on a pitch approximately 137 m (150 yards) long and 82 m (90 yards) wide. The goalposts are the same shape as on a rugby pitch, with the crossbar lower and wider than in rugby, slightly higher and narrower than in soccer.

You may strike the ball on the ground or in the air. Unlike hockey, you may pick up the ball with your hurley and carry it an unlimited distance on the hurley, one of the many skills of hurling – this is called the 'solo run'. You may then catch the ball and carry it in the hand for not more than four steps. After those steps you may bounce the ball on the hurley and back to the hand, but you are not allowed to catch the ball more than twice. To get around this, one of the skills of hurling is running with the ball balanced on the hurley – this is called the 'solo run'. To score, you put the ball over the crossbar for a point or under the crossbar and into the net for a goal, the latter being the equivalent of three points – striking must be done with the hurley, handpassed scores are not allowed.

Goalkeeper

Right-corner-back

Full-back

Left-corner-back

Right-half-back

Centre-back

Left-half-back

Midfielder

Midfielder

Right-wing-forward

Centre-forward

Left-wing-forward

Right-corner-forward

Full-forward

Left-corner-forward

Each team consists of fifteen players, lining out as in the diagram on the page opposite.

A game is played over two halves of 30 minutes (at club level) or 35 minutes (at inter-county level).

Players wear a jersey of their team colours with their number on the back. The two competing teams must have different colour jerseys on the day, which means a change of jersey where a clash occurs. The goalkeeper's jersey must be different to the jersey of any other players. Referees normally tog out in black jerseys, socks and togs but there are official alternatives where there is a clash with either of the competing teams.

Goalkeepers may not be physically challenged whilst in possession of the ball inside their own small parallelogram, but players may challenge for possession when the ball is 'close' or harass them into playing a bad pass, or block an attempted pass.

Teams are allowed a maximum of five substitutes in a game, not including blood subs. Players may switch positions on the field of play as much as they wish but this is usually on the instructions of team officials.

Officials for a game comprise of a referee, two linesmen (in inter-county games, these are also qualified referees; they indicate when the ball leaves the field of play at the side and to mark 65-m free shots when a defender puts a ball wide on his own end) and four umpires (to signal scores, assist the referee in controlling the games, and to assist linesmen in positioning 65-m frees).

A goal is signalled by raising a green flag, placed to the left of the goal. A point is signalled by raising a white flag, placed to the right of goal. A '65' is signalled by the umpire raising his/her outside arm in line with where the ball crossed the endline. A 'square ball', when a player scores having arrived in the 'square' prior to receiving the ball, is signalled by pointing at the small parallelogram. That score is then disallowed.

Donal Óg Cusack in typical pose.

Goalkeeper
The Gamekeeper

Noel Skehan (Kilkenny)
Seamus Durack (Clare)
Donal Óg Cusack (Cork)
Christy O'Connor (Clare)

According to those who chose the GAA hurling Team of the Century (1984) and the Team of the Millennium (2000), the best goalkeeper of all time was Tony Reddin of Tipperary, or Martin Charles Reddington from Mullagh in Galway, to give him his original name and parish. Universal agreement on these matters is always impossible, so that down Kilkenny way you would get serious argument for one of their own. But, which one? Ollie or Skehan?

So famed are both that single-name identification is enough, but, even in that, there is a clue as to which was more popular; there's first-name familiarity and there's surname respect. Ollie Walsh was probably the most flamboyant hurling goalkeeper of all time; dash and panache, cavalier blond hair flying as he plucked the high dropping ball from a forest of flailing ash, then danced and dodged his way to open prairie before launching a 100-yard clearance. That was Ollie. During his fifteen-year inter-county playing career (1956–71), and at a time when the goalkeeper was still fair game for inside forwards who were chosen as much for their strength and ferocity as for their hurling ability, Ollie won four All-Ireland senior medals with Kilkenny in the number one position. He was named hurler of the year in 1967 and left an indelible impression on all who witnessed his derring-do.

For nine of Ollie's fifteen years, Noel Skehan warmed the bench for Kilkenny, watched in admiration and in frustration as his cousin (Noel's mother, May, was a first cousin of Ollie) won plaudit after plaudit, his own true worth unknown, never getting a chance of expression. During that period, Noel collected six Leinster medals, three All-Irelands, and they are appreciated to this day. What he most wanted, however, was a chance. Finally it came, 1972, and when it did, never was a man more ready!

NOEL SKEHAN
(b. 1944, Bennetsbridge and Kilkenny, 1963–85)

AWARDS & MEDALS WON
1 Hurler of the year (1982)
9 All-Ireland senior (a GAA record; 1 as captain)
7 All-Star awards
4 National Hurling League
4 Railway Cup
3 Oireachtas
6 Kilkenny county senior

First position
As a young fella I always preferred playing out the field. I played there for the vocational schools and for the 'Bridge minors. I was even called for a minor trial for Kilkenny, but I missed out when my lift never called. The next year, they came around again, but I was now a goalkeeper.

The transition
When I was a young lad, Bennetsbridge had a very good senior team. They'd be training, backs and forwards. I'd be in the middle of the field pucking the ball into them. More and more lads would come, I'd be going further and further back the field. Next thing, someone would tell me, 'Go into the goals there, we'll have a full practice match.' I didn't want to, but I would be told, 'Get in there or feck off home!' Of course I wanted the few pucks, so in I'd go, but I wasn't too happy about it! That's how it started.

Bennetsbridge had a junior team as well as a senior team. I played in goal for them, then in goal for Kilkenny minors. Actually, I was still only playing in goal for the Bennetsbridge junior team when I was a sub on the Kilkenny senior team. When I made the club senior team, I was playing outfield and I won two counties playing there. I played outfield a few times for Kilkenny as well. When I was the sub-keeper, I played [outfield] in New York one time when we were short. [On another occasion] I was sub-keeper for a Rest of Leinster team against Wexford. They were short players though and I was put in at half-forward and scored the winning goal. Pat Nolan [Wexford keeper] stopped a high ball coming in and I just knew it was going to drop, and where it was going to come. Come it did and I was ready.

Making the breakthrough with Kilkenny

The thing that kept me going was that I felt I was sub to the best goal-keeper in Ireland. When I went training I never went with the idea that it was a waste of time: 'What am I doing here? Leinster championship starting again, but I'm only going to be on the bench again. No chance of a game.' I didn't think like that, I went in and trained like a demon. I'd be in the opposite goal to Ollie and I'd train at least as hard as he trained, if not harder. You never knew the day you'd get in. You never knew what could happen and you had to be ready to take your chance.

I never felt that I was going to push him off the team, not that I can remember anyway. I played a few matches in 1971, maybe even in the All-Ireland semi-final – Ollie had gone into hospital for an operation. But when Ollie was there, I was number two. He was probably starting to lose a bit of sharpness in '71 and the operation wouldn't have helped, but as far as ousting him – no, never.

1972, you finally got your chance. Did you feel pressure?
Oh it was enormous. Not alone were you trying to prove a point to your-self, that you could in fact do this job, you were also trying to prove a point to the supporters, both inside and outside the county. Bad enough if you were just replacing the best goalkeeper in Kilkenny, but you were replacing the best goalkeeper in Ireland, and the most popular. It wasn't easy, I'll say that, it was hard going, and I'd like to pay tribute to Fr Maher [former Kilkenny coach] – Monsignor Maher as he is now – for the help and encouragement he gave me.

The biggest thing was concentration. He always said to me, 'Don't ever let your concentration drop. If a ball comes in in the first minute and ends up in the back of the net – forget about it, don't let it affect you. Concentrate, stay concentrated, all the time.'

Another thing he said, 'Don't be trying to make saves look spectacu-lar. Don't be waiting until a shot is taken then dive to make the save. Position yourself early, get your body behind the shot. There are times when you have to dive, when you're beaten all ends up and you have to dive to get it. But more often than not, when a shot is taken, especially from outside the 21, you should be able to get your body in the right position to make the save without doing anything spectacular.'

Good advice, advice I'd pass on to any young goalkeeper. One thing I would like to note is that I was coming onto a good team. Some great backs, the likes of Jim Treacy, Fan Larkin, the Hendersons, Pa Dillon. Great names, all legends of the game, still familiar today. That was a great help to me. There's something else as well, and a lot of people don't know this; Ollie stayed on in 1972. He was the sub-keeper that year and he was a great help to me, very encouraging [Ollie won his fifth All-Ireland medal that year].

So, having waited since 1963, you win your first All-Ireland on the field of play in your first year as a starter, and you're team captain to boot, Bennetsbridge having won the Kilkenny senior county in 1971 – ten years to become an overnight success. What about the following year, 1973, Limerick's last All-Ireland win, and that controversial goal?

Yes, the first pushover try in Croke Park. I will always feel aggrieved about that goal. The ball broke in front of me, I went down, a number of players came in and someone picked up the ball, carried it over the line and dropped it there – I haven't a clue who did it. And definitely, it was picked up. I know, because the ball was right in front of me and I was trying to pick it up myself! I ended up in the back of the net when the push came. It should never have been allowed, certainly wouldn't be allowed today.

I don't begrudge Limerick that win though, they were due a title. They had a very good team with the likes of Grimes, Hartigan, Cregan – great hurlers.

Towards the end of that game – Limerick had it won – Joe McKenna [young Limerick forward] says to Larkin [experienced Kilkenny defender who loved the banter]: 'Fan, I think they're looking for you on the sideline!' He was going to be taken off, like. A year later in 1974, the final again, two minutes to go, Kilkenny well in control, Fan turned to McKenna: 'Joe, I think they're looking for you on the sideline.' And they were too!

The qualities needed to be a top goalkeeper

Number one, you have to be brave and you have to be confident about what you're at. You wouldn't want to be a worrier. If you're goalkeeper

'It's behind you, Kevin!' *Noel Skehan knocks the ball away from Cork centre-forward Kevin Hennessey, watched by Brian Cody (Kilkenny) on his left and Seánie O'Leary on the far right.*

and a worrier, every little mistake you make – and you will make them – is magnified and will become worse and worse in your head. Learn from it and forget it. Don't make that mistake again, and definitely not in the same match!

Concentration is a big one. Talking to umpires, anyone like that, is totally out of the question. I remember when I was a young fella, Seán Ó Ceallacháin interviewing Christy Ring. There was something Ring said I never forgot: 'Keep your concentration. If the ball goes up into the Hogan Stand, I'll follow it [with my eyes] up into the Hogan Stand'. I never forgot that and when I was playing, I would do the same. If there was a penalty being taken for us at the other end of the field, I would watch that ball the same as if it was a penalty being taken against us. I hate to see lads turning their backs to the ball, in any situation, but it happens all the time, even at inter-county level.

Control is critical, I worked very hard at that. Fr Maher was a stickler for it – batting balls out, dropping them off your chest or letting balls off your hurl – losing control. Eventually I became pretty useful at bringing down the high ball into the hand. That was done by killing the ball in the air, using the wrists, angling the hurl backwards slightly and deadening the ball, down into the hands. It's in the wrists really. The squash was a great help to me in that. I was playing a bit at the time, but as the 1970s went on, I got more and more into it, played a lot. There is a lot of wristwork in squash, a lot of reaction, short little sprints.

In general, I'd say the control of the ball afterwards is as important as the save. You could stop a bullet, but if you don't control the rebound, it's straight back out again, and that's where any forward worth his salt is waiting. Stop it and control it, it's a different story.

Reflexes and sharpness are very important. Hard bloody work, that's how you improve those. I never took anything for granted, I didn't rely on experience or skill. I trained, and the older I got the harder I trained, harder and harder as the years went by. For the reflexes, squash, I continued to play squash. A hard game, but a great one. Great for the eye, great for the reflexes, great for being quick off the mark, always on your toes – ideal training for a keeper. I did that all through the winter. Even on the day before an All-Ireland final, the Saturday, I'd play for half an hour with a friend of mine.

Hurley size, there are those who say you played with a half-door…

Five-and-a-half inches was the width of my hurl all the time and that's the truth. I wouldn't have been able to control anything bigger, to be honest. It was an inch shorter than the normal, about 35 inches, which probably made it look wider. The important thing to me was balance. If it was too heavy on the heel, I wouldn't be able to bring it back up as fast as I'd like, I wouldn't be able to use it.

I think Ollie's hurl was a little smaller than mine, though it looked bigger in comparison to the normal hurl. That might have been because the normal hurl didn't have as big a bas then as now. Look at the Cork outfield hurls now, big bas, curved at the bottom as well. That's for balance and that's a nice hurl.

The kind of ball most hated

The ball coming high across the face of the goal, right to left or left to right. It's a ball you should control and the place to take it is at the near post. Don't let it cross the face of the goal, but doing that is taking a big risk. There are players coming in, others coming across you. All it takes is a little nudge to put you off, or a little touch on the ball, a deflection – gone. I hated it, really hated it.

The kind of forward I hated was the guy who could take half a chance. He was a worry the whole time, you could never leave him out of your mind. The Cork lads – Jimmy Barry Murphy, Charlie McCarthy, Seánie O'Leary – were like that: flick it, touch it. You had other forwards – good forwards – who needed the complete chance.

The ball least feared

I loved the ground shot. I was really strong on the ground. Ollie hated those!

The forward I least feared was the guy who would never give a pass, was always anxious to take his own shot, go for his own glory.

Tricks

I hadn't a whole lot really. The dummy handpass was one, sell the dummy. Another one was to dummy to hit on the weak side, then swing around and clear with the strong side.

Most people still don't know this, but my left side was my stronger side. When I started off with the Kilkenny minors, I was pucking the ball out left-handed, I wasn't able to hit it right-handed. My uncle, Dan Kennedy, who captained Kilkenny in 1947, came along to me – 'You've got to be able to hit the ball with your right hand.' I worked, worked, worked, and when I came onto the Kilkenny team in the middle of 1963 as a sub, I was equally good on both sides.

Another trick I had; if a lad was going to handpass a goal, just as he glanced up, I'd let on I was going to charge out to meet him. I wouldn't though, I'd stay back and that gave me a better chance. It didn't work all the time, but it worked enough.

Tricks seen

I saw so many tricks outside me, over the years. The flick on the hurl was a great one, used by backs and forwards. Fan [Larkin, Kilkenny back] was a great one. Before we'd play Cork, he'd say to me, '[Ray] Cummins is playing full-forward today. Everything is coming into you. I'll make sure he doesn't get hand or hurl to the ball, but you make sure you're coming out to take it!'

And that was the way it happened. The high ball would be coming in, Ray would be way up there, Fan would be down there, waiting [Cummins was nearly a foot taller]. I'd be saying to myself, 'Is he going to go at all? I'm going to be caught in no-man's land here!' But every single time he did what he said he'd do: a little touch on Ray's shoulder, on the catching hand, and the ball came in to me.

Primary advice to a promising youngster, above all else, to master the goalkeeping position

Number one, ask yourself: 'Do I want to play here? Am I here of my own free will?' If not, if you're half-hearted, that's a bad start. You have to want to be there, you have to want to master the position. Do everything you can. You have to train hard, train as hard as anyone out the field. You do the same running, the same physical training. Everything they do, you do. And then you do more. You arrive at training before anyone else, half an hour before, and you have someone with you. Then you practise your shot-stopping, you practise your control.

What are you doing between official training sessions? That's an important question for every player, but it's especially important for the goalkeeper. It's the half-hour they do on their own on the nights when there is no official training, that's what's important. I'd recommend something like squash or racquetball, very beneficial. It has to improve you as a goalkeeper. But you must do something, you must do some other activity to keep your eye in. If you're going to represent your county, no matter what position, you want to give your best all the time. You want to put yourself in the situation where you can give your best. Give yourself the chance, that's what I always felt, give yourself the best chance. Don't be lazy about it; put in the effort, do the training, reach the best possible standard you can reach. Be happy with yourself. If I wasn't happy with myself, I'd know there was something I wasn't doing: I wasn't training hard enough, I was missing out somewhere. And I'd work harder again until I was comfortable going into the next match; then I'd have no worries. If I had, I was letting myself down and I was letting down my fourteen teammates. I'd never play injured, never, no matter how bad I was. You'd think you could do it, but you couldn't. Someone in full health is surely better.

Through all the years when Noel Skehan was winning All-Ireland titles and All-Star awards, the man closest to him in goalkeeping recognition was Seamus Durack of Clare. Seamus won three All-Star awards during this period, a remarkable achievement given that Clare didn't even get out of Munster in the championship through his whole career. Would he have earned greater recognition had his county been more successful? Without question, yes.

SEAMUS DURACK
(b. 1951, Feakle and Clare, 1969–83)

AWARDS & MEDALS WON
3 All-Star awards
2 National Hurling League
2 Railway Cup
3 Clare county senior
1 Clare county intermediate
2 Clare county junior

First position
I started at midfield/wing-forward. I always wanted to be a forward and it was only by accident that I wound up in goal. I was on the Clare minor panel as a wing-forward. I played all of my under-age hurling at midfield/centre-forward/wing-forward, including U-21.

The transition
We played a league game in Newmarket-on-Fergus, against Westmeath or Kildare or someone like that. I was wing-forward. We won that game and our next game was against Antrim, which I'll never forget.

The game was in Loughiel, in north Antrim. I travelled on the basis that I was a sub for the forwards. We arrived at the hotel in Dundalk, checked in, came down to the dining room for a bite to eat. I was sitting at a table with the chairman of the county board. 'I hope you brought your goalkeeper's hurley,' he said to me.

I had played a few games in goal for my club Feakle at this stage, but thought nothing of it. I had been in the forwards, but no matter how fast we were scoring at one end of the field, the goals were going in faster at the other end so I would be put into goals.

'I didn't,' I said, and I hadn't. It was never my intention to play in goals for Clare. 'Sure, isn't Paschal O'Brien in goals?' Paschal had played for Munster a few months earlier, so he was an automatic choice.

'We're just after hearing that Paschal wouldn't travel, the distance was too far for him. We have no other goalie, you're going to be playing in goals.'

I was about nineteen or twenty, and I was lucky, Antrim weren't very good at that time, though you still had to pay them respect. They were an inter-county team playing on their own patch. A lot of the lads went to the disco in the hotel that night, but I went to bed early. This was a new development, I wanted to make sure I was right. You can make your mistakes out the field but not in there.

We won, but only by a couple of points. A tough game, a wet and windy day, and I think I played well enough. We went out the next day and because I had played well the last time, they couldn't very well drop me. I played better again that time seemingly, so I was in goals for the next day again.

In the meantime, Paschal still hadn't turned up, the league continued, and we got to the quarter-final, against Wexford. I happened to play very well in that game.

At the time, one thing you could expect as the Clare goalkeeper was plenty of action. A lot of ball coming in; there was never a situation when you had nothing to do and I was getting plenty of opportunity to show my wares. At that stage people were beginning to say, 'Well, here we have a new goalkeeper,' even though a lot of people would have expected – as I did – that Paschal would be an automatic choice again for the championship.

It then came around to the championship and we came into Flannan's for training. John Hanley, who was principal of the school in Clarecastle and chairman of the county board, was training us. He called everyone together in the middle of the field and picked two teams. Whether by accident or design I don't know, but I was picked on the A team, the best team. The best forwards were playing in against me, on the best backs, and it happened that nearly all the play was up at my end of the field for the first twenty minutes, nothing happening at the other end.

Paschal O'Brien had turned up for that training, but what was going through his mind at this stage, I have no idea. I remember halfway through the practice looking down at the other goals, pucking out the ball, and there was no goalkeeper. I looked around.

'What's happening?' The dressing rooms were about 200 yards away from the goals and then I saw him, going around the corner. He went in, togged out, went home, and that was the last we saw of him. From then on, I was the Clare goalkeeper. I think that was 1971 and typical GAA, no one ever went back to Paschal. He had decided to walk and he was left alone.

Like Noel Skehan, you were another frustrated forward?

I suppose, yes. At that time I was playing inter-firm with a chipboard company in Scarriff. Séamus Shinners, the Tipperary goalie, was also with us. We had a good team, won Munster and All-Ireland inter-firm titles, but neither Séamus nor myself ever played in goal, we were more valuable out the field. He was centre-field, I was wing-forward or centre-forward. We had a few very good club goalkeepers who played in goals for us, but we always played out the field. Wing-forward was my favourite position but I never got the chance there, apart from the U-21 championship against Tipp in 1971.

The qualities needed to be a top goalkeeper

There's a half dozen and without them you're nothing. First of all, you need to be brave. You can't be windy, you can't be yellow, you never show the white feather. Number two: you've got to have two sides of equal ability. Three: you've got to have good feet. You've got to be able to go left or right with the same ease. Four: you've got to have great hands. In particular, you need to have an excellent catching hand. Five: above all, you've got to have nerves of steel, which basically means you've got to be able to control the pressure that is bound to be there. Six: and a lot of people would overlook this – your fitness levels have to be good. You've got to be fast coming off your line and to a certain degree that depends on your fitness level.

I always competed with [Colm] Honan and [Johnny] Callinan in our sprints in training. There was a battle between us as to who would be first, hence if I had to come off my line for a ball, even against the likes of Jimmy Barry Murphy, they'd never gain an inch on me. Those are the six.

*Seamus Durack in classic puck-out pose, big wind-up,
everything going into this ball on 25 May 1983.*

You've got to talk – and I talked. You controlled your area, from midfield back. I used to slag the half-backs in training: 'Lads, can ye hear me at all?'

'Of course we can hear you. We'd hear you down at corner-forward!' But you had to take charge; you're the leader. You'd be eating them to get into position, but you'd be wicked, you'd be high inside there, in a zone of your own. And you're not doing it for yourself, you're doing it for the team. You had to be looking at their forwards and you had to be thinking a move ahead, anticipating what they were doing. You're not just making the saves, you're preventing the shot, if you can.

Hurley size

My hurley was slightly bigger than the normal. It wasn't any longer than normal, about 36 inches, but the bas would be slightly bigger. I used different hurleys on different days, depending on the weather. On wet days I used a stronger hurley with a slightly heavier bas, more rigid than usual; in dry weather I used a lighter hurley with much lighter timber in it, but with three times more spring.

You need a bit of spring to be able to kill the ball on the hurley. No matter how good your hands were, if you didn't have a bit of spring on the hurley it made it much harder to kill the ball stone dead, it would rebound out those two yards for the forward coming in. You've got to kill it dead, down into your hand.

The favourite ball that time was a Cummins ball, almost like a base-ball. It was better to play with, more consistent, very sure, but it was also very lively, travelling faster than the normal. To control that speed you needed a hurley with real flexibility in it and I had a hurley that time, you could nearly bend it back on itself, touch the handle to the bas! During the fine weather, on the hot days in Thurles, I used that hurley, but I used it sparingly. It was so difficult to get that kind of ash, you had to mind it.

I had loads of hurleys, for goals and for outfield. I never used a big hurley out the field. For puck-outs I had one special hurley, a normal one, but I could really hit that ball with it. In an All-Star game against Kilkenny in San Francisco, a short pitch – about 114 yards – I scored a point from a puck-out. I think I also scored a goal. All the players from both teams turned around and gave me a clap, but it was one of those days when everything felt right. My timing was perfect, I felt strong, I had a beautiful hurley.

The kind of ball most hated

The ball just under or over the crossbar. It was always tempting to bring it down, but you always wondered if you should leave it off, if it was going over. Jump up to catch it and you could hit your fingers off the crossbar or they could be bent back. Mick Malone [Cork forward] used to say, points keep you in matches, goals win them. You didn't want to give away goals.

The ball least feared

The ground ball never bothered me, even though a lot of goalkeepers hated it. You counteract the bouncing ball with speed of foot. You got across in front of it, covered it with your body, so that even if you missed the catch or the touch, it hit your legs. If you're diving, your hurley is your last chance saloon – miss and it's a goal. Get across.

Tricks

I'd always try to get the centre-back out of position for the puck-out. One of the things I'd try to do was to shape my body as if I was going to hit it one way and then, when you saw him moving in that direction, hit it the other way, with the wing-forward on that side already moving. I'd sometimes put my hand down by my side before I pucked out the ball, which meant I was going that side. I'd then pretend to go the other way.

We never really got into signals and plans though, it was just a co-ordination that developed. I had Jim Power at full-back, we had our own understanding. Jim wouldn't stop the ball coming through, he'd let it off to me, give me the couple of seconds to control. The backs had to trust you implicitly and you had to trust them. That was critical.

Primary advice to a promising youngster, above all else, to master the goalkeeping position

A guy won't be worth the proverbial damn to you unless he wants to be a winner. You can be a great competitor, you can be a great sportsman, but you must be a winner, nothing else matters. Other players, other supporters, recognise that quality. Fanaticism is a different thing again, I don't think that's healthy.

What was the best advice you ever got?

Be fair, be balanced in your approach to things, don't hit anyone unfairly and walk off the pitch with the respect of your opponents. I got that advice from many different people over the years. You've got to listen, especially to the older generations; pick up a bit here, a bit there. I learned from Gareth Howard, from Donie Nealon, from Mick Mackey, from Con Murphy, a whole learning process. To me, the complete player always is a gentleman. The man that's a thug on the field is a thug off it, you can never trust him. Character stands out a mile, on and off the field, quality stands out like a beacon.

Over the last decade or more there have been several standout keepers – Davy Fitzgerald from Clare, Brendan Cummins from Tipperary, Damien Fitzhenry of Wexford. There is one, however, who has attracted more attention than any. Since his first full senior season with Cork in 1999, Donal Óg Cusack has never been far from the public eye.

An intelligent and articulate individual, passionate about his sport, about his club, about his county, but passionate also about fair play for inter-county players, Donal Óg has been to the forefront on and off the field. Off the field, he was one of those most vocal during the Cork hurlers' strike of 2002, at the end of which the Cork county board were forced into making a number of changes to the manner in which players had been treated. He was there at the end of the 2007 season when the players again took on the Cork county board, this time after they had attempted to revert to the pre-2002 system of appointing senior hurling and football selectors. Again, the players got their way.

In the meantime, and still off the field, he is one of the leading lights of the Gaelic Players Association, the GPA, an organisation formed several years ago primarily to look after the interests of inter-county hurling and football players. To many of the more traditional members of the GAA, the GPA is anathema. It is seen as greedy and destructive, full-blown professionalism its ultimate goal (despite several definitive statements to the contrary), with Donal Óg as its most public face. To those more rational, however, the GPA is simply a long overdue body, ready and willing to work with the GAA for the common good of all in the association, though – obviously – with the players as its priority.

On the field, Donal Óg has been almost as controversial. Since 2003, with a very obvious Newtownshandrum influence (three Cork senior titles won in the 2000s), but with the full embrace of the whole panel, Cork have adopted a style which is very much the opposite of all that was held dear by generations of hurling supporters both inside and outside the county. Where once Cork were direct, first-time, no-nonsense, now they were playing a running, carrying, passing, possession-type game.

Even when it worked (and it did, two All-Ireland titles won in 2004 and 2005) it drove the purists to distraction. When it broke down, however – and given the nature of hurling, that was bound to happen at least as often as not – it drew condemnation by the truckload. As goalkeeper, as the man who started so many of those short-passing moves, Donal Óg has drawn down no shortage of opprobrium on his head. Despite this, he perseveres.

DONAL ÓG CUSACK
(b. 1977, Cloyne and Cork, 1996–present)

AWARDS & MEDALS WON
3 All-Ireland senior
3 All-Star awards (2 Vodafone, 1 GPA)
1 All-Ireland intermediate
2 All-Ireland U-21
1 All-Ireland minor
1 National Hurling League
2 Railway Cup
1 Oireachtas
1 Cork county senior (with Imokilly)
1 Cork county intermediate

First position and transition
I played out the field with Cloyne at underage. I was in the forward line up to minor and U-21, but I played in goal for the school, Midleton CBS, all the way up to Harty Cup [captained them to win that title]. I played there [in goal] for Cork minors and for Imokilly seniors [won Cork senior championship].

The qualities needed to be a top goalkeeper
Obviously you need a bit of aggression, but you also want calm. You must be calm to keep things settled. Courage is fierce important also, but I think it's critical to have the mental side right in goals. If you're not right there, if you're not happy there, then it's an awful place to be. You must be totally happy there, you must be mentally very strong, able to overcome the setbacks and get back up on the horse immediately.

Is size important?

I don't think so, and I think David Fitzgerald [Clare] has proved that. I stood behind him in 1999 when Clare played Tipperary and he caught several balls under the crossbar, with forwards coming in around him. It looks easy but it's a fundamental part of goalkeeping. That was a high-intensity game, but all the basics were there with him. Everything he did that day was positive: he made that save from Shelley, he scored the penalty; but for me, it was those catches under the crossbar – that was the complete display.

Hurley

Important for a goalkeeper. And mine are all the same size, I don't have a special hurley for puck-outs. I used to have when I was younger, but not anymore. I don't want to change the feel of the hurley in my hand at any stage during the game. You're making saves, making clearances, but if you then have to change the weight and balance of the hurley in your hand for the puck-out, that's throwing things off. You're playing with a light hurley one second, then using a heavier hurley, then back to a light hurley. I'm looking for consistency as much as possible. My hurleys are light, but the balance is the most important thing.

Tricks

Changing the ball. Jimmy McEvoy [kit-man] used to always stand beside the Cork goals and when we wanted to change a ball, Jimmy would roll in an All-Star ball – the one we preferred. I'd get rid of the other one, the O'Neill's ball, the one sanctioned by the GAA. There was one problem though – what if there was a penalty against us?

The Cummins ball travelled much faster than the O'Neill's ball and we'd look right stupid if we were beaten by our own stunt! In that situation we'd try to swap them back again. In the 2005 Munster final Tipp got a penalty. Jimmy rolled in an O'Neill's ball ['Not necessarily a new top quality one either!' Diarmuid O'Sullivan interjects] and I hit it out to Eoin Kelly [Tipp free-taker]. I'd say he knew what was going on, but he was such a powerful striker of the ball he didn't care. He must have felt confident he'd score anyway. He didn't, and we went straight up the field and scored a point at the other end.

There was a follow-up to that story though. I was flying out to London next morning, then on to Germany. I was sitting beside these two fellas on the plane: Tipp men, one of them a priest, and they were playing tough.

'Cork won yesterday,' one of them said.

'They did,' I said, but didn't say anymore.

'Were you there?'

'I was there alright,' but I knew that they knew well who I was.

They talked away anyway, and they were obviously trying to get me to give in, to say who I was, so they could get stuck into me, but I said nothing. As we were coming in to land, however, they couldn't stand it anymore.

'Did you change the ball?' They told me that one of them was Eoin Kelly's uncle and that they had been talking to Eoin the previous night and he was adamant that the ball had been changed.

'Not a hope!' I said. We shook hands, parted, and they were probably thinking to themselves, 'That cute Cork hoor!' They knew well, but why should I tell them? Has Babs ever admitted that Tipp changed the ball in Killarney against Limerick in 1971?

I checked that out with Eoin, he had this to say:

In 2004, in Killarney, Cork tried the same trick. We got a penalty, next thing a commotion starts, but while it was going on, Cusack went to his bag of balls and threw one out, but I had copped him. I picked it up. It looked like someone was after sewing an extra rim on it, an extra strip of leather, the rim was that big on it! I hit it straight out over the stand and got another ball. They still saved it anyway. In 2005 though I think he really codded me. The guy he met on the plane was Johnny White who played minor football with Tipp in the 1950s, and when he said it to Cusack, Donal just started laughing. My uncle was probably with him alright, yes.

Donal Óg continues

There was a huge difference between the two balls. A few nights before the game we were practising and Ger Cunningham [goalkeeping coach] made me stand for a penalty from Sully [Diarmuid O'Sullivan], with the All-Star ball. I had a bit of an argument with him, said it was too close to the match, I could get injured. But he was the boss. I went

Left: The pic that tells a litany of tales: *the changing of the ball during the Cork/Tipperary Munster final in 2005; the two number 12s side by side (Timmy McCarthy, Cork, and Tommy Dunne, Tipperary; the three in the Cork goals (Ronan Curran and Diarmuid O'Sullivan flanking Cusack) with similar 'goalie' hurleys; the save being made by Cusack after Eoin Kelly (13) has let fly.*

Above: *Note the bruise on the inside of Cusack's right thigh. It was sustained during practice before the match.*

in, Sully hit the penalty, a rocket, straight at me, hit me in the inside of the thigh and laid me out. Sully was roaring laughing, I was mad and went away home.

There's a picture from that game of three of us lining up in goal and it tells a number of stories. There's a black and blue mark on my leg, that you can see plainly. That was the belt from Sully's penalty. You can also see the two number 12s, Timmy McCarthy and the Tipp man, standing shoulder to shoulder, which – for a hurling man – doesn't make a lot of sense. But that was part of a tactic we had developed. After the goal Paul Flynn got in the 2004 Munster final [35-yard free, caught everyone unawares] we developed a tactic where we brought everyone back for those frees. We worked on the premise that if the penalty was stopped and we got possession, we'd use the call 'Forrest'. That was the signal to keep your composure and run with the ball like Forrest Gump! Work the ball up the field, into a scoring position; and it worked.

We made the save, worked the ball up the field and scored. That was a double psychological blow for Tipp – deny the goal and score at the other end. Every player who was involved got a great kick out of that. [You can also see in the photo that] the three of us in the goals had the same hurleys, goalie hurleys with the same colour grip that the boys were to use for penalties.

A fella gave me a gift of that photo and also gave one to Sully. Just before Christmas, Sully came to me with a present, all wrapped, and I was a bit embarrassed. I mean we're good friends, but we wouldn't normally be giving each other Christmas presents! It turned out to be the same picture!

Last Man Standing isn't just a brilliant book on hurling goalkeepers, it is as good a sports book as you'll ever pick up. Insightful, revealing, brutally honest, it is built around interviews with several of the top goalkeepers of the last fifteen years, from those with the best counties to those with the weakest, but all with the same drive.

It was penned by Christy O'Connor, himself a top-class keeper, number two in Clare behind Davy Fitzgerald for a number of years, winner of an All-Ireland club title with St Joseph's Doora-Barefield in 1999. Christy's expertise and knowledge goes beyond that again, however; a keen student of the position, he is now – along with being a top GAA journalist with the Sunday Times *– a goalkeeping coach, working with several top goalkeepers. Here are his thoughts on the position.*

CHRISTY O'CONNOR
(1973, St Joseph's Doora-Barefield and Clare, 1999–2002)

AWARDS & MEDALS WON
1 All-Ireland senior club
2 Munster senior club
3 Clare county senior
1 Clare county intermediate
1 All-Ireland colleges

The qualities needed to be a top goalkeeper
The first thing you have to be is a good hurler, you have to be skilful. It's a seriously demanding position – you won't get away with being a mechanical hurler inside in goals. So much of what happens is off the cuff, you're reacting to situations all the time. You need all the skills of any outfield player, all the ball control. You need huge mental strength.

We played Athenry in the All-Ireland club semi-final in 1999 and were playing with a near hurricane in the first half. Only a minute gone, Eugene Cloonan [Athenry and Galway forward] went for a point but the ball held up in the wind and dipped at the very last second. I thought it was going over the bar, but I couldn't take a chance so I tried to control it on the stick. The ball went away from me and I shoved it out; an Athenry forward picked it up and buried it.

My dream was to play in Croke Park, now I was afraid my mistake was going to cost me that dream, and cost my own club and my best friends the potential opportunity of a lifetime. I'm telling you, the mental torture I went through in that game, I wouldn't wish it on anyone. I know some people endure horrendous tragedy and this is only sport but that moment was absolute nightmare. I was trying to keep my focus and concentration, but the demons kept coming back into my head. 'Jeez man, if we lose this, how am I going to live with myself?' And I kept banishing them.

Half-time was really tough, but I kept thinking of Davy Fitzgerald and how he recovered after making a bad mistake in the first half of the 1995 All-Ireland final. I had to stay positive. We were six points ahead at the break, but we were facing a hurricane in the second half and I remember thinking, 'No matter what happens, I have to mentally stand up to this test, whatever the cost.'

The second half was a total nightmare, especially when they levelled it with fifteen minutes remaining. The good thing was that before the end I made possibly the best save of my career, which I felt made up for the mistake at the start, but it was still hard going. We led by a point at the very end when Brendan Keogh [Athenry forward] latched onto a mis-hit shot. He was less than ten yards out and with only me to beat he went for glory. I just charged off my line and tried to cut down the angle. I remember just focusing on the ball and thinking, 'If this is going to hit you in the eye, you're taking it.' I actually stopped it with my hurley, but the ball was still alive and I still felt sheer terror that it would end up a goal because Athenry forwards had converged and were trying to smuggle it into the net. When the whistle blew seconds later, I got down in my knees and screamed at the top of my voice, 'Thank you Jesus!'

You need to be brave, that's hugely important. You need a good eye, you need agility. Different keepers have different ranges. Fitzy – Davy Fitzgerald – made a save in a league game in 2005 from Jerry O'Connor [Cork], he was diving one way to make the save but the ball took a deflection and somehow he got the hurley back to it. That was agility and reflex in one – very few players would have that kind of instant hand-eye coordination, in any sport.

Look at how goalkeeping has gone in recent years. It's a case now of playing further off your line than ever before, and I've studied this fairly extensively. Most goals now are scored from one-on-one situations. It's very seldom shots are taken from the 21 now or outside that. That means a lot of the saves are made with the body. It's become a question of geometry, cutting down the angle, moving off the line. Look at James McGarry [Kilkenny]. The cornerstone of his achievements in goal was cutting off the danger, organising his defence, basic stuff like that.

Look at hurling now. How many shots per game do you see a keeper getting to save? Apart from the qualifiers or the league, when you can have a turkey-shoot, when was the last time you saw a keeper making five or six saves in a match? Cummins in 2006 in the league in Thurles was an unbelievable display of shot-stopping, but that was the league. How often do you see that in championship? Cummins played really well that day, but I think he'd tell you himself, he's made much better saves than that but saves that were less spectacular.

A goalie will always know himself, when he's made a great save or when he's missed one he should have got. Cusack against Waterford in the Munster semi-final in 2005; he came out that day among three or four bodies, hurleys flying everywhere, and caught a dropping ball. Go to the video and you can actually see Dan Shanahan was pulling right across Cusack's hurley, but still he made the catch. A goalie gets way more satisfaction from making a save like that than from the diving save, the save that looks flashy but, really, is bread and butter.

You'll read reports of fantastic saves but to a goalie they're not really fantastic, they're fundamental, straight-forward blocks. It's the save where the ball is coming in – high and straight, or from the wing, where you have a couple of forwards waiting inside, or coming on the run; you can see all this but you still go, make the catch or the block – those are the great saves, from a goalkeeping point of view. Someone takes a shot, even from inside the 21, you have time to see it coming and react, block it, deflect it, knock it out. That's often called a great save but it's not. If a goalie lets in a goal like that he won't be blamed, but deep down he knows he should have blocked it, whereas a ball that's coming down out of the sun and drops under the bar, he's deemed to have made a huge mistake. A goalie gets more satisfaction out of catching that kind of ball, especially under pressure, than he does making a block. Does that make sense?

I would put this on the record: Damien Fitzhenry, Brendan Cummins, Davy Fitz are three of the greatest keepers to ever play the game, no question. I've seen a lot of keepers, studied a lot of keepers, and I would argue that with anyone. But now I'd say Cusack is definitely in that bracket. No one has ever changed goalkeeping as Cusack has. He has revolutionised the position. Look at puck-outs; people are beating him up for years over his puck-outs – the short puck-out especially – but look at how hard it is to win possession from a Cork puck-out. He has moved the parameters that define goalkeeping. He has re-shaped his body, he has worked very hard on the core work. His level of preparation, his analysis of the position, of the opposition, his whole outlook on goalkeeping – he has definitely become the brand leader. Cummins was the number one, no question, very closely followed by the other two, but I'd say now that Cusack has taken over. He has set a standard for everyone else to reach.

There was a time when he wasn't valued even in Cork, and that's still the case among a lot of Cork fans, but how can anyone question his value now? Go back to 2001, the famous day when the police escort never showed, Cork players had to make their way to Páirc Uí Chaoimh through the crowds and all that. Barry Foley won that game for Limerick with a late sideline puck from under the covered stand. It was a ball that went just over the bar and you could see Cusack letting it off, he didn't have the confidence to bring it down.

Go forward to 2006 against Waterford in the All-Ireland semi-final; stopping that late point, batting it at an angle well away from the danger area, that's the kind of improvement I'm talking about, that change from 2001 to 2006 won an All-Ireland semi-final for Cork. People go on about saving points, that it's a risky business – the reason Cusack does it with such confidence now is that he practises it, over and over. That goes back to the whole thing I was talking about, with goalkeeping; it's not just about the spectacular saves. There's a saying, 'Don't tell me – show me!' That's what Cusack is doing.

There's all this training now: strength training, stamina training, speed training, skill training; but how many teams have specialist goalkeeping training? I think everyone agrees that it's a unique position but

'Not yet, let me warm me hands.' Christy O'Connor (centre) faces a penalty with
Liam Doyle (left) and Anthony Daly (right) on 27 February 2000.

how many teams have specialist training? From what I see with a lot
of goalkeeping training, it's technically flawed. You should be training
to do what you'd do in a match. What's the point of diving all over the
place, doing stuff that looks fancy, when you're going to be doing very
little of that in a match?

The goalie should always be concentrating on what's happening in
front of him, always, but what does he actually get to do? Ninety per
cent of the time, it's the puck-out; so what should he be practising? The
puck-out. Why then do so many goalkeepers go to training and never
practise this crucial element of their game? It makes no sense. They
should learn to master every kind of delivery, they should practise hitting a target – a standing target, a moving target, short-range and long-
range.

People have to accept that the short puck-out is here to stay. The reason the Cork puck-out is so successful is that everyone on the team has
bought into it, they're working as a team to create space. The guys who
are making the dummy runs, time after time, will never get the credit
for it but they know what they're doing, they know the contribution
they're making and that's enough. Nothing is ever perfect, sometimes
it goes wrong; usually though when that happens the keeper gets the
blame. Even if he has put the shot right on the button and the receiver
fluffs it, lets it over the sideline or loses possession, the keeper gets the
blame. But that's the problem with being the keeper – you're always in
the line of fire, even when you're taking the puck-out.

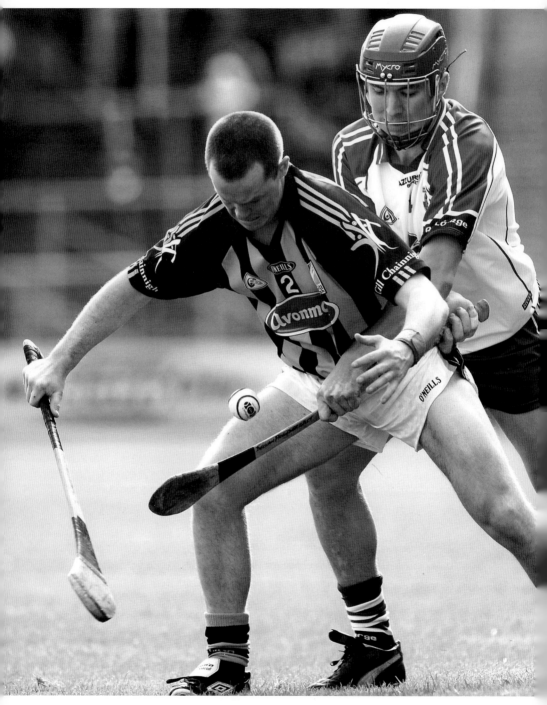

'My ball,' says Michael Kavanagh and there's nothing Waterford's Declan Prendergast can do about it during their match in the Allianz National Hurling League played at Nowlan Park, Kilkennny, on 16 March 2008.

Right-Corner-Back
The Terrier

Phil 'Fan' Larkin (Kilkenny)
Brian Murphy (Cork)
Michael Kavanagh (Kilkenny)

From all the interviews for this book, all the talk about positions in general, when it came to right-corner-back there was almost a consensus: right-corner-back is a specialist position. It requires a specific state of mind. The right-corner-back is a spoiler, a negative hurler, in fact 'doesn't have to be able to hurl at all', reckoned one outstanding wing-back. He's sticky, he's aggressive, barking, snapping at the heels, heedless of his own safety, courageous to the point of recklessness.

He is Phil 'Fan' Larkin, top All-Star award-winner in this position with four credits. He is the middle generation in a family with a unique record in hurling. His father, Paddy, won four All-Ireland medals with Kilkenny in the 1930s; Fan won five; and his son, Philly, won two in recent years.

PHIL 'FAN' LARKIN
(b. 1941, James Stephens and Kilkenny, 1962–79)

AWARDS & MEDALS WON
5 All-Ireland senior
4 All-Star awards
1 National Hurling League (as captain)
6 Railway Cup (1 as captain)
2 All-Ireland senior club (1 as captain)
4 Kilkenny county senior hurling (1 as captain in 1975)
3 Kilkenny county senior football
   (2 with Clann na nGael, 1 with The Village)

First position
I started as a left-half-back with the school, played centre-back for Éire Óg, then I went to corner-back and finally, to full-back. I was twenty-seven at that stage, there was no one else to play there. I first played full-back for Kilkenny in the 1972 Leinster Final. Pa [Dillon] didn't play, so I was picked. It ended in a draw, 6-8 apiece. Some introduction, but I felt I did alright. The man I was on scored nothing anyway, that's what I was most worried about.

Were you happy at right-corner-back?
I wasn't happy or unhappy – you play where you're picked. My favourite position though, and I never played there for Kilkenny, was number six.

The qualities needed to be a top corner-back
I'd say the most important thing is to be first to the ball – anticipation. Know where the ball is breaking, know where your man is, get there first. The way the game is played now is completely different to the way we played it. No one seems to care now what score is got off them, whereas in our day that was the most important thing. Stop your man from scoring; if you never hit the ball in the hour, but your man scored nothing, you were doing your job. If you hit a hundred balls and your man scored two goals, you didn't play well. That was the way we were taught anyway and that was the way I always thought.

Where to stand in relation to your opponent

I'd always stand goal side when I was corner-back, and when I was full-back I was side-by-side, ready for the break. I'd stand on the catching-hand side, so you wouldn't be pushed off, ready for the break when it dropped. With Cummins [Ray Cummins, multiple All-Star at full-forward for Cork, almost a foot taller than Fan] you stood on his left [caught with his left], with Doran [Tony Doran, huge bustling Wexford full-forward] you were on his right [caught with his right].

What about the man who was ambidextrous, could catch with either hand?

You met very few of those. Kieran Purcell [Kilkenny full-forward] was the only one I saw, a brilliant player for a man who didn't train that hard. But it was different then, fellas enjoyed it a lot more. I'd come down here before All-Ireland finals and sit up there at the bar in the village with my father. Often I wasn't drinking but if I wanted a pint I could have one, no problem. I learned it all from him, wasn't that the secret of it?

Did you pass that on to your own son Phil?

Well, sure, I talked to him alright, but whether he listened or not is another thing! But Philly played most of his hurling out the field, played senior at sixteen. I never saw my father playing, and he never saw Philly playing.

Tricks

Maybe a little shove at the right time, and you'd see lads who pulled jerseys, shoved the helmet down over the eyes. With Cummins you'd be shoving his hand while he was trying to catch it, leave it into Skehan. The referee wouldn't usually spot that, especially with a small man. But I was lucky with Cummins, very lucky. My plan was to get the ball to the ground, I knew I'd have a better chance of winning it then. Ray was used to having lads standing shoulder to shoulder with him, big men, strong men. I'd be under him, trying to shove him off the ball as he was trying to catch it, let it drop. Once it hit the ground I'd strike.

Primary advice to a promising youngster, above all else, to master the corner-back position

Enjoy it, that's the most important thing. After that, first to the ball, and in that respect, I think anticipation is more important than speed. The problem is, you can't coach either of those. You either have it or you don't. I was never fast over 100 yards, but I'd go 10 or 20 yards with anyone, and that's all you need at corner-back.

Line-up of the legends *– the Kilkenny team who played Limerick in the All-Ireland Senior Hurling Final at Croke Park, on 2 September 1973. Front row (left to right): P. Broderick, P. Lawlor, M. Brennan, L. O'Brien, P. Delaney, N. Skehan, C. Dunne, F. Larkin. Back row (left to right): N. Orr, P. Cullen, B. Cody, P. Henderson, M. Crotty, F. Cummins, J. Lynch.*
Note: On the extreme right, on crutches, is corner-back Jim Treacy who missed the final through injury, as did Eddie Keher.

While Fan Larkin has the most All-Star awards at right-corner-back, Brian Murphy is surely the most decorated. Brian is a dual star with Cork and he has won practically every honour the GAA has to offer. He was right-corner-back in both hurling and football in a career that extended from the 1960s to the 1980s. A quiet individual, he was the cornerstone of Cork's three-in-a-row of 1976–78, during which time he also won a three-in-a-row of Railway Cup football medals – a unique achievement. A Garda detective in Kilkenny, he and Fan Larkin are on the best of terms and share a lot of mutual respect.

BRIAN MURPHY
(b. 1952, Nemo Rangers and Cork, 1971–83)

AWARDS & MEDALS WON
4 All-Ireland senior (3 hurling, 1 football)
4 All-Star awards (2 hurling, 2 football)
3 All-Ireland U-21 (2 hurling, 1 football)
3 All-Ireland minor (2 hurling, 1 football)
3 National Hurling League
4 Railway Cup (1 hurling, 3 football)
4 All-Ireland senior club (all football)
1 Cork intermediate county (hurling)
7 Cork senior county (all football)
2 All-Ireland colleges (both football)

First position
I started off around the half-back-line with Nemo Rangers and played a lot of my hurling there. The first time I played for Cork was a league match against Tipperary in the old Athletic Grounds; corner-back, on Babs Keating. That was the league of 1971–72. I did well that day, but I always had great admiration for Babs, a super player.

What was your favourite position?
I preferred half-back, played there a lot in both hurling and football with Nemo, but fell back into the full-back-line with Cork. I always felt half-back was easier, you always had a chance of recovering and

generally, there was someone behind you anyway. The full-back-line is more difficult.

Was there a difference between playing in the two corners?

No, I wouldn't think so. I didn't mind either position. I played full-back as well, never liked it there to be honest but you're glad to play in whatever position you're picked to play in, with club or county. I think a full-back needs a real physical presence and I didn't think I had that. I remember one year at full-back playing on Roger Ryan of Tipperary, Ned Rea of Limerick and Liam Canning of Waterford. You also had Joe McKenna in Limerick, Kieran Purcell and Pat Delaney in Kilkenny – big strong men at full-forward, who were not easy to handle. But, you get on with it.

Were you strong off both sides?

Well, some people would tell you I wasn't even strong off one! But yes, I think I was.

Was your main focus the man or the ball? Denis Coughlan says that after the 1978 All-Ireland final, the third of the three-in-a-row for Cork, you were walking down Grafton Street and you told him you had touched the ball seven times in all over the course of the three finals?

I don't recall telling Denis that, but in the third final I was on Matt Ruth [Kilkenny], and certainly there wasn't a lot of ball coming in to that corner. That's all very fine too, but if only two balls come in during the game and the forward wins both and bangs in two goals, you're in trouble.

The ball is always the focus really, but you have to be that bit tighter in the corner than you would be at wing-back. The margin for error is lessened. You have to be tight; you have to try to get to the ball first, but if you don't manage to do that, you have to be sure your man doesn't get inside you. You must put him under pressure striking. These are all basic things you'd be telling young fellas – put him under pressure, force him to shoot under pressure, get the hurley in, try to block him down, that's all vital for a corner-back. It's also vital for every part of the field, forwards, especially, are inclined to forget that part of their duty is to prevent easy balls from coming out.

Another legendary line-up – the Cork team and All-Ireland champions in 1976. Front row (left to right): C. McCarthy, B. Cummins, G. McCarthy, R. Cummins, M. Coleman, P. McDonnell, S. O'Leary. Back row (left to right): J. Barry Murphy, M. Malone, J. Crowley, P. Barry, M. O'Doherty, P. Moylan, B. Murphy, D. Coughlan, Fr B. Troy (coach).

Was there a tendency for the ball to end up in one corner rather than the other?

I never noticed that, to be honest. A lot depends on who the opposition have in the corner, the way they're playing, who's hitting the ball in. The ideal ball for a corner-forward is out in front with a bit of space, especially if the corner-forward isn't that physically strong. If they feel the corner-forward isn't that strong they probably won't give him much ball.

The qualities needed to be a top corner-back

You certainly need to be able to read the game, that's number one. Then you need pace, a burst of speed. Getting to the ball first is critical, because if you can do that, get the ball out to the half-back or whatever, your man is not going to score. It's hard to beat pace. You must be able to read the situation with your full-back and half-backs. You must be conscious of those around you, know when to go, know when to offer support, make yourself available to take a pass.

John Horgan, left-corner-back for Cork, says you had an understanding with Martin Doherty, the Cork full-back of that period?

Yeah, the corner-back must be conscious always of where the ball is. He must be watching out for the fellas alongside him. If you know that even if you miss the ball, those alongside you are going to cover across, that gives you more confidence. That works vice versa also – if they miss, you're covering across. The guy who just minds his own corner to the exclusion of everything else, that's very negative, that's not good team play. The full-back-line is a combination and I had that in nearly all of the teams I played on, especially when you played together for a while – you developed an understanding. The goalkeeper played a big role in that, he's the last line of defence, he has the best view of the whole situation, must be making the calls to alert everyone to what's happening.

Where to stand in relation to your opponent

Goal side, always goal-side. That would be the ideal scenario, though it might have to change as the forward moves around and the good corner-forward will move, but you would always be conscious of standing on the goal-side.

Tricks

I didn't have any, really. You'd see the odd tug on the jersey – by backs and forwards – that sort of thing, gives a fella a slight advantage, but that was all.

Primary advice to a promising youngster, above all else, to master the corner-back position

Work on the skills, improve yourself and enjoy yourself. No matter who's over your team, no matter what advice you get, it's what you do in your own time that will really improve your game. Practise the skills any chance you get, and enjoy it. It's good to have a winning mentality, but don't put too much emphasis on it. Enjoy it first, especially as a youngster, that's most important.

There are several modern outstanding personifications of the right-corner-back, but now that Wayne Sherlock of Cork has retired from inter-county hurling, the one who springs most readily to mind is Michael Kavanagh of Kilkenny. The game has changed since the days of Fan Larkin and Brian Murphy, positions constantly evolve, but some things never change. The right-corner-back is still very much his own man, still needs an attitude that differs slightly from everyone else on the field. Michael Kavanagh, the longest-serving member of the current Kilkenny panel, fits that bill and is a worthy heir to the two above.

MICHAEL KAVANAGH
(b. 1979, St Lachtain's and Kilkenny, 1998–present)

AWARDS & MEDALS WON
7 All-Ireland senior hurling
4 All-Star awards
5 National Hurling League
4 Railway Cup
12 Leinster senior hurling (one as a sub)
1 All-Ireland U-21
1 Oireachtas

First position

I started in primary school, probably corner-back, and right through school and college I stayed around the full-back-line, though I'd have done a stint all over the field, even in the forwards. I remember a game where my brother James was full-back and I was in the corner. Chunky O'Brien's son – I think he was called Chunky as well – was coming through with a ball and we made a sandwich of him, the two of us – a chunky sandwich! That's one of my earliest memories.

Nearly everyone I've been speaking to says Kilkenny defenders are the toughest of all. Are you given specialist coaching in back play?

No, I wouldn't say we are. I suppose you grow up looking at the county players from previous eras and how they played, and you try to play the same way. You'd be working on things like blocking and hooking, on getting out in front, on discipline, not fouling your man – playing on the edge really, getting on the ball. But I don't think there was any specific backs' training; you just tried to adapt your game, work on your weaknesses, play your own game. After a while, I think everyone learns whether they're a natural back or a natural forward, and you're told quick enough anyway, and labelled quick enough. Not too many players have the versatility to play at both ends of the pitch.

Most young lads want to play in the forwards, that's where the glory lies, that's where the scores are got.

I suppose, yes, it is the glamour end. At a young age everyone just follows the ball all over the pitch, you just want to play, run around, get involved, but as you get older, you get to know your position. If you can't hack it in the forwards, if you can't score, if you can't create scores, lay on scores, if you can't do the work for the others even, you'll be told quickly enough to get out of there, get back down the field.

Is forward a tougher position?

It's certainly not an easy position, at any level. When I came onto our [club] intermediate team for the first time, I was only fifteen or sixteen and I was at wing-forward, so I got a taste of what it's like for a forward. It's great when you're scoring, but if the ball isn't coming your way, or if you're on a strong marker and not managing to get away, that's when the natural forward instinct should take over. You take up the good positions, you're patient. But certainly it's a tough position to play, I feel for a lot of forwards [believe that if you like – DO'F]. I don't really envy them, but some of the lads make it look very easy.

Are you the kind of corner-back that didn't care if he never saw a ball, as long as your man didn't score?

Well, it's true that some of your best work at corner-back goes unseen and you would prefer it that way, because if you're not being seen, then your man is probably not being seen either. That means you're keeping tabs on him, he's being quiet, and if he's not scoring it's increasing the chance that your team is going to win. If the opposite applies, if you're hitting a lot of ball, then he's probably hitting a lot of ball which means he's probably scoring also. For the good of the team I suppose the quieter the better, that has to be your primary aim.

You've played wing-back also – what's the difference?

You need better legs out there! I enjoyed it when I was there and Brian [Cody, Kilkenny manager] would often put me out there for a while in training as well, give me a bit of freedom, away from the corner. You can express yourself a bit more out there, you get to go forward and that's one thing you really miss when you're in the full-back-line – the attacking element is gone, setting up the play. You're a lot more restricted in the full-back-line, safety first. I enjoyed myself out there, but there's too much competition in the half-back-line in every county, a lot of top-class hurlers out there. Corner-back would be my best and my favourite position, at county level.

Did you ever try left-corner?

When I started with Kilkenny seniors, they already had a top-notch left-corner-back in Willie O'Connor – I knew there was no point in going for that position anyway! There is a difference between the corners, definitely; I played left-corner-back with St Kieran's in an All-Ireland final against St Colman's, that was probably the only campaign I ever had there. The difference is in the side you're going to be striking off. I think the left corner is more suited to left-sided hurlers. In the modern game though, with so much switching and chopping and changing among the forwards, you have to be able to play both corners, because more than likely you're going to end up there for a while in every game. We try to hold our positions as much as we can in Kilkenny, we try to hold our shape.

The qualities needed to be a top corner-back

You need to be a very good reader of the game and you need to be very concentrated, very clued in on what's happening. Be ready for the breaks, be constantly alert, reading your own man, reading the other forwards, what's happening around the field, and be out in front whenever possible. And you have to be patient. Patience in the tackle is the big thing, restrict the fouling; you do need to live on the edge but without fouling. Be strong and aggressive, let him know that you're bossing that corner, that this is your patch and you're going to win it. You need to be out in front; a good burst of speed is needed, especially the way the game is gone, the pace of the forwards out there now. You need to

Getting the stick in – *Michael Kavanagh makes things awkward for Waterford's Paul Flynn during the National Hurling League game at Walsh Park, Waterford.*

be quick-thinking, but you need to be cool-thinking, be controlled in your play; things can get fairly hectic in there at times, so a cool head is required. Don't panic, don't be lunging into tackles. Be patient, let the game take its shape, let it pan out; don't be rash.

Do you tackle the man or the ball?

The ball usually, but you can take both. Keep your eyes on the ball at all times; even if the forward wins it, he still has a lot to do. He's not going to throw it up in front of you, he's going to have to try to take you on. Work on being patient, be nimble, be ready to move in any direction; force the forward into taking a few steps, invite him to come at you with the solo, but don't lunge in and foul, which can be costly, an easy score conceded. Make him work for it. Step back, force him to take a few extra steps, maybe over-carry the ball.

Where to stand in relation to your opponent

I'd always try to position myself within an arm's length of my man, maybe right behind. Certainly you're trying to read the game as well and if the opportunity arises, you break out in front of him. You can't be afraid to attack the ball. But keep him close at all times, don't let him get away. You might have to give him the odd tug or the odd dig to let him know you're still there, that you're not letting him off. If the ball is coming in from the other side of the field, you have to be willing to gamble occasionally, you have to be ready to tidy up around the goals. Don't gamble too often or too big though. Know where your man is at all times, but know also where the danger is likely to come from, what's likely to develop. You have to make your decisions fast, err on the side of caution. It's not a position for fancy stuff, for heroes.

Tricks

You're always learning the game, always picking up new things. Playing behind Tommy Walsh you'd wonder how a small lad like him can catch so much high ball, but he has that trick mastered. He can sweep everything away while he makes the catch. He has perfect timing, perfect awareness, knows exactly when to make his move. A great man to sweep up as well.

He's not that small?

No, I suppose not. He's not that much smaller than myself actually! And he doesn't even jump, just gets his hurl up to protect his hand, make the catch. I wouldn't mind having that in my armoury! It looks great, lifts everyone around him.

Primary advice to a promising youngster, above all else, to master the corner-back position

The tackle; any good corner-back must be able to tackle. Don't panic, don't foul, don't lunge. Be patient. When the forward wins the ball, he still has a lot to do. Be aware of that.

Stephen Lucey getting the stick in against Jackie Tyrrell (Kilkenny) in the Allianz National Hurling League on 12 March 2006.

Full-Back
The Gatekeeper

Pat Hartigan (Limerick)
Brian Lohan (Clare)
Diarmuid O'Sullivan (Cork)
Stephen Lucey (Limerick)

For those of us who spent much of our hurling lives on the edge of the square, trying to manufacture scores for ourselves or for the two girls in the corners, the full-back holds a special place in the memory. He was the guy who blocked your path to goal and blocked it in no uncertain fashion. He was the gatekeeper, the doorman, the bouncer. And just as the normal rules of society don't seem to apply to bouncers, the normal rules of hurling don't seem to apply to the full-back either. What others further afield would be whistled up for, perhaps even sent off for, the full-back was applauded for, and usually, you were the unfortunate at the receiving end.

Funny, then, that the man who has more All-Stars in the position than anyone else (five straight from 1971 to '75 inclusive) was probably as civilised a hurler as ever swung ash. A man before his time, Pat Hartigan made history in 1968 when he played for Limerick at eight different levels – minor, U-21, intermediate and senior in hurling; minor, U-21, junior and senior in football. His career was eventually cut short when he received a serious eye injury in training. Pat was also an international athlete and represented Ireland on many occasions at the shot-putt.

PAT HARTIGAN
(b. 1950, South Liberties and Limerick, 1968–79)

AWARDS & MEDALS WON
1 All-Ireland senior hurling
5 All-Star awards
1 National Hurling League
2 Railway Cup
3 Limerick county senior
1 All-Ireland Colleges
2 All-Ireland club athletics titles

First position
I played full-back for Limerick CBS in the Harty Cup in 1967 and '68. I then progressed to the Limerick minor team and played corner-back and full-back in '67 and '68. I was on the U-21 panel from 1966 to '71, played corner-back in '68, centre-back in '69, '70 and '71. When I joined the senior team in October of 1968, for the league, I started off at right-half-forward, believe it or not, and I was there for the senior championship in '69, at full-forward, still only eighteen years of age.

The transition
In 1970 I played my first game for Limerick at full-back, that was in Corn na Cásca in the old Athletic Grounds in Cork, against Cork. From then on, while I played the odd game at centre-back, my position was full-back. I played Railway Cup from 1971 to '78, won two titles, one at full-back in '76, and one at centre-back in '78, when Martin Doherty was at full. I had a reasonable amount of speed for my size, so I had the range for centre-back.

How did your athletics career affect your hurling?

It's funny, but they talk nowadays of doing weights programmes. My brother Bernie [Limerick selector in 2007/08] and myself were both international athletes, shot-putting and hammer-throwing. Bernie had converted his garage into a gym with a lot of home-made weights in it. We were in that gym every Monday, Wednesday and Friday from 1 October to the end of the following February. At that time inter-county teams trained on Tuesday and Thursday, out in the muck and the mud, doing stamina work. We were doing these weights all the time and they stood to us, obviously. My level of strength, Bernie's level of strength, was much superior to most of those who were playing hurling at that time. We were built like tanks naturally, but doing those weights three nights a week made us even stronger again. Then in the spring and summer we were doing all that running in hurling training which was building up our speed and aerobic fitness. It meant that the hurling training was making us better shot-putters and hammer-throwers and the athletics training was making us better hurlers.

Having said that, our weights programme, while it involved a lot of reps, also involved very heavy weights which made us much bulkier, which wasn't ideal for hurling. If I was doing it all over again I'd do more reps but with lighter weights. What it did do for me, though, was that it meant I was able to take all sorts of physical punishment. Apart from the eye injury I never really got injured – no breaks, no muscle pulls, nothing.

You were known as a bit of a gentle giant, but did anyone ever take you on physically?

No, never. One thing I regret though, I don't think I ever fully realised my own strength at the time and definitely I didn't fully utilise it. I watch the rugby guys now, the power they have, the speed allied with strength, I see the bigger guys hitting the smaller guys and hurting them – I wonder what would have happened if I had done the same? I look at someone like Diarmuid O'Sullivan with Cork, I don't think he's as strong as I was when I was playing, but he's far more aggressive. He has the bulk power, he uses his size far more effectively than I did. I remember when we were training in the Gaelic Grounds, no one could touch me in the physical stakes. There was one exercise in the winter, cones laid out, you'd run up to a cone side-by-side with someone and when you got to the cone you had to give a shoulder; no one could shift me, ever, and I don't think anyone ever really wanted to run with me.

Who was more powerful, you or Bernie?

I'd say Bernie; he was shorter, about 5 foot 10 inches, but he was very strong and very fast. I was nearly 6 foot 4 inches, a lot of upper body weight, a lot of muscle in my legs, but Bernie was more explosive. I was stripping at over 15 stone at twenty years of age and that was with no body fat, but there was nobody there to advise me on how I could marry what was a serious amount of muscle to speed. That's where the coaching of thirty years ago failed me. I was raw, but I was willing, if there was someone there who could have taken me further. I was doing all these power exercises – bench-pressing, clean-and-jerk, squats – but I was doing them without expert advice and that's critical with weights.

Everything was homemade. We had a bench for the bench-press, a railway sleeper at an angle on which we'd also do our stomach exercises, maybe five sets of ten. We had another couple of lads used to come out to us and it was often a case of who'd collapse first! But the stomach muscle I had after that, what they call the core strength now, was phenomenal.

The qualities needed to be a top full-back

My situation was that I married two eras together. I played in the 1973 final when the old rules were still in vogue, when the goalkeeper could be challenged inside the square and often was, and buried in the back of the net. He was game for everybody. In 1974 then, he could have had an armchair inside, he had become almost untouchable.

Having said that, the way I played in '73 and prior to that was the very same as I played after '73. I played out in front, went for the ball always. I reasoned that if I could draw the full-forward out, then even if the ball breaks behind me, the goalie had it covered. There was enough distance between us, whereas if I stayed back, played like the trad-itional full-back, I was inviting the full-forward to take on the goalie. What was important too though, was that I had full confidence that I could deal with any ball, high or low, that came to me. I was big enough to take almost any high ball and if it went over my head, it was probably too high for the full-forward anyway. If it was a low ball, I was out in front and I had good control, kept it in front. I had worked out for myself, even at that young age, what was the point of hanging back around the square with a big, strong, heavy, experienced full-forward who was just waiting to pull on the first thing that comes, break the ball, then get in on top of the goalie? Why would I do that when I could go out and intercept the ball 20 or 30 yards out?

I think I developed a new style of play for the full-back before 1973, and I think it might even have been instrumental in accelerating that rule change for the keeper. People could see that you didn't have to have these mad scrambles around the goalmouth, that my style of play was more effective, and more attractive. I often found myself out behind the centre-back collecting the ball, and driving it straight back down the field, which made for a much more open game, a much more exciting spectacle.

I think I pioneered the modern style, in that respect, though you still had to be able to play the old style. When we were training for the 1973 All-Ireland, Ned Rea [big, muscular Limerick full-forward] and myself used have pure murder, pure unadulterated murder. I had always seen Ned as a kind of father figure on the Limerick team. I had first seen him in 1964, when I was only fourteen and he was corner-back. When he went to full-forward in '73 though, it was tough. We gave it hard in training – you had to – but it got to the stage, before the final, that Jackie Power [trainer] came over to me one evening and said, 'You're on the team for the All-Ireland final, but we want Rea there as well!' In other words, don't kill each other.

We're great friends, always were. He played with Faughs [in Dublin], I played with South Liberties. In 1976/78 we played in the Kilmacud Sevens; Ned came in full-forward, I was full-back for Liberties. I was thinking, 'Nice weekend in Dublin, our first time at the Sevens, we'll enjoy this, have a bit of craic.' I tried to have a bit of a chat with Ned, but got no response. That was all very well, it was really open play – as Sevens is – but the first ball that came to us Ned went out, turned, came at me, threw the ball over my head, went around, collected, and stuck it in the back of the net.

'Okay,' I thought, but said nothing. Ned said nothing, just passed me back out the field. Next ball he was out first again, came at me again, but this time I was moving too, straight out at him. I saw no ball, just ran into him, full belt. He was wide open, creased him – talk about full use of my weight training!

Pat Hartigan at a celebration to commemorate the thirty-fifth anniversary of the Vodafone GAA All-Star Awards in Croke Park, Dublin, on 7 November 2006. Pat was a member of the 1971 Limerick Hurling All Stars team.

Limerick were already out of the championship, I was back full swing into the athletics training so I was strong, very strong, and hard. I hit him with my chest, my knees, everything – he was stretchered off. I hurt myself as well, fell awkwardly, was limping as he was being carried off. I was worried about him and apologised.

'Ned, I'm sorry. To tell you the truth that shouldn't have happened but Ned, when you did that to me the first time it was bad, but if I'd let you do it a second time, I'd have been a pure fool.'

'I thought you were a cleaner player than that,' he says to me.

'Ned, if it meant saving a goal for South Liberties or for Limerick, I'd kill you! We went through all this already when we were training for the '73 All-Ireland final, when there was no love lost, so you should know that by now!'

We had words then, but we were friends again soon afterwards, and we're friends to this day.

To sum up, I'd say the greatest quality needed in a full-back is that he shouldn't be afraid to attack the ball, he shouldn't be afraid to play from the front. Read the angles at all times, get yourself in position, cut off the angle of attack. Don't confine yourself to just that little area around the goals, expand it, push the full-forward out and leave the space inside to the goalie. Play the ball and don't be afraid. When I was playing I'd spend hours and hours in the ball alley sharpening my stroke, building up my confidence.

A friend of mine, Joe O'Reilly, was a tennis player. We'd go into the alley, he'd have his racket, I'd have a hurley. We'd use a tennis ball and we'd play matches, handball rules and scoring! Now that was a hybrid game for you! But it was great for sharpening you up.

Where to stand in relation to your opponent

On the left shoulder as much as possible, but the worst position is behind. Usually, all you can do there is foul, after he has won the ball. The best position is in front, but the danger there is he can snap a ball, and he's gone. Side by side, that's the safest. I'd love to be full-back in front of [Donal Óg] Cusack. I'd give anything to experience that. Skehan was the best keeper I've seen, but I've great admiration for Cusack. He's a backman's dream.

Tricks

One thing I used to do, and I did it a fair bit with Cummins – had to because of his range – was stand on his catching side. I couldn't take the risk of letting him catch the ball. He had a great leaping ability, but just as he'd be about to take off, I'd step on his foot, pin him down, keep him land-bound. Another thing I did then, was to put my left hand on his left shoulder and just press him down, try to force his hand down. He was a great man to protect his hand, so pulling wasn't an option.

Tricks seen

Seánie O'Leary [Cork forward] throwing the ball into the net. That was some trick, and I saw him do it so many times, making it look like it was handpassed. Then he'd run into the net, throw the arms in the air, create a fuss, confuse the umpire and referee, and the score would stand.

Primary advice to a promising youngster, above all else, to master the full-back position

Keep your eye on the ball at all times; never take your eye off it. If you know where the ball is all the time, the man only comes second, but if you're juggling between the two, you're losing concentration. Christy Ring often said to me, 'When the ball was in the referee's pocket before the throw-in I'd have my eyes on that, and I'd never take my eyes off that ball 'til the final whistle.'

Never, ever, turn your back on the ball. Focus on it from the start and you're a split-second ahead of your man all the time. Remove that focus and you're playing catch-up. As a full-back, remember that it's not enough for your man to just win the ball, he has to do something with it. Put him in the most awkward position possible, all the time, make it difficult for him to do anything.

Pat Hartigan was a gentleman full-back. The next three – all from the modern generation or the generation just past – are throw-backs, the kind of full-backs who like their meat raw. The first of those is Brian Lohan, the guy who was there when Clare won those unforgettable All-Ireland titles in 1995 and 1997, he of the famous red helmet.

BRIAN LOHAN
(b. 1971, Wolfe Tones and Clare, 1993–2006)

AWARDS & MEDALS WON
1 Powerscreen hurler of the year 1995
2 All-Ireland senior hurling
3 All-Star awards
5 Railway Cup
2 Clare county senior
1 Munster senior club
2 Clare county intermediate (football)

Tony Considine, a selector during that golden era for Clare hurling, tells a revealing story

In 1997, we were training for the Munster final against Tipperary, the be-all and the end-all for us. We had won the All-Ireland in '95, but we hadn't met Tipp since 1993, that famous day [Clare were hammered]. We had a training match one evening in Cusack Park, Eamonn Taaffe had scored a few points off [Brian] Lohan, and we went across to the Sherwood afterwards for a bite to eat. Bear in mind now that you weren't allowed get any points off Lohan, at any time.

The seating arrangements in the Sherwood meant that some people would be back-to-back, so there we were: Lohan on one side with Daly maybe, Doyle [Anthony and Liam, two players], then there was [Ger] Loughnane, maybe Colm Flynn, [Mike] Mac[Namara] and myself [all management] on the other. I could see Lohan's red hair, his back to me, and I gave Loughnane the wink.

'Jesus,' I said, 'wasn't Taaffe mighty this evening? What did he get, 1-6 or 1-7?'

Three-in-one shot *– the red helmet, the single-minded focus, the eye on the prize: Brian Lohan in action against D. J. Carey in the Allianz National Hurling League final in Semple Stadium, Thurles, on 2 May 2005.*

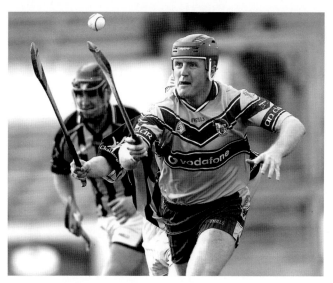

'*This ball is mine! This space is mine!*' *Brian Lohan leaves a few Kilkenny forwards in his wake on 20 March 2005.*

Loughnane copped what I was doing. 'I don't think he got any goal, but he got a good few points alright.'

All the time I could see Lohan's neck stretching, the head coming back. We were training again the following morning at seven o'clock. I was first in. Who was second? Brian Lohan. He didn't salute me, he growled at me. Loughnane and Mac came. We had two teams picked for a training match. Taaffe full-forward again on Lohan.

I said to the lads: 'By God, I'd hate to be Taaffe today!' Well, he beat him up and down Cusack Park the same as you'd beat an ass out of the bog. Absolutely destroyed him. We knew then, Lohan would be okay.

First position

My first position was left-corner-back. I wasn't really making the underage teams and when I did, it was always left-corner-back, for some reason. I wasn't big as a young fella, didn't really make the team at U-12. I played U-16, minor, U-21, corner-back all the way.

Did you go straight to full-back then for the Clare senior team?

No, I was right-corner-back again. I made my debut there in 1993, up in the Park against Limerick. Sparrow [Ger O'Loughlin, Clare forward] scored 1-6. We played Cork then, corner-back again, on John Fitzgibbon, his last game for Cork. I have his jersey upstairs, a prize possession. After the game, which we won – Daly had an awesome game at full-back – I went up to Fitzgibbon, asked him to swap jerseys. He took off his jersey, handed it to me, says 'You played well today.' I went to hand him my jersey, he said 'No, no,' and off with him.

When did you get the red helmet?

When did I get it? In 1988 or '89, I'm not sure which. I still have it, thrown outside in the garage.

The transition

The first time I played full-back was U-21 for Clare, 1992. Loughnane put me in there.

Did you get an explanation?

No.

Did you like it?

I did, yes. In the club at home, we had a fella called Derek Collins, another lad called John McPhillips, and those guys played full-back for

Clare U-21s. John was only one year older than me, which meant that I didn't really have the opportunity of playing full-back. I was in the corner beside one of the two lads.

I moved to full-back for Clare seniors in 1994, after we got hammered by Tipp in that famous Munster final of '93, when English [Nicky, Tipperary forward] was supposedly laughing, throwing the ball around. I met Loughnane shortly after that game – I knew I would. I was walking home from training and he passed me on the road. He turned around, came back for me. 'Hop in.' I hopped in. He dropped me up home, told me I'd be full-back for the next year and Seánie McMahon would be centre-back.

I didn't even know McMahon at that stage, had heard of him alright, but he hadn't made the U-21 team – he was a sub, on the same panel as Frank [Brian's brother]. I think what Loughnane was really saying to me was, 'Gear yourself,' and I did have a lot of work to do to get myself into shape for full-back. I wasn't strong enough for the position for starters, and I had to improve my speed. I did a lot of weights, had to do a lot of extra work anyway, because I was always under pressure with my hamstrings. It only increased my speed a little bit, but a little bit at inter-county level can mean an awful lot. There was a gym on the Ennis Road in Limerick, I'd do it on my way out from college, hitch home afterwards. No car that time. Get in, do it, get home, always hitching.

The qualities needed to be a top full-back

The biggest things are speed and skill. You need both. A lot depends on who you're going to be on. There are many different kinds of forwards out there.

What about aggression?

I think you have to be aggressive in any position on the field, no matter where it is. I don't mean being stupidly aggressive, hitting people, giving away frees, but aggressive on the ball. You'd know even in challenge matches, club matches, even in training – if someone is taking it handy, they'll probably take it handy in a championship match as well.

You might get away with not being aggressive in other positions?

I don't agree. I think you have to be aggressive in all positions.

What about concentration?

Yeah, it's not something I've ever really thought about, but yes, if you're not tuned in for even a few minutes in a game, it's a goal, the way for-wards have gone now. If you're not tuned in to the corner-backs around you, to the goalkeeper behind you, to Seánie [McMahon, centre-back] in front of you, you're in trouble. A lot of that comes down to training. If you feel you have that extra bit of work done, then come the big day you're going to be able to fall back on that. You won't be susceptible to nerves or anything like that. You're not going to be beaten by someone who has done less work than you.

You attacked the ball – were you told to do that or was that how you decided to play?

That's just the way I played. We were always told in training, even as youngsters, get out first to the ball. We did drills where the ball was hit hard at you, you'd be running at full pace. That was all about attacking the ball, getting out as fast as you could, winning possession, winning control. That was how I played, at full-back or corner-back.

Where to stand in relation to your opponent

On his shoulder, and generally on his catching side. If you were on someone like Rabbitte [Joe, giant Galway forward], you'd nearly have to be in front of him. Try to block the ball. No full-forward should beat a full-back by catching the ball, but that's what makes Shefflin [Henry, Kilkenny] so hard to play. His skill level is such that he can get up to the highest point of the ball and bring it down to himself. He's big and strong. You could see that in the goal he got against Stephen Lucey in the 2007 All-Ireland final. Lucey has obviously done a lot of work in the gym, a big, strong man, but he couldn't hold Henry out for that goal.

Tricks

I didn't have any. The only time, maybe, was the All-Ireland final of 1997. I was marking Eugene O'Neill, got a clip early on from Leahy [John, fiery Tipperary forward], a good shot, in the first ten minutes. He knew what he was doing and, fair play to him, he got away with it, but I was struggling after that. I knew I couldn't go [sprint], so for the second half I just grabbed O'Neill by the jersey, held him into me and didn't let go. He should have turned around and let me have it but this was only his second game for Tipp. He was young, inexperienced.

Tricks seen

We had that big rivalry with Tipp, especially after that beating in the Munster final of 1993. Then we played them in '99, drew with them, a game they should have won. The following week in Cork we met them again and Loughnane walked out of the dressing room, as if he'd had enough of us after our performance the first day. He left us inside on our own, just the fifteen of us. We heard Tipp going out onto the field anyway and just as we were about to follow them, Loughnane came back in.

'I'm only going to say one thing to ye, I've just heard Nicky English giving his dressing room speech to Tipp and his last three words were "kill wounded animals".' And he walked out. I can never remember speeches, whether before a game, at half-time, after the game, or who gave them, but I'll always remember that one – 'Kill wounded animals.' Whether it was true or whether Loughnane was just pulling a stunt, it worked [Clare subsequently hammered Tipp].

They truly were three wise men in that setup, Loughnane, Considine, Mike Mac?

They were extraordinary in that everything was timed to the last. The logistics were always taken care of to a tee. Never a problem with anything. From the minute we met to the minute we went home, everything was planned. It was extraordinary.

Primary advice to a promising youngster, above all else, to master the full-back position

Skill – work on the touch, get onto the ball at pace and control it.

From Brian we go to the man he named as the best full-back he has seen: Cork titan Diarmuid O'Sullivan.

DIARMUID O'SULLIVAN – 'THE ROCK'
(b. 1978, Cloyne and Cork, 1997–present)

AWARDS & MEDALS WON
3 All-Ireland senior
4 All-Star awards
1 National Hurling League (as captain)
2 Railway Cup
2 All-Ireland U-21
1 Young hurler of the year
1 Cork county senior (Imokilly)
1 Cork county intermediate
1 Munster senior football

First position
I started at wing-back, but I could be played anywhere these days with the club. I'd pick myself at centre-back. I think that's where I'd be most effective, but my favourite position is left-half-back [his usual club position]. You have that bit of licence to do more.

The qualities needed to be a top full-back
The most important thing a full-back needs is two good midfielders to stop good ball getting into the full-forward line! Seriously though, I'd say the ability to adapt immediately to all kinds of situations: high ball, low ball, diagonal ball; big full-forward, small full-forward, fast full-forward. One corner one minute, the other corner the next, then dragged out 40 or 50 yards. That's the modern game and you have to be able to adjust to all that.

You need luck too. The 2004 Wexford replay, no matter what I did it seemed to work. I remember I tried to catch a ball over my head, missed, it dropped and I just put my hand behind my back. It fell into it! Another ball, Larry Murphy was in front of me, and I reached around in front of him, blind – again, the ball fell into my hand. There are days like that when everything seems to go right, and that was one.

Cork's Diarmuid O'Sullivan bursts from defence chased by Tipperary's John Carroll during the National Hurling League semi-final at Páirc Uí Chaoimh in 2000.

Tricks

There was one that Donal O'Grady showed me. We were beaten by Kilkenny in the 2003 All-Ireland final, Martin Comerford [Kilkenny full-forward] played very well. We were meeting them again in 2004 and Donal came to me.

'Don't worry about him,' he said. 'He's the easiest fella in the world to put off his game. I'll tell you what to do. Walk up behind him and open the strap of his helmet. See how you get on.'

After ten or fifteen minutes, your man was going wild. He was looking out to the sideline, shouting at Cody [Brian, Kilkenny manager]: 'That fella should be doing this, this fella should be doing that.' He had lost it, all because of a simple little trick. So effective – unreal.

The next year they changed the rules. That sort of thing became a foul. In fact I was the cause of two rule changes in hurling: the helmet rule and the blood-sub rule. In the 2002 Munster final replay, I came on as a blood-sub and Cork had used their five subs at the time, which made me technically illegal. The rule was changed after that.

Finally, we come to the man who was voted by his peers in the GPA as the All-Star full-back for 2007 (Tipperary's Declan Fanning got the Vodafone version). Like O'Sullivan, Limerick's Stephen Lucey is a convert from further out the field.

STEPHEN LUCEY
(b. 1980, Croom and Limerick, 2000–present)

AWARDS & MEDALS WON
1 GPA All-Star award
2 All-Ireland U-21 hurling
3 Munster U-21 (2 hurling, 1 football)
4 Dublin county senior (3 hurling, 1 football)
1 Walsh Cup (captain of UCD)

First position
I've played at three, six, nine and eleven. I wasn't a natural forward, but would be thrown up there to do a job. Physicality, that was me. I was always put somewhere down the middle, so if a centre-back was dominating, I'd be thrown up centre-forward. For a while after I came on the inter-county scene, Limerick had no natural centre-forward. Gary Kirby had finished up, Ollie Moran was tried there once or twice. Then they tried me, a stop-gap. It was a real shock to the system. In 2006 I was full-back, played Cork in Bruff and pulled my hamstring. When I came back, they had pulled T. J. [Ryan] back from full-forward to full-back, put me up at centre-forward and I was there for the rest of the year, 'til the wheels finally came off.

The transition
Everyone is telling me that full-back is my best position and I suppose I'm beginning to accept it myself at this stage. At the start of 2007, I went to Gary [Kirby, Limerick selector]. 'Well Gary, what's the story this year? Will I get a chance out the field?' Centre-back, midfield – that's what I was getting at.

'No!' he said, and said nothing else.

I waited, then, 'Is that a "No" as in "No, never" or is there a maybe?'

'No, never. You're full-back this year. That's it, get used to it!' and he walked off. He did more or less the same with Ollie Moran at centre-forward.

I get dog's abuse from the lads in Croom over it. They know I love to play out the field and every time I'm picked at full-back the sniggering starts. I hated it before, but I'm finally used to it now. When I realised I had a job to do and began to settle into that job, it became easier. And we have a settled unit now, that's very important in the full-back-line.

2007 was the first year I went a full season without playing midfield. I was full-back for the club as well, which pissed me off a bit to be honest. You're back there, things are going wrong out the field and you can do nothing, only sit back and watch. You're fuming, champing at the bit, but it's a bit like being goalkeeper – there's nothing you can do. You have no input, no impact on how the team is attacking. Out the field, you're more involved.

The qualities needed for the various positions
Centre-forward

Centre-forward was frustrating for me. As a back you're used to facing the ball, playing against it and that's easy. All you have to do is force the forward out of the way, get a hurley to the ball, belt it away. Now you have to turn around, do the opposite. As well as winning the ball, you have to try to create something, or score. A different game. Eventually I think I knew what I was doing up there, scored a good few points, but I was ever only a stop-gap, no future in it.

Midfield

I loved midfield. I played there with UCD, played there also for Dave Keane with the Limerick U-21s, really enjoyed it. You always felt you were contributing. There was so much involved in midfield – you broke up the play, won ball, helped the forwards, dropped back to defence. You imposed your strength, and again physicality was important, though that's changing now. You look at Jerry O'Connor, Tom Kenny, it's about going from box to box. The likes of Seán O'Neill, George O'Connor [Limerick and Wexford respectively, strong men], that's going out of it a bit. Now you have the runners, the distributors like Cha Fitz [Kilkenny midfielder].

Waterford's Paul Flynn feels the pain as Stephen Lucey collects during the All-Ireland semi-final in Croke Park on 12 August 2007.

Centre-back

Centre-back was probably the nicest position of all to play in. You have fellas all round you to help out if you're in trouble. The ball inevitably comes to you, you get to play a lot of ball, constantly involved. At centre-back you can show your skill, all your skill, which is not the case at full-back. You get ball in the air, on the ground, you get to hit it short, long. You have to be strong. You have to hold your ground. Centre-back is one position where you can't go missing because if you do, the hole opens up for the midfield runners coming up the middle. You need to have an understanding with your wing-backs. Support them, support the full-back-line.

Full-back

I've changed my game for full-back, had to. My attitude is different, my style. Safety first, that's my attitude – don't allow goals. I don't care if I don't hit a ball in the hour; I'd rather stop a good full-forward, keep things tight, solid, safe, than clear a hundred long balls. Back in 2000 I remember a game in Croke Park, Seán Óg Ó hAilpín [Cork] at wing-back on Johnny Pilkington against Offaly. Seán Óg had a pain in his hand from clearing ball, but Johnny scored several points the same day, won about four balls, scored four points, and Offaly won.

You have to be more aggressive there. The best advice I got was from Richie [Bennis, manager]. 'Pull like a tinker!' he told me, and you have to. You can't pussyfoot around back there. Look at Brian Lohan, Diarmuid O'Sullivan, Noel Hickey. You have to be borderline, which I wasn't before.

It's vital to have a good relationship also with the two corner-backs. The square is the thing, we all have to cover for each other around there. One in front, one behind. Know which way the ball is breaking. A runner from the wing, the corner-back has to go, you have to cover his man, sort of a drift defence. If the other corner-back is miles away, the goalkeeper has to come out and take the full-forward in that situation.

Encouragement across the line, that's important, developing a unit. The zone of terror, that's what you want that area to be. 'This is my space – invade and I'll f***ing kill you.' That's the attitude you need in that area. You hear the old stories about the Tipperary full-back-line, Hell's Kitchen. That's what it's got to be.

Mental attributes are similar for a lot of hurling positions, but if you're in a central position, leadership qualities are very important. You learn this as you go along. Some fellas are born leaders, you'll follow them naturally, without thinking. Ciarán Carey was like that, Mark Foley today. They talk, you listen. Roy Keane did both. He talked, but he also gave leadership on the field. Keith Wood is the same, a very good speaker. Seamus Hickey is young, but I see that coming through already. There are guys who don't say a whole pile, like Peter Lawlor, but they're excellent leaders on the field.

Mental toughness, calmness under pressure, I think that's the key for any inter-county player. T-CUP: 'Think Clearly Under Pressure', that's very important. Pat O'Shea, the Kerry football manager, had us for minor football and he was brilliant, an excellent trainer. He didn't just train us physically, he spoke to us, coached us mentally. We'd get into a huddle, he'd go through what we were doing, elaborate on it. He always talked about composure on the ball. You don't have to do everything at a hundred miles an hour – look up, see what's around you, see what's on offer, take stock, be aware. Presence of mind, pick someone out with a pass, maybe someone coming around the back, rather than just giving the ball away. Maybe someone coming around the back, unmarked. Mental preparation – get yourself ready.

Tricks

I have a few tricks I won't be giving away, not yet anyway. One thing I did learn to do, always stand at the side of the full-forward under the high ball. Use your body to shift him out of the way, legitimately. You have to be in the right position to contest it, the catching-hand side. I marked Joe Brady of Offaly in Nenagh, stood on the wrong side of him, he caught the ball and I had to pull him down – penalty, goal.

Another thing you can get caught with if you play from the front, the tip on your hurley. Kilkenny are excellent at that, Tommy Walsh especially. I tried to play from the front when I was centre-forward, but I often got clipped. We were playing the Fitzgibbon Cup in 2004, [I was with] UCD, a good team, won the Dublin championship that year. We came up against WIT, Keith Rossiter of Wexford was having an outstanding game at centre-back and I was thrown in to centre-forward. He got me. High ball, I went for it, he tipped my helmet from behind, down over my eyes, my face guard down below my chin. No idea where the ball had gone. That was good play by him, very clever. Got away with it.

Left-Corner-Back
The Lurcher

John Horgan (Cork)
Martin Hanamy (Offaly)
Ollie Canning (Galway)

Maybe it was the long blond hair that made John Horgan stand out so much from his peers or maybe it was that a mere corner-back wasn't meant to be flashy or dashing, cutting a swathe through opposition forwards as he came swash-buckling out to make yet another huge clearance. But there was a lot more to John Horgan than met the eye. There was steel to the Corkman, he was a corner-back of genuine defensive talent, with genuine defensive attitude.

The unmistakeable blond locks of John Horgan (sixth in line) as Paddy Barry leads the Cork team around Croke Park on All-Ireland Final day in 1970.

'BLONDIE' JOHN HORGAN
(b. 1950, Blackrock and Cork, 1969–81)

AWARDS & MEDALS WON
1 Hurler of the year (1978)
5 All-Ireland senior
3 All-Star awards
3 All-Ireland U-21
1 All-Ireland minor
3 National Hurling League
2 Railway Cup
3 All-Ireland senior club (all as captain of Blackrock)
5 Cork county senior

First position

I played three years for Cork minors and started off at centre-back. The first year, 1966, I was in the crowd in Killarney for the first game, watching Cork against Galway [Galway played in Munster then]. The next thing I got notification to go for a trial. This was in an era when it was very rare for a fella from a country area to wear the red jersey. I was only sixteen, and one evening shortly after that trial, Seán Geary, a great Passage clubman, came in the door.

'John, you're on the panel for Sunday.'

My mother, who loved the game, was absolutely thrilled. Then, just as he was going out the door, he turned. 'By the way, you're on the team.'

Not in my wildest dreams – and I really mean this – did I think I'd get on that minor team that year; in a couple of years maybe, but at sixteen? To this day that's probably the best news I ever got in hurling – my mother in tears, dinner gone out the door. We reached three All-Ireland minor finals, 1966, '67 and '68, and won the middle one.

The transition

I can't remember when exactly I was switched back to the corner, or why, but I suppose it was because I played better hurling there. It suited me, it suited my style. I played full-back a few times as well and didn't mind it. But if you're flying, hurling with nonchalance, afraid of no one, feeling fit and on top of the world, then centre-back is a great place to be. You're on the ball a lot, covering across, covering back, sweeping up everything.

Back in the corner though, it's different. You cannot afford to take too many chances. When we won the three-in-a-row, beat Kilkenny in 1978, I was marking Mick Brennan for the first twenty minutes and I couldn't take my eyes off him. He was very dangerous. We were just holding one another really, breaking even. Then he was moved out the field and some other fella came in, not as dangerous as Mick at all, and I got more pucks in the next twenty minutes than I would normally get in a whole game. I could afford to take chances because I knew I had it over your man. Then Kilkenny brought Brennan back in and that was that, it was back to the unspectacular. He didn't get too many pucks, but I didn't either. When you're out the field you have more freedom, more safety, because there's always someone behind you. Not at corner-back though.

The qualities needed to be a top corner-back

No matter where you play, you have to work at your hurling skills. It's fine to say that it comes naturally to some people, but everyone has to put in the work. With due respect to other sports, anyone can kick a ball, but it takes many hours of practice to master the hurling strike. I did huge practice, but looking back on it now, it was probably unknownst to myself. We lived in a row of houses – five houses then a break, five houses, another break, five houses. Fair play to the neighbours, they left me use the two gable ends between rows, almost back to back, and that's where I'd practise.

A variation on the old theme of a ball and a wall – you had a ball and two walls?

Exactly; I'd hit it off one wall, double it to the other wall, back to the first wall, left and right, right and left, always trying to keep it moving. There was a rim on the wall, a flat rim, flat plaster, and I'd aim for that then. That was for accuracy. Sponge balls, the odd tennis ball, if you could come across one. Those were hard times, money was very scarce, you had bugger-all really.

When I was a youngster P. J. Mahony in Killeagh was the big name in hurley-making. If you got one of those hurleys, by Jesus you were made. The college in Rochestown was a boarding school that time and we'd go up there sometimes, to the hurling field. There would be lads there from the college, training. They might go away to do a few sprints or something, leave their hurleys down. We'd 'find' those! And if you found a P. J. Mahony hurley – well, put it this way, you wouldn't go home the main road anyway, you'd head across the fields with your treasure!

You must be able to read the game. You see one of their corner-backs or wing-backs coming out with a ball, plenty of room to get in a long strike – you know that ball is coming down to your corner, you must be moving out to meet it. Try to get there before the corner-forward, beat him, get in front of him rather than run with him.

Right or left corner, was there a difference?
I preferred left corner, always. I wasn't the strongest off my left, preferred to turn into the centre to clear off my right. Left corner suited me perfectly. I don't ever remember playing in the right. Maybe it was a comfort thing.

Where to stand in relation to your opponent

On the three-in-a-row team, myself, Brian Murphy and Martin Doherty [Cork full-back-line], with a high ball coming in, we'd never be in a straight line across. We'd always be diagonal, one covering the front, the other covering behind. You'd never cover all the angles, but you did the best you could. A lot of it was instinctive too, knowing where the other fella was from having played together for so long.

For the high ball coming in you'd read a fella. If he was the kind of fella that liked to double on the ball, he was easier to handle – out of a hundred balls he might hit one. But the fella who liked to catch it, you had to be really careful of him. If he was around your own size he was going to catch a few, so you couldn't let him inside you. You had to be careful that you stood goal-side. You wouldn't want to stand too far goal-side though, you didn't want to give him too much room either – a good corner-forward would take advantage of that. I'd take an occasional gamble, that would be my nature anyway.

Where did you get the distance from?
I don't know, I think you just have it. Did you ever see the bowlers in

action? It's not all power at all, they just whip it. The same with golfers, it's in the speed of the swing, the whip. But I had a big, heavy hurley. I liked weight on the hurley.

Tricks

One I used a lot was in striking. If there was a fella in front of me trying to block me down, I could throw the ball behind me, well away from me, and still hit it, arms fully extended – you can't block it. That came from all the training on those gable ends, hitting the ball with the arms fully extended. Size was important there. I was around the 6-foot mark, not huge but big enough. That one often got me out of trouble.

Tricks seen

I saw Ringey one time against Waterford; Cheasty or Grimes or one of those guys had put the ball down for a sideline. He ran up along the line, stamped down on the ball and stuck it into the ground. You couldn't touch the ball yourself that time, the linesman placed it for you. Stood on it, buried it and it was there then, they had to try and hit from there.

Primary advice to a promising youngster, above all else, to master the corner-back position

Never take your eye off the ball, never, even if it's at the other end of the pitch. A long clearance, if you're watching and he's not, you have the advantage, you're gone [for the ball]. If you're not watching and he is, he's gone and you're lost. Keep your eye on the ball.

John Horgan was one type of left-corner-back, Martin Hanamy of Offaly was quite another. Where John stood out, a colossus, Martin stayed back. A lot like Fan Larkin in the other corner, the less you saw of Martin Hanamy during a game, the more he liked it, because more than likely you weren't seeing much of the corner-forward either.

MARTIN HANAMY
(b. 1966, St Rynagh's and Offaly, 1986–99)

AWARDS & MEDALS WON
2 All-Ireland senior (one as captain)
3 All-Star awards
1 National Hurling League
1 Railway Cup
1 Oireachtas
4 Offaly county senior

First position

Wing-back. I never hurled corner-back, any grade, 'til I was put there for the county. Even when I started with Offaly, in the 1986 league, I was wing-back. Ger Coughlan or one of the usual wing-backs must have been injured in '86, which was probably why I was out there.

The transition

The 1987 championship came, they were stuck for a corner-back and Georgie Leahy [manager] threw me in there. Pat Fleury had retired from the corner, they had tried a few fellas and maybe they were stuck. That was the first experience I had of corner-back, I came on against Laois in the Leinster semi-final, a sub.

Obviously you were being tutored for weeks and weeks beforehand on the nuances of the position, had studied all the handbooks?

Ah yeah. 'Get out there to f*** and stick tight to your man!' That's all I got.

Were you that type of player anyway, sticky, a man-marker?

I suppose I was, yeah. I was never the swash-buckling kind of defender that loved going forward. Even at wing-back I was a man-marker. I wasn't interested in scoring three great long-range points while my man was scoring 1-6, that kind of thing. In my opinion, a back's job is to keep his man scoreless, a corner-back especially. By hook or by crook, that's what you did. I often went through a whole half of hurling, thirty-five minutes, without ever even touching the ball; go through a whole game only touching it once or twice. That wouldn't worry me – as long as my man never touched it either, I was fine with that.

Did left-corner-back become your favourite position?

It did in the wind-up, because I never again played anywhere else for the county. Cregan tried me at centre-back when he came in 1992, but he only gave me one game there. I was saying to myself, 'Jaysus, let me back into the corner!' A different ball-game out there. You have to be looking left and right all the time, minding; whereas in the corner you're only looking to one side – goal-side. You have only the sideline on the other side.

The qualities needed to be a top corner-back

As the fella in the pub might say, you need to be bull-thick and ignorant! But you need awareness there. You need to know where everything is happening around you. Anticipation is a huge thing. I wouldn't have been too blessed in the speed department, and in fact I'd say that applied to most corner-backs of the time.

Awareness, anticipation, cuteness, that's what it took. Anticipate where the ball is going to break and be gone before the corner-forward. Of course the longer you play, the better you become at that. You must be prepared to sacrifice your own game. I think I was a much better hurler than I was made out to be! Seriously, a bad hurler doesn't get to play at inter-county level, but there's something I've noticed over the years – a guy is picked to do a specific job at inter-county, he comes back to his club and feels he has to be a star, that he has to start doing things he never did, and he goes off the boil for his club. Fellas trying to shoulder too big a burden.

Were the yarns about the Offaly team of that time true, how laid-back they were?

A few of them might have been true, yes. We had a few fellas who were hoors to drink and smoke. Sure, Pilkington and John Troy would be smoking at half-time, even in All-Ireland finals. Imagine that nowadays!

Ball firmly in his grasp, Martin Hanamy personifies Offaly's determination against Cork in their shock All-Ireland final win of August 2000, Ben O'Connor doing his utmost to hold back the tide.

And now, neither of them are smoking! But I could be drinking away in Cloghan and no one would say a word. I wasn't a heavy drinker, but I'd have a couple of pints. Poor ould Johnny Pilkington could go into a pub and drink a mineral, but the word would be out straight away. Give a dog a bad name – a lot of it was like that.

If you're known as an early riser, you can stop in the bed all day?
Exactly!

Offaly played a very intelligent game?
I suppose we had to. We didn't have the same pick as everyone else, but we were very closely knit. Everyone had their own job, knew what they were to do. I just had to get the ball out to Kevin Martin, he took care of it after that. We were very together in that sense. We played very simple, straight-forward hurling and didn't it work? I think it would still work today. The game is crying out for a team that will just move the ball first time, double on it, keep it going fast up to the forwards.

Where to stand in relation to your opponent
Always on his right, goal-side, I'd be conscious of that all the time. The likes of Ollie Canning [Galway] could stand on any side because he had pace. I couldn't take that chance.

Tricks
What, apart from pulling the jersey, the togs? Tipping the hurl I suppose, that kind of thing – I didn't really play the hand. If a ball was going wide, I'd always pull with it, never against, let it off. I don't know if that was legal or not, but I got away with it anyway. Hit their hurl. High ball coming in behind the wing-back/wing-forward, my man in front of me waiting for the break – I'd crowd up to him, push him into them just as the boys were clashing, then the ball would break back to me. I got caught a few times with that but it worked more often than not. That was a good one.

Tricks seen
More of the same, really, playing the hand, playing the hurl. Johnny Dooley was a hoor for playing the stick, just tipping it out of the way when he went up to grab the ball.

Ollie Canning is the modern manifestation of an inter-county hurling corner-back, right or left. A hurler to the core, superb stickman with outstanding control, he is also lightning fast. Gone are the days when the corner-back was simply a spoiler. Today, and as personified by Ollie, he wants the ball as much if not more than any corner-forward, and will fight him for it. Preventing scores is still the priority, but the method has changed, as has the profile of the corner-back.

OLLIE CANNING
(b. 1977, Portumna and Galway, 1996–2006)

AWARDS & MEDALS WON
4 All-Star awards
4 National Hurling League
3 All-Ireland senior club (two as captain)
1 All-Ireland U-21
2 All-Ireland minor
2 Railway Cup
5 Galway senior county
1 Galway county intermediate

First position
My first position with Galway was centre-back, at U-14. Fergal Healy was on one wing, Brian Higgins on the other, and I can remember my dad saying it was probably the smallest half-back-line he'd ever seen, even at U-14! With the club, I started at wing-back with the minors, only thirteen or fourteen. I also played at corner-back in a county final. Generally speaking that's how it developed. At schools level I played in the forwards at different stages. I broke onto the club senior team at a young age, sixteen, and I was stuck in at corner-forward, which is natural enough at that stage. Generally the backs are older, well established, and management don't like to take a chance on a young fella. I had no problem with that, in the forwards. As time went on, with the club I went centre-back and was there when we won the championship in 2003, but I was actually playing in the forwards with the county.

The transition

It was when Mattie Murphy took over in 2001. I was with the minors in 1994 when Mattie was manager, playing out the field, but he moved me back to the corner for the final against Cork and we won that. In 2001 then, with the seniors, he moved me back there again, and that's where I stayed.

Do you like it there?

I don't mind where I play, to be honest; anywhere I can do a job for the team, I'll do my best. Growing up, I loved the half-back-line. I enjoyed centre-back when I was there. That's the nicest position, I think. I played midfield but the game can pass you by there, which can be very frustrating. At corner-back though, you can have a great game for sixty-five minutes, then make one mistake and it's all gone. It's a very unforgiving position.

The qualities needed to be a top corner-back

At inter-county I always felt that reading the game was very important. Depending on how the ball was coming, I was never afraid to take a step out in front of the corner-forward. I'm not saying I was the fastest man around, but generally speaking if I did get caught when I went forward, I always felt I had the pace to get back, to recover. When you're reading the game, you know when the midfielder or half-back is going to send the ball into your corner and you can take that chance, anticipate. I think that worked well for me over the years. I could turn quickly, get back. I never felt I was going to get caught. Obviously there are some very fast corner-forwards out there and you have to adapt accordingly. I think the position is changing. Corner-forwards now tend to be faster, less rugged, and corner-backs are the same.

Did you work on pace?

No, it was natural. Training has changed a lot lately, however, even at club level. You have this speed/agility/quickness programme, fellas working on their break over the first five yards. As I've got older I'm probably concentrating a bit more on that, but not in former years. It was just there, and I was lucky in that respect.

But you can work on your speed, on your quickness – running downhill, increase leg-speed, length of stride?

Yeah, but when I started it wasn't that scientific. Even in the last five years things have changed dramatically. You're shortly going to reach the stage that, not alone will you have sport-specific training for hurlers, you'll have position-specific training, everyone doing their own thing for much of the training session. It's coming already, with goalkeepers, but you're going to see it for every position, more and more.

What about the dispossession game, the Kilkenny game, did you work on that, the flick?

Yeah; something I always worked on – and it was always very effective – was to just shadow a guy 'til he showed the ball to hit, then get the flick in, get the ball away. Don't slap across him, don't give away the free, but once the ball leaves his hand it's fair game. Get the hurl in. That's very effective, and it's a killer if a guy thinks he's just about to hit the ball over the bar, score a point. Follow up with the clearance, that's a great feeling. Block-downs, hooks – the basics, that's what I always concentrated on.

Sometimes, a couple of inches, a split second, can make all the difference. In the All-Ireland final of 2005, when Ben O'Connor got the goal, I was just after blocking down Niall McCarthy. I had lost my hurl in the process – gave him an ould jab as well, you can see it on the video. The ball broke to Fergal Healy, he first-timed it off the hurl, down the field. I was still in a heap on the ground, beside McCarthy, Ben inside me. I was looking around for my hurl, saw it, had to take two steps down towards the Cork goals. By the time I turned, Ben was already gone, about ten yards away and running. At the other end big Diarmuid O'Sullivan came thundering out, just grabbed the ball and sent it as far as he could, a low trajectory into Ben's path. Straight away I knew I was in trouble. I can still see Derek Hardiman [Galway half-back] at full stretch trying to get to the ball and I was praying – 'Please Derek, just get a touch. Deflect it away from O'Connor.' He missed, barely. I don't know where the full-back and the full-forward had gone, but Ben was now in pole position. He got on the ball, delayed just a split second to make sure of the pickup and I thought – I have him! I was visualising the ball leaving his hand, the swing, tried to time the flick to get the ball away. We both ended up in a heap on the ground, but I actually thought

Ollie's going to get you *– Cork's Joe Deane is about to have his pocket picked by Ollie Canning in the Allianz National Hurling League game against Galway in Pearse Stadium, Galway, on 7 April 2003.*

I had succeeded, I thought I had got the ball – next thing the roar of the crowd, and I knew Ben had scored the goal for Cork. But I knew I was in trouble from the moment I had to take those two steps out the field to get my hurl. Ben read it and moved, and that's the difference at the top level.

Where to stand in relation to your opponent

Goal-side, generally, but I preferred to be on his catching-hand side, which gave you direct access to the ball. If he was a left-hander that meant he was going to catch with his right, which was fine, but a right-hander caught with his left, which could leave you exposed. The name of the game then was not to let him catch it. Generally I'd go for the flick, try to get my hurl in front of the catching hand, get a touch. I rarely went for the big pull because players today are just too good at protecting their hand. Look at any of the Kilkenny lads, they'll protect the hand. But no matter how tall a guy is, you can get the hurl up there as high as any hand. Stay cool, time it right, knock the ball down, then get onto it. And you're on the right side for that. Brute force won't always work. I wouldn't be able to knock a fella off the ball anyway because of my size. Just stay cool, get your hurl in there. And never panic. A guy could have 1-1 got off you very quickly and you could fall apart – don't.

Tricks

You'd sometimes see fellas doing fancy flicks, the ball up into the hand, but generally speaking in championship you don't see too much of that. I never spent any time devising tricks, anything like that. Maybe the odd foot-trip alright, make it look like incidental contact, fool the referee. The other thing, I often played for the free, ran across a fella's feet on the way out with the ball, fall down, but I don't do that anymore, obviously!

Tricks seen

I've seen guys opening guys' helmets before the ball dropped, opening the clip under the dropping ball. I've seen Joe Cooney put the ball under his armpit in training, fooled a lot of fellas like that. I was a young lad, thought it was great. I remember seeing P. J. Molloy [former

Galway forward] going through [with a ball] one day. He stopped, went down, pretended he was fouled. Everyone stopped playing, he got up and roofed it! Old foxes, all they need to do is take your attention away for a second.

Primary advice to a promising youngster, above all else, to master the corner-back position

Patience is crucial at corner-back. Skill level is very important in there, work on the hand-eye coordination, work on speed of hand, speed of foot.

Pete Finnerty (left) chases Tipperary's volatile wing-forward
John Leahy in the National Hurling League final of 1989.

Right-Half-Back
The Sweeper

Pete Finnerty (Galway)
Brian Whelahan (Offaly)
Liam Doyle (Clare)

To most hurling followers the half-back-line is the crucial line in any team, club or county. 'Aerial goalkeepers' is how they've been described, the first official line of defence (in any team worthy of the name, when the other team has the ball defence starts in the full-forward line). If they can hold the line, their team has a good chance of success. If they can dominate, tá siad ar muin na muiche. Few were more dominant at right-half-back, ever, than Pete Finnerty. Broad-backed, barrel-chested, bould-faced, his physique and attitude were more all-in wrestling than hurling, yet he made the position his own. This interview took place in the company of Tony Considine.

PETE FINNERTY
(b. 1964, Mullagh and Galway 1983–94)

AWARDS & MEDALS WON
2 All-Ireland senior
5 All-Star awards
2 National Hurling League
4 Railway Cup
3 Oireachtas
1 All-Ireland U-21
1 Galway county intermediate

First position

With Galway it was full-back, but when I started with the club, centre-forward. Then we were playing a Feile semi-final and they asked me to go back full-back and I did. Played there all the way up along underage with Galway. I played two All-Ireland minor finals at full-back.

The transition

Michael Bond put me out wing-back for the U-21s of 1983. My first time there, but I think I was still more or less earmarked as a future full-back for Galway. I was a big, strong central-type player. Then [Cyril] Farrell picked me at wing-back in 1985, which was as much of a shock to me as it was to anyone else – I was still training for full-back. I was probably fortunate as well. I burst a blood-vessel in my leg in 1984 and had that not happened, I'd have been playing corner-back, marking Joe Dooley in the All-Ireland semi-final, and I'd probably never have been heard of again! It's an ill wind – sometimes you can be fortunate to be injured!

Did you get any explanation as to why you were going to wing-back?

No, and I never bothered looking for one either. I loved the freedom out there, rather than just marking a man at full-back. The first day I played there was the All-Ireland semi-final against Cork in 1985. A dirty wet day in Dublin, about 8,500 people at the game, Cork as red-hot favourites. [Gerry] McInerney wasn't playing that day, but Tony Keady was centre-back, Tony Kilkenny on the other wing. Someone said beforehand that it looked like a half-back-line that was pulled out of a hat! I had never played senior at wing-back, Keady hadn't played centre-back, but it all fell together on the day. Galway got the great start, held on.

Did you bring the full-back attitude to the wing?

Well, I'd be a more traditional defender in that I'd be more worried about what my man would score than what I would clear. If I didn't hit a ball in a game, but if he didn't hit a ball either, I'd feel I had done a good job. Now, a John Gardiner or a Brian Whelahan would love to go forward and score, but I'd say in my entire career with Galway I didn't hit three wide balls. Going for the long 90-yard spectacular point was never a priority of mine. I always believed in first, keeping the number of scores I gave away to a minimum, and second, giving early ball to the forwards. That's the way I was. I wasn't loose, I was a traditional old-style marking wing-back. Mac on the other hand [McInerney] – I remember one All-Ireland final where he scored two points from play, but Declan Ryan [his opponent] scored four. Two incredible points they were though, especially for a man who could hardly hit a ball! Mac would solo 50 yards to handpass five, where I'd just hit the ball the 55 without moving at all. I figured that was a lot easier, and I didn't have to run back to my position either! So yes, I did bring the full-back attitude to wing-back. I was a stopper first, a man-marker. I never tried to develop the game any further than just marking my man, keeping him scoreless, and anything that came after that was a bonus.

When did that famous Galway half-back-line of Finnerty/Keady/ McInerney fill out?

That was in 1986. McInerney joined us against Cork. I think he was just out of U-21, was only playing club. I'd say he was picked on his ability as an underage player because he wouldn't have been seen much with his club at that stage. He was over and back to America, would play the odd match – make this one, miss the next one. Then they picked him on the other wing, 1986, against Kilkenny in the semi-final I think. That was in Thurles, and that was the three of us in place.

Tony Considine: Did he buy the white boots in America? [in an era where black was the colour, Gerry was famous for his white boots]

Oh he did; I was there with him when he got them. They weren't called 'boots' at all, they were called 'cleats', the baseballers wore them. I remember saying to him, 'You might as well buy the whole uniform and make a right clown out of yourself!' But nothing would do him only to wear them; even in the dressing room before we went out, the first day, I was still saying to him – 'Are you really going to wear them?' 'I am, I am, they're lovely, they're lovely!' But d'you know, I think a lot of people actually thought he played in his socks, because we had a white base to the socks. But that was Mac, everything about him was flamboyant, he had different ideas to everyone else. We were coming back from Lanzarote one time after a short break, getting ready to play Cork; they had already beaten us twice and Mac came up with this idea that if we wore white jerseys with maroon dots the Cork lads would be so bamboozled that we'd be four or five goals up before they knew what was happening, then we'd hold on to win!

The qualities needed to be a top wing-back

You're the linkman between defence and attack. You have to be able to feed off people, work off people, work with people. Your ability to be able to assess your own players' abilities is essential. You have to decide, in an instant, whether you're needed more in attack or in defence. I might be thinking, 'Coleman is okay [Michael Coleman, Galway midfielder]. I'll go here for the pass.' If you don't have that ability to read the game in front of you as it's happening, you'll find you're going for the pass when there's no pass coming, because you've left a man in trouble. You should have gone in to help.

I always man-managed my own patch. I considered my area to be from ten yards one side of Keady, ten yards in front of Sylvie [Linnane, right-corner-back for Galway], then out to the halfway line. Inside that area – for puck-outs, whatever – I took charge. For long deliveries, like from Ger Cunningham [our keeper], I'd establish in my mind where his longest puck-out would land. I'd mark that line across my area and I'd never be beyond that line when he was taking his puck-out. I'd always come into the ball because it's far more difficult to try and deal with a ball when you're going backwards. The main thing for a half-back is that you stop the ball; however you do it – whether it's with the hand or with the hurley – you must stop it, nothing should pass you.

The aerial goalkeepers?

Yeah, I'd agree with that.

Could you have played left-half-back?

I probably could, but I wouldn't have been as comfortable there, even though I had two good sides, another essential at wing-back. On the right wing, if I have a choice I'll pass my man on the right, down the wing, using my free hand to push him away while getting ready to swing the hurley. That way I'll be throwing the ball away from him. For McInerney on the other side, he had to work a lot harder to make room for himself to get off the strike, even though he was an unorthodox hurler [right hand below left on the hurley]. A right-handed hurler will always feel more comfortable on the right wing. Out there, when I'm swinging my hurley, there's only the linesman outside me.

Tony Considine: Something I noticed about the Galway team of your era – yourself, Keady, McInerney, Lynskey, Hayes, Sylvie – they all had huge hands.

Every one of those players you named – and this has changed, to the detriment of hurling in Galway – worked physically. None of the current side, for example, works on a farm. We grew up with shovels, pikes, we were picking stones from fields from a young age. If you look at us, yes, all of us had big paws on us, we'd all be physically wider than today's players. They're doing all this training, training, training, but they're all pushing pens, Mammy and Daddy want them all going to college.

I remember the first time I went to Dublin to play in Croke Park, it was the minor final, the oul' lad got up on the Saturday morning. 'We'll bring in those few cocks of hay down the hilleen.' I was the tallest, that meant I had to do the piking. So okay, say nothing, here I am, standing on the mudguard of the tractor as the barn was filling up. Then up onto the roof of the cab to go higher again. I looked at my watch. 'Jaysus,' I said. 'It's twenty past one.'

'But sure you're not going 'til two o'clock!' he says to me.

'I know, but by the time I change, get ready ...'

'Sure what changing is in it?' he says. But he knew what he was doing. He was keeping my mind off the game. We finished anyway, I thought we'd never get to Ballinasloe, but we did. I got up to Dublin that night and where other fellas were getting sick, all nerves, I could hardly keep my eyes open, slept like a baby. It didn't knock a stir out of me for the next day either. It was a lot easier than piking hay, I can tell you! But strength yes, and size. Farrell always said, give me a good big fella over a good small fella.

Did you have preset plans for defending the left-wing with Sylvie Linnane?

No, there was a system alright where if Sylvie ever had to leave his position, go across to take a man coming through the middle, I'd drop back to the corner, automatically. We didn't mind a fella getting a point from outside, but we wouldn't allow the free run on goal. We went up to play Offaly in a tournament game in Dunshaughlin. It was before the All-Ireland semi-final of 1985 or '86, we were still trying to establish a team. Mick Coughlin was playing centre-back for Offaly, Eugene [his brother] was gone to full-forward. Mick got a ball and went off on a lazy solo run, passed midfield, passed Mac on the far wing, then the little terrier [Sylvie] left from behind me, took off. I went back to his corner to cover the defence. Mick saw Sylvie coming from ten yards away, handpassed in to Brendan Bermingham who put it over the bar. At the same time as the ball was going over the bar, Sylvie was meeting Mick, doubled him over with a huge hit – he had never stopped running. Mick was on the ground, writhing in agony. Eugene came running out.

'Linnane, you're a filthy bastard!'

Sylvie looked at him. 'Don't you ever forget it!' In fairness to Eugene, all he could do was laugh.

I remember though when I got the number five jersey first, and Sylvie got the number two, he wasn't really too impressed at what he saw as demotion [Sylvie had been going for wing-back himself].

'You have it now,' he said. 'You'd better be ready to look after it.'

I'll be honest with you, I was half afraid to make a mistake there. Sylvie was a bit of a legend, I was afraid he'd come out and clock me! But he was a great corner-back.

Where to stand in relation to your opponent

Under their puck-outs I'd always start behind the wing-forward – whether I finished behind him or not was another thing. I'd always put him between me and the ball to start with, then anticipate whether Coleman [Galway midfielder] was going to win it. If he needed help I'd be in front of my man, but I'd never be more than a yard away from him, if I could help it. I'd never be one to drift. If he wasn't going anywhere, I wasn't going anywhere.

Did you try to bully your opponent?

Physically I would, yeah. I'd breathe down a fella's neck, impose myself on him if I could. I would always have a presence around him. I wouldn't talk, though meself and Leahy [John, star Tipperary forward renowned for getting 'involved' with the opposition] would have a good chat alright, but he talked with everyone, everything came out. In fairness to him though he wasn't as bad as he's often portrayed to be. He was like a good dog, if you knocked the dog out of him you had nothing – take that aggression out of him and you had nothing left. Leahy was at his best when he was playing in your face, when he really hated you. He was a great hurler.

Tricks

The only trick I had was to come straight out through fellas. Route one, that was the Finnerty sidestep! I remember we played Kilkenny in an All-Ireland final, some fella came on me, hit me a flake right across the shin, off the ball. The next ball I got, I came out and there he was, facing me, his little bony chest stuck out. Well I hit him, drove him five yards back and he was rocking there like someone who was hit with a stun-gun. I never heard of him again afterwards. I just hit him the once, a square solid shoulder, I could hear his bones crunching! But I didn't have jersey-pulling, anything like that.

Tricks seen

Niall McInerney [a Clare-man who played for Galway] was brilliant at the little jersey tug and brilliant at getting inside someone's head. If someone was out in front of him, he'd give him a little tip in the back just as he was catching the ball. Nothing serious, just a tip. I remember he was coaching us in the vocational schools final, he'd tell us: 'Stand on the side of his shoe when the ball is coming. Put him off.' He'd also tell us: 'When you're going up to catch the ball bring the hurley up to protect the hand, but bring it down as well!' You see the Kilkenny lads doing that now, but they bring it back. Tommy Walsh is brilliant at it, when he goes up for the ball, he brings everything down on you, everything, and he does it with skill. A great player.

Primary advice to a promising youngster, above all else, to master the wing-back position

If he has all the tools, then you need strength, power, physique, and in the modern game, you need a big engine. You have to be able to take punishment; you must be able to dish it out. Rambo with a hurl!

Ball in hand, the glance upfield *– where's Johnny Dooley? Brian Whelahan in action against Eoin Quigley, Wexford in the Guinness Leinster Senior Hurling Championship Final in Croke Park, Dublin, on 4 July 2004.*

Where Pete Finnerty was an enforcer at right-half-back, Brian Whelahan was the stylist. They had a lot in common, but each commanded their position in very different ways. They both had Lamborghini engines, plenty of horse-power, but Pete was the Lamborghini tractor, Brian was the sports car.

BRIAN WHELAHAN
(b. 1971, Birr and Offaly 1989–2006)

AWARDS & MEDALS WON
1 Team of the Millennium (right-half-back)
2 Hurler of the Year (1994 and 1998)
4 All-Ireland senior
4 All-Star awards
2 All-Ireland minor
1 National Hurling League
2 Railway Cup
1 Oireachtas
4 All-Ireland senior club
7 Leinster senior club
11 Offaly county senior

First position
I started with Birr at corner-forward with Johnny Pilkington [another famous Birr and Offaly star] in the other corner. It looked at that stage as if those were going to be our permanent positions. We struck up a great partnership, even though we were both very young. As we got older, we grew into more central positions. I only started hurling in the backs when I was a bit older and a bit bigger. I went to centre-back with the club, Johnny to midfield, and we stayed there. I was hurling minor at centre-back in 1989, there as well in '88, but pushed out to the wing. I played at corner-back for the U-21s, before progressing to the seniors.

The transition
In 1990 Paudge Mulhare took over the Offaly senior team and for the first few games in the league, I was at corner-back. Martin Hanamy was

in one corner, Eugene Coughlan at full-back, and they were looking for another corner-back. They were wondering if Aidan Fogarty, who had played there the previous year, would rejoin the panel; I played a few games there, then progressed to the wing and was left there. We hadn't a great year in the league in 1990, but we beat Kilkenny in the championship and that set me up.

What was your favourite position?
I always preferred centre-back. I played there for the club, but with the county it worked out well on the wing. We had Hubert [Rigney] at centre-back and he played a very physical role, everything that came up the centre was stopped in its tracks.

Martin Storey [Wexford centre-forward] said that also
Yeah, he'd kill you. My father [Patjoe] is from Banagher, my cousins lived beside Hubert, so I'd have known him from very early on. We'd go to Banagher and give them a hand with their turf, or whatever. They'd have done the same with us, though that wouldn't stop him from giving you a clip if we were playing each other! Just before an U-21 game one year, I had damaged an arm on the Friday beforehand and there was a big hullaballoo about whether I'd be playing or not. I cut the plaster of Paris around the fingers so I could catch the hurl. I was going fairly well early on, in at corner-forward. Hubert was in the other corner, [and] after about ten minutes he came over on me. The first ball that came I went to pick it, it flew away from me, the left hand in the cast. As sure as night follows day Hubert was pulling, right down on the cast! We had a few words, but we got it sorted.

He apologised?
Oh he did, yeah! Hubert was the kind of fella that didn't like to let you pass him, but I always felt he was a very fair player. Let's just say that if he got a knock he felt was unfair, he wasn't shy about giving it back. You had to respect that in a player.

The qualities needed to be a top wing-back
In the modern game you have to be strong in the air. Secondly, you have to be a good reader of the game. Pace is important too but really, you have to be an all-rounder. In the modern game you could find yourself anywhere in the back line, especially if you're asked to do a specific job on a specific player.

Would you follow or would you stay zonal?

I'd recommend following a man from one wing to the other, but I wouldn't change lines. I don't like to see a wing-back ending up in the corner, for example. A wing-back addresses the ball totally differently to a corner-back. The first reality for someone in the full-back-line is to be strong, secure his position. A wing-back needs to be aware of his man, has to help out his full-back-line, but he's also the launch pad for attacks. He's got to be a good distributor. The half-back-line breaks down attacks, sets up attacks and very often it's the quality of the ball coming from the half-back-line that will decide a match. There's no point in you having two half-backs playing in the corners and two stoppers on the wings, still doing their own job of marking their men but not doing the rest.

Where to stand in relation to your opponent

Under a high puck-out I stood just inside his catching shoulder – he couldn't push you off. Nine times out of ten you were on a good ball-winner, so it wasn't about winning clean possession, it was about breaking the ball down to your own advantage. The low ball situation, I'd try to read whoever was hitting the ball and break accordingly. You took a calculated risk – you couldn't take an out-and-out gamble, because if you missed you were in trouble. Again it's a reading situation. If a ball is coming from left to right your aim was to be in position to cut out that diagonal ball. I wouldn't be goal-side all the time, but I'd be aware. I'd be trying to get that edge you need, take a step towards where you think you need to be but always being aware you might have to step back. At county level a step is enough, for the back or the forward.

How important was Michael Bond [new manager, came in from the blue after Babs Keating had resigned] in Offaly winning the 1998 All-Ireland final? A lot of people give him very little credit.

No one knew Michael Bond. The first training session, I was late. I didn't even notice him, got togged really fast and someone told me this lad had been appointed, Michael Bond. 'Michael Bond me arse,' says I, 'Who's Michael Bond?' Went out on the field and the first thing I saw was the white cap that he wore. He called us together and he had this expression in Irish [he was a teacher], '*Mar sin, mar sin* – like that, like that.'

We did a few exercises and he called us together and announced, 'Now lads, we have nine weeks to get ready to win the All-Ireland …' With that there was a loud, spontaneous burst of laughter – from everyone.

'In the name of Jaysus, where do you think you're going? We're the laughing stock of the whole country and he thinks we're going to win the All-Ireland?'

But he kept saying it and in those nine weeks he instilled the confidence back into the team that had been totally eroded [heavy Leinster final defeat]. The second night he was with us, he told us he couldn't believe our demeanour, a team that had played in two of the previous three All-Ireland finals and won one, how lacking in confidence we were. He brought that back to us.

Tricks

Martin Hanamy had a habit of tapping a fella in the elbow when the forward was going up in front of him, about to catch the ball; or he'd pull the jersey back, by the arm. Little tricks like that, that the referee wouldn't see. Tap down on the hand, the hurley hand or the catching hand. I think players learn themselves what they have to do to survive at the top level.

Tricks seen

Everyone had their own little trait and if you watched them long enough you'd see it repeatedly. Paddy Delaney and Ger Coughlan had a great understanding from playing with their club. Delaney would go up, make it look like he was going for the ball, but he was actually letting it through for Coughlan to pick up. He got criticism for that, fellas thought he was missing the ball but it was deliberate on his part, good play, his wing-back there to collect.

Brian Corcoran [Cork centre-back] hardly ever went to bat a ball. I think he tried to catch everything and one thing we learned was that trying to pull against him was useless. He was one of the best men you ever saw to protect his hand. If you went up to catch with him though, that was totally different. Go back to our game in 2000 [Offaly had a surprise win over Cork, then the reigning All-Ireland champions] and Gary Hanniffy, after trying to pull on the first ball and getting nowhere, went to catching, and had a field day. You just have to read players, read their tricks.

Primary advice to a promising youngster, above all else, to master the wing-back position

Obviously they should be looking at the top hurlers in that position. Study them, try to emulate them. When you're out the back of the house, try to visualise what Tommy Walsh or John Gardiner – or whoever you aspire to be – did in the last match and try to master that skill. Also, the big thing is you have to have a hurl in your hand every day, particularly as a youngster because you won't have the time as an adult. You have to be going out to the wall every day practising the ball skills. It has to be something you love doing. If you love it, you'll repeat the exercise over and over again. If you don't, you won't improve as much.

Liam Doyle was the quietest of the three heroes who manned the half-back-line for Clare during the heady years from 1995 to 1999, but his value was recognised by all his teammates, by the team management, but most of all perhaps, by a succession of opponents who struggled to make any headway against a man who combined pace, power and hurling skill in one potent package.

LIAM DOYLE
(b. 1968, Bodyke and Clare, 1989–2002)

AWARDS & MEDALS WON
2 All-Ireland senior hurling
2 All-Star awards
1 All-Ireland junior
2 Railway Cup
1 Oireachtas
1 Clare county intermediate
1 Clare county junior

The qualities needed to be a top wing-back

I suppose most people would say speed, although this didn't apply in my own case! You have to be thinking the whole time, watching the play, and you have to be ready to break, take a chance, a calculated risk. Anticipation is very important in that case, you're hoping the ball will come to where you're breaking. Skill is important, as is man-marking. You have to be on your guard the whole time. The handpass is used very often around this area and if you lose your man, if he gets a handpass a few yards away from you, you're probably not going to catch him.

Where to stand in relation to your opponent

The ball would dictate that. If it was a high ball, you'd stand behind him, a low ball you'd take a chance on breaking in front. You'd have to weigh up every situation, make a split-second decision; I had no set place where I'd stand in every circumstance.

***Clare's unsung
hero** – Liam Doyle
breaks free, while
Tipperary's Paul
Shelley is held up by
Seánie McMahon.*

Tricks
Oh, none. I was very naïve, I always played the ball! I suppose I pulled
the jersey once or twice, especially if a fella had a yard start on me,
just a tug. A couple of times too, under the dropping ball, I might have
lowered the swing a couple of inches. John Power [Kilkenny centre-
forward] didn't mind getting a dig or two before the ball landed – well,
neither did I, nor did I mind giving them either. But you wouldn't get
away with as much now as you used to, it's a lot more exposed.

Tricks seen
Brian Quinn in Tulla, when he was corner-back he always had the
jersey caught, always.

Primary advice to a promising youngster, above all else, to master the wing-back position
Attack the ball; work on your first touch so you have that confidence
to attack.

1968 National Hurling League final – *'The Day Tipp Attacked' as one Kilkenny media-man put it. Ted Carroll (Kilkenny) on left, and Pa Dillon, with the hurley posed over his shoulder, in conversation with their Tipp opponents – Babs Keating, in Pa's case. Meanwhile, Jim Treacy looks to the fallen Ollie Walsh. Although neither was actually sent off, Ollie and Tipperary's John Flanagan were later suspended for six months each following an investigation into events surrounding this incident.*

Centre-Back
The Pivot

Pat Henderson (Kilkenny)
Pat McGrath (Waterford)
Liam Dunne (Wexford)
Seánie McMahon (Clare)

The most decorated All-Star at centre-back is Ger Henderson from Kilkenny, with four. There are those, however, who would argue that, magnificent and all as he was in that position, Ger wasn't even the best in his own house! Ger's big brother, Pat, won just two official All-Star awards at centre-back, but then Pat was already a household name before those awards began in 1971. Between 1963 and 1967, Pat won three Cuchulainn awards, sort of pre-All-Star all-stars: two of those at corner-back, one at wing-back. Considering that there were no awards of any description between 1968 and 1971, when he was at his peak, that's some achievement. Centre-back on the Kilkenny Team of the Century (chosen in 2000), by his own admission Pat wasn't as physically powerful as Ger, but then few were. He was strong, however, had both size and strength, and he had hurling – oh, he had hurling.

PAT HENDERSON
(b. 1943, Fenians of Johnstown and Kilkenny 1964–78)

AWARDS & MEDALS WON
1 Kilkenny Team of the Century (2000, centre-back)
1 Hurler of the year (1974)
5 All-Ireland senior
2 All-Star awards
3 Cuchulainn awards (pre All-Stars)
1 All-Ireland minor
2 National Hurling League
5 Railway Cup
3 Oireachtas
1 Leinster senior club
5 Kilkenny county senior
1 Kilkenny county intermediate (football)

First position

The club I came from, we almost started it ourselves. We started a junior club, a poor junior club – in fact there were three junior clubs in the parish, none of them any good. I was a student at Thurles CBS, playing Harty Cup and I could almost decide myself where I was going to play. Initially I played anywhere there was a need to play. I started off when I was only sixteen, corner-back on a veteran, a fella about 6 foot 2. He was a real gentleman – minding me and playing on me at the same time! In 1968 two of the junior clubs joined together to form Fenians, joined by the third club eventually. I don't think the question even arose as to where I'd play, I went into centre-back. The first game I played with Kilkenny was in New Ross, I was centre-back on Jim English. Tony Doran came on for Wexford, also a young lad – that was 1963. I was twenty-one, Doran was probably about nineteen.

In college I played in a variety of positions but I felt most comfortable at centre-back. Comfortable also at corner-back, but more so at centre-back. The switch from centre to corner is far easier than from centre to full. You're picking up a lot of broken play at centre-back, from your wing-backs and midfield – at corner-back you're doing the same. At full-back you're in a holding position, you have to protect your goalkeeper, you can't be as adventurous. At corner and centre you can read the play and go for it, you can take chances, take on the breaking ball. At full-back that is often too big a risk, the consequences if you fail are far more severe.

The qualities needed to be a top centre-back

The most important one is to have good ball control. You're meeting the ball in the air and on the ground, but if you let that ball behind you you're giving a fierce advantage to all the forwards – the wings, the full-forward coming out, the corners. You must have good ball control and by that I mean being able to stand into the dropping ball and take it, either into the hand, or break it back to midfield with the hurl. If it's coming low and hard, you've got to be prepared to go and meet it, block it, even if a guy is pulling hard on it – you can't let it through.

There were exceptions – Liam Dunne didn't have the size, so he'd often play to let the ball through and have his wing-backs pick up the ball behind. We did a bit of that as well, but as a rule I'd like to see the centre-back stopping that ball.

Defence is an art. Learn how to block, to hook, to get in the way. Tommy Maher, the old coach here, told us a hundred different ways to block someone, and then he'd tell you, 'Don't make the mistake of trying to rise it after blocking it – get rid of it!'

Where to stand in relation to your opponent

Under the opposing puck-out I'd stand under the ball, try and anticipate the drop and let him worry about me. I always liked to position myself so I was coming into the ball, not backing back. The ball dictated where I stood, the centre-forward was irrelevant. If he went to the sideline, I wouldn't go with him, leave him off.

Tricks

One of the lads I really hated playing against was Kieran Purcell, here in Kilkenny. He was as strong as me, if not stronger. We were training in the park one day, Purcell was catching everything. I tried every-thing, couldn't push him out of the way. I flaked at the hand as he was going up, no difference. Then I got a tap on the shoulder – Pa [Dillon, full-back]. 'You're pulling on the wrong hand!'

102 Hurling – The Warrior Game

'What do you mean Pa?'

'Pull on the other hand, the one that's not catching the ball and see what happens!'

The next ball I just tapped the other hand, on the hurl – the ball dropped behind me. That broke his concentration. It wasn't about playing a dirty stroke, it was about breaking his concentration. There's so much involved in catching a ball – the timing, the jump, the catch. There's lots you can do to break into that sequence. Even just rubbing against a guy's back before he makes the catch, anything to break his concentration at the last second. Once the ball drops you're in a position then to do something about it.

When we were playing Cork, Fan [Larkin] on Ray Cummins, I'd drop back under the high ball for the set pieces, blind him [Cummins]. You could nearly have considered every ball Con Roche got as a set-piece, because you knew he was going to burst out and blaze it down on Cummins, so you'd be making your way back straight away. Once it was on the deck Fan was the master.

In 1964 I was only starting off on the team, played wing-back. Then one day, against Tipp, Fan was dropped, Pa got dropped – the whole frigging full-back-line was dropped. I was picked in the corner, on Seán McLoughlin. Coming out of Mass that morning, I got a light tap on the shoulder.

'C'm 'ere boy,' an old lad said to me, 'You're going up to Thurles to play against McLoughlin today. How are you going to hurl him?'

'God I don't know, sure we'll take it as it comes.'

'You won't,' he said, 'He'll make an eejit of you! When he puts up the hand to catch the ball, don't mind the pulling, just put your hand up beside his as if you're going to catch it as well and give his hand a little tip – the ball will go wide!' And that's what I did. These lads didn't hurl at the highest level, but they studied the game, they had the knacks. Nothing done with the hurl, done with the hand. Fan used to do that with Cummins, just push his arm aside, at the shoulder.

Tricks seen

Willie and Eddie O'Connor were brilliant at what I call the half-free – the little push in the back, the tip. Then there was Fan, coming out with the hurl up like a hatchet, like he was going to split the forward, then stopping at the last second – that put many a forward off his stroke! We played Galway in Thurles in a league semi-final, Fan was on Paraic Fahy. There was often a bit of needle between Galway and Kilkenny in those years and they had a bit of a boxing match, Fan and Fahy. John Moloney, the referee, comes down, 'Fan, I'm putting you off.'

'Oh Jaysus John!'

'No Fan, I'm putting you off. You hit him a box – it was the manly thing to do, but I'm putting you off!'

Primary advice to a promising youngster, above all else, to master the centre-back position

Never let the ball pass if you can. Stop the ball in the half-back-line and half the work is done. If you can take it cleanly, fine, but block the middle, put your body on the line, don't let it through.

Jim Treacy on the ball, Fan Larkin about to hold off Frankie Nolan from Limerick and Pat Henderson with a watching brief in the All-Ireland Senior Hurling Championship final in Croke Park, Dublin, on 1 September 1974.

I don't know if it was the best individual display I've ever seen, in any position, but it certainly made the biggest impression: a league game in Waterford, 1981. I was full-forward for Cork (an abbreviated inter-county career), Pat McGrath was centre-back for Waterford – he gave an exhibition. Everything that came down the middle, whether in the air or on the sod, was his, gathered in with a flick of the wrist then sent back whence it came with added interest, every clearance acclaimed by the huge crowd. One trick he performed that day I'll never forget. In the midst of a crowd of players, having lost his hurley, he stood over the ball, back-flicked it up in the air between his heels, then handpassed directly out to a colleague, who belted it downfield. The crowd? Went wild. Cork? Went home subdued, beaten.

PAT MCGRATH
(b. 1953, Mount Sion and Waterford, 1971–86)

AWARDS & MEDALS WON
1 National Hurling League (Division 2)
4 Railway Cup
7 Waterford county senior

First position
Corner-forward when I was younger, then I moved out to midfield. I started off in the local street leagues when I was about six. When I was about eight, I played U-14 at corner-forward.

The transition
Up to minor I was midfield but from about eighteen on I was in the half-back-line, with the club and the county. Left-half-back to begin with in the early '70s, Jim Greene was centre-back but when he went I moved to centre-back. I preferred wing-back, you can attack more; at centre-back you have to watch your position.
What's the difference between the wings?
I don't think there's too much in the difference really. It's just that I was started at left-half-back and you tend to stay there then. But any position in the half-back-line would do me, and I played in all three.

The qualities needed to be a top centre-back

You have to be able to tackle. In my time anyway you couldn't just stand out of the way and let a fella through, you had to be able to tackle.

When you say tackle, did you tackle the man or the ball?

Well, you could take both! At times you had to tackle the man. You were centre-back, you couldn't just let a man come running through, step out of the way and stick the hurley out – he'd just break through that. You had to stand your ground, put the shoulder down and hit. You had to time your tackle right too. Centre-forwards were all big strong men, if you didn't get it right they'd just burst you out of the way.

You had to be able to read a game. I remember Seamus Power used to tell us, if you had a centre-back who was a bit slow, the two wing-backs had to cover for him. Let him look after the centre, anything coming behind let the wing-backs get it, two fast fellas or whatever. And that understanding in the half-back-line is critical.

Where to stand in relation to your opponent

I liked to stand beside him, but at certain times you had to stand behind. If the ball broke short you had to be ready to break out as well. I preferred to stand on his left, don't really know why. I suppose you could guard against him, push him off. I held the hurley in my right hand, was stronger off my right, though I could strike off my left.

Tricks

Under the high ball you had to know how to block a hurley and go up for the catch, and you learned that from experience. Even the ref throwing in the ball for a hop ball; getting the hurley down, block his pull, get down on one knee and pick the ball as the ref is throwing it in. All that kind of stuff. I did a lot of handpassing in the half-back-line, the dummy handpass where you catch it again, but sometimes you can look like an eejit, accidentally hit the ball.

Tricks seen

I saw Philly Grimes catching the ball behind his back and I did it a few times myself. Not in inter-county games, but in club games you'd try it, try and catch the ball behind your back while you were running; it looks good when it works.

Pat McGrath, former Waterford star centre-back
and father of Ken and Eoin on the current side.

Diarmuid O'Sullivan did it against Wexford?
Yeah, but Grimes did it deliberately, and I did it a lot in training. A fella hits the ball, you take off, catch it behind your back, keep going. I remember Seamus Power saying to me, 'Feck sake Mac, you could hit the ball from anywhere!' and maybe sometimes I overdid it. You might want to make it look too fancy maybe.

Primary advice to a promising youngster, above all else, to master the centre-back position
He'd have to learn how to read the game. It comes naturally to some kids, and you can see that even when they're very young. But I think it could be taught also. Get out there with the young fella, have a makeshift game, show him the different things that can happen around centre-back, how

he should deal with it. Get him thinking about his game the whole time, anticipating rather than reacting, judging what's likely to happen.

What's the biggest change from your day?

I think fellas have more hurling now, better strikers, they're hitting the ball a lot further. Different ball too, different game. Television has changed things. In our day if someone was acting the maggot you could sort things out off the ball – you can't do that anymore, it's shown on telly over and over. A lot of the dirty play is gone out of the game which is a good thing, but sometimes it goes too far. I don't mind hard hurling, but even the shoulder is gone.

Ken [Pat's son, current Waterford star] is a handy centre-back but I tell him, 'If a fella is coming through, put the shoulder down and let him have it.' He won't do that, he's not great to give a shoulder. 'Alright,' I say, 'Just stand in front of him then and if tries to run through you, you're going to get a free. He's charging you.' The problem is that a lot of the time you don't get that free. A fella running through with the ball, you should be able to stop him, stand in his way and stop him. Some fella coming straight through, how do you stop him shoulder to shoulder? Are you supposed to just get out of the way?

One of the questions I asked in every interview was about picking a team, and in almost every interview, the name Liam Dunne came up. Why? Well, because almost everyone felt that centre-back was the pivotal position, and that it needed a man of stature, a physically commanding figure. Liam Dunne defied that logic. He wasn't tall, nor was he particularly powerfully built, but Liam Dunne won three All-Stars in the half-back-line, all on the wing. In 1996, however, when Wexford finally made their All-Ireland breakthrough, Liam was the man in the number six shirt, as he had been for some years before, as he would remain for years afterwards. You don't have to be tall, do you, to be a giant? Liam Dunne was that.

LIAM DUNNE
(b. 1968, Oulart-the-Ballagh and Wexford 1988–2003)

AWARDS & MEDALS WON
1 All-Ireland senior
3 All-Star awards
2 Railway Cup
6 Wexford senior county
1 Wexford hurler of the year (2003)

First position

I started at left-half-back, [Martin] Storey was at right-half-forward, and fellas were constantly on to me why I always cleared the ball over to his wing. Apart from the fact that diagonal ball was usually the way to go anyway, Martin was the man up there most likely to win it! Then he was moved into the centre, I was moved into the centre, and that suited us as well. That was the first time I ran into John Power of Kilkenny – he was one hardy boy!

The transition

I started with Wexford in 1988 at wing-back, then was gone for two years, came back to wing-back in 1990. I finally moved into the centre in 1991, but that was after they had tried everyone else there. Mick Jacob from my own club would have been the last really established centre-back for Wexford, but when he left they had problems replacing him. So many different fellas were tried, but no one seemed to last very long. I remember one night saying to George O'Connor, 'Jaysus Christ, would they ever try me in there?' I was already playing there for the club and doing alright, but I suppose when they looked at me they didn't see a centre-back. I'm 12 stone now, but I was only 11 stone then, and not tall – hardly the ideal centre-back. If I got a euro for every time a fella has said to me since 'God I always thought you were a bigger man, you togged out bigger anyway!', I'd be a rich man. Power was only a light fella as well, but he was up around the 6 foot mark, gangly, a raw hardy farmer and I felt the full whack of that many times!

What was your favourite position?

Centre-back, you were in the thick of the action the whole time. Fellas told me I was able to read the game but often you took a chance, tried to be in the right place at the right time, hope the ball would break your way. But I was fortunate too in the fellas I had alongside me, fellas like Seán Flood and Larry O'Gorman. I said in my own book [*I Crossed the Line,* with Damian Lawlor] that Larry was as good a hurler as I ever saw. He took a lot of the pressure off me at centre-back, especially under the high ball. He was the catching man, he'd come in and take it while I got out of the way, wait for the breaks. Sometimes you'd make a balls of it too but that was the understanding we had. When Larry came in I'd never go for the ball. It worked the other way too; if I was going for a ball they had no business coming in and if they did, I'd spend a few minutes afterwards eating them.

My brother Tomás was on the wing for a while, Seán [Flood] went back to the corner and I worked things out with Tomás as well. You get the centre-field man to come back and help you. Often you'd find yourself on the likes of a John Power or a Declan Ryan [Tipperary] – good men, and you needed help, you needed that understanding. In the All-Ireland semi-final of 1997 I remember standing behind Declan Ryan at one stage and trying to look up the field. I couldn't see anything! He was so big, wide, a huge man. I had to stand well to one side of him, but he was a very effective player.

The qualities needed to be a top centre-back

Oh, size and strength! That's what I was always told anyway, size and

No messing, first-time ground clearance by Liam Dunne against Dublin in the Guinness Leinster Senior Hurling Championship semi-finals in Thurles, Paul Codd leaps out of the way.

strength! My mother got me Tim Flood's book for Christmas – a fine book too *[Autobiography of Tim Flood]* – goes right back to John Keane of Waterford, the Rackards, all those, and he singles out Mick Jacob at centre-back. But he has a bit in it that he couldn't leave the centre-back position out without mentioning myself – 'He was fearless, brilliant and dangerous!' The way he [Flood] finished was that if you're good enough, you're big enough.

I think the big thing is being able to read the game. It doesn't always work out for you, but you take the chance. Over the years I'd have people saying to me, 'The ball always seemed to be where you were,' but it was the opposite case. You always tried to be where you thought the ball was going to land or to break. It wasn't accidental.

Did that come from knowing the fellas you were playing with and against, or purely from instinct?

A bit of both, really. From knowing the fellas up the field you'd know from early on what was likely to happen in different situations, but I would have been watching games all through the years, games in which I wasn't involved at all, watching how other defenders were playing, what they'd be doing. It might be Kilkenny against Offaly, other fellas would be following the game but I'd be studying the backs on both sides, watching what they were doing when they won the ball, where they were likely to clear it. When we met them, that's the kind of thing you needed to know.

People will say to you, 'Sure it was easy for you, hurling came natural to you,' but they ignore all the hours of practice you did, hitting a ball off a wall, all the years of hard training to reach the level you were at. They see you in the winter, struggling in league games, but then come the spring you get back into the swing of it again. Natural ability is fine but you have to really work on it. Watching other players is the important thing, learning from them, picking up things.

Communication is vitally important also, talking to everyone. Kilkenny were masters at splitting defences, a forward racing to the wing or the corner, two defenders running after him, and next thing they're coming up the middle, into the space. You'd learn more from watching Kilkenny than from anyone else, they were masters at it. We learned to deal with that, so that when a Kilkenny-man went, whoever went after him – whether it was Tomás, Seán, Larry – one of us would immediately take his man. Didn't always work, but they were good at that.

Where to stand in relation to your opponent

That depended on the game, on the opponent, on the situation. In 1994 we went eleven points down against Dublin in the second half, but we equalised at the end. I got the last point. I was standing behind Ciarán Barr that day, he was just pushing me all over the place. The next day, after getting advice from Tom Neville [star Wexford defender of the 1950s], I stood back about eight yards under their puck-outs, and now

I had the advantage. I could come in and bat the ball, or tip it down or whatever, and he didn't know where I was coming from.

Tricks

The dummy handpass coming out, that would be one I suppose, and the sidestep, put a lad the wrong way. It might go the wrong way for you too and you'd end up being crucified coming out!

And what of the ones the referee didn't see?

Well, I always got caught! Martin Storey always played the hurl, last second under the high ball. Even in training he does it.

I was hurling in the Railway Cup against Connacht one day in Ballinasloe, on Joe Rabbitte. Brian Whelahan was at right-half-back and Willie O'Connor at left-half-back. I was wondering how I was going to handle Rabbitte, Whelahan came up to me before the match – Willie was there as well.

'They're going to pump everything down on top of yourself and Rabbitte,' he said, 'And he's going to try to catch everything. You just come in behind him as if you're batting the ball and hit his shoulder, the catching hand, and put him off. We'll be coming in to pick up the break.'

I did, it worked, and Joe wasn't happy, he got awful mad. But that's the kind of thing you do.

Primary advice to a promising youngster, above all else, to master the centre-back position

We brought a young lad to centre-back with the minors last year [Liam is involved with Wexford minors], only a chap, sixteen, but he was the best we had to catch a ball. As the games went on he was meeting hardier fellas, but he got good experience. I didn't have to tell him an awful lot, but there were times he was going in on top of the wing-backs, going for ball that wasn't his. I got him to think a bit more about that. But centre-back has to be the boss, he has to be the organiser of that area.

'The Bertie Ahern of hurling' was how Ger Loughnane described Seánie McMahon in his book, **Raising The Banner.** *'The most cunning and the most ruthless of them all!' And Ger wasn't done. 'If Seánie was in the mafia,' he continued, 'he would be a killer. He'd be a babyface killer.' Without question, Seánie was the linchpin of an outstanding Clare defence, the backbone of those two All-Ireland titles in the 1990s, but a killer? When you meet him in civvies that's not at all how he strikes you, not remotely. Soft spoken, the innocent face, and yet, and yet – there's many a transformation takes place when a man crosses the white line. Some grow, some diminish, some become lambs, many a pub blusterer exposed over the generations, and then there are those whose whole personality changes. Seánie McMahon, the Incredible Hulk? Incredible alright.*

SEÁNIE MCMAHON
(b. 1973, St Joseph's Doora-Barefield and Clare 1993–2006)

AWARDS & MEDALS WON
1 Hurler of the year (1995)
2 All-Ireland senior
3 All-Star awards
3 Munster senior
1 Railway Cup
1 Oireachtas
1 All-Ireland senior club
2 Munster senior club
3 Clare county senior
1 Clare county intermediate

First position
When I was younger I played in different places, but it was at about nineteen that I went into the centre, and I loved it. I felt I didn't have the legs for wing-back, a different position. In the Munster final of 1994, against Limerick, I started at centre-back but was switched to the wing at half-time. Mike Galligan got five points from play off me in the second half! I suppose I wasn't aggressive enough, but that match

Shall not pass. Will not pass – *Seánie McMahon stands strong against Waterford's John Mullane in the Allianz National Hurling League game played in Fraher Field, Dungarvan, County Waterford, on 26 March 2005.*

taught me a lesson. The ball could be coming down the middle, the centre-back and centre-forward contest it, the ball would break and the wing-forward would just take off, be gone. The wing-back has to see that break. Someone like me would be just standing there, waiting, and that's how all the scores were got off me that day. The other time I was moved out of the centre was in 2002, against Tipp, on Tommy Dunne, only about ten minutes to go. A ball broke off the centre-back, Tommy was gone like a shot, over the bar – I was still waiting. There's a big difference between centre-back and wing-back.

The qualities needed to be a top centre-back

I'd say you need physique anyway, definitely did going back to our day, though I think the position has changed a lot in the last few years. Go back to 1997 and '98, you had a Declan Ryan, Joe Rabbitte, at centre-forward, and more often than not the ball was going to be pucked down on top of you. Today you have a Niall McCarthy, dragging you to the sideline, the ball being driven to the other sideline. But you need physique. You need to be able to read the game also, that's probably more important. You look at someone like Liam Dunne; he was physical, but he wasn't big, relied on reading the game. There's a few things that can overcome lack of size: skill, determination, aggression, all of that helps. If you're reading the game well, that's a huge advantage. Look at Tommy Walsh [Kilkenny star]!

Where to stand in relation to your opponent

Ball and man would decide that, a combination of the two. Generally if it was a high ball you'd like to position yourself to attack it, but you'd probably be behind, regardless of whether you were on a big lad or a small lad. I wasn't that great to catch a ball so I'd probably be using the hurley. For a low ball I'd like to be standing beside the centre-forward at least.

Tricks

I had one, again with my friend Joe Rabbitte. He was a big man, good in the air. When the ball was in the air but going over our heads, instead of dropping back immediately I'd hold my ground, keep him outside. It kept me out of the play as well, but I knew one of the two boys [Doyle or Daly] would be in the vicinity to sweep up.

Another trick is if you were on a fella who liked to catch the ball, just put an elbow on his shoulder at the last second, keep his arm down.

Primary advice to a promising youngster, above all else, to master the centre-back position

Master the skills, and that applies to every position. The most important thing is reading the game but I don't know how you coach that. After that, the skills – catching, striking with left and right, good delivery.

Cork captain Ray Cummins prepares to make his speech after being presented with the Liam MacCarthy Cup by GAA President Con Murphy following Cork's victory against Wexford in the All-Ireland Senior Hurling Championship final in Croke Park, Dublin, on 5 September 1976. Also pictured are: (front row – left to right) Pat McDonnell, Tom Cashman, Charlie McCarthy, Denis Coughlan, Eamonn O'Donoghue and Mick Malone; (back row – left to right) Cork County Board Chairman Donal O'Sullivan, John Horgan, Martin Coleman, goalkeeper, Gerald McCarthy, Brian Murphy, Seán O'Leary and John Allen.

Left-Half-Back
The Artiste

Len Gaynor (Tipperary)
Denis Coughlan (Cork)
Anthony Daly (Clare)

How unlucky can you be? Len Gaynor won two All-Ireland senior hurling medals and he's grateful for both, as well he might – it's a proud addition to any sporting CV. Had Len been born a few years earlier, however, he might have ended up with five or six of those precious Celtic Crosses. In 1961 and 1962, Tipperary won the All-Ireland; 1963 they were beaten by a very good Waterford team, but in 1964 they were back, won Munster and All-Ireland again. That year Len Gaynor was just coming on the scene, however, he won an All-Ireland U-21 with Tipp [the first U-21 championship].

By the following year, still U-21, he was on the senior team and another senior All-Ireland crown was won by Tipperary, the first for Len, the fourth for most of his team-mates. He would wait until 1971 for his second, but it was only then the real drought was to start. It would be another eighteen

119

years before Tipperary won its next senior All-Ireland.

During his own career, however, Len was recognised as one of the finest half-backs around. He won three Railway Cups with Munster when that was still a hugely prestigious competition, in 1968, '69 and '70, the second of those as captain.

LEN GAYNOR
(b. 1944, Kilruane McDonaghs and Tipperary 1964–74)

AWARDS & MEDALS WON
3 All-Ireland senior
1 Cuchulainn award (pre All-Stars, no awards in 1968–70)
1 All-Ireland U-21
2 National Hurling League
3 Railway Cup (1 as captain)
4 Oireachtas
3 Tipperary county senior
   Managed his club to 4 Tipperary county senior and
   1 All-Ireland senior club title (1986)

First position
I started off at corner-forward, went down to St Flannan's and was corner-forward there.

The transition
I remember one day in Flannan's the trainer came to me and says, 'We're going to try you at wing-back.' I said fair enough, went to left-half-back. There was no particular reason, maybe because as a right-hander you were moving into the centre to strike. But that was it, I never moved out of there again. I really loved it, a smashing position to play. You had a man to mark but at the same time you were free and easy, covering the centre, shoot down the troublemakers. I felt that if you really studied the play you could come to anticipate a lot of the action, a lot of the trouble, whether down your own wing or diagonally across. You could really get yourself in to position early to clear the danger.

The qualities needed to be a top left-half-back

Sharpness. First of all, you had to be very sharp, very alert. Half-back was the first line of defence in those days. If the ball passes you, the team is in trouble, you're in trouble. You're facing the wrong way, you now have to chase back after the ball, try to retrieve, where the forward is headed in the right direction. Stop the ball at source before it got past you, be nippy enough to do that.

Is it critical to be a good hurler here?

Yeah, you needed that bit extra. You had to stop your man from scoring but you were also probably the primary source of supply for the forwards. If you got any sort of decent clearance at all, you could reach all the way up to the full-forward line, so you needed to be a good all-round hurler. You needed left and right, a sharp swing to be able to clear the ball under pressure.

Where to stand in relation to your opponent

Behind, if I knew it was going to be long and high – if I missed the ball I wouldn't miss him, I knew I would be able to hold him anyway. I remember against Kilkenny one day, Ollie Walsh, a fierce wind, I actually started back at the end-line when he was taking the puck-out, got to it around the 21, and won it. I was moving towards it, which gave me the advantage. If Ollie was there today, he'd be scoring points! I saw him one day, ball going well over the bar, he reached up with the hurley, one hand, killed the ball stone dead down into his hand, cleared it. Ah, he was a great one. Great feet also, as had Skehan – probably a better keeper, but didn't have the same feet.

Tricks

No tricks! I remember one day alright we were to play an inter-county match, cold enough ould day, and before the ball was thrown in I was shuffling in my position, just sort of jogging on the spot. The fella I was marking started doing the same. 'Is this fella taking the Mickey now or what?' I thought. 'Is he just mocking me, trying to psych me out of it?' I kept shuffling but started moving forward a few steps, backwards a few steps. He started doing the same. 'Alright,' I thought, 'if that's what you want, let's go,' and I then started going around in little circles, tighter

*Len Gaynor (right) gets between Jimmy O'Brien and the
ball in the 1965 senior All-Ireland final against Wexford.*

and tighter – he did the same. I'd stop suddenly, turn and go the other way – he followed. And I had him, now he was dancing to my tune!

There was another one; with the club one day, coming out with the ball hopping on my hurley, there was a fella running with me and I knew he was going to pull. Just as he did I hopped the ball a little bit higher – he went under it with the pull. I kept going, felt him coming again, felt the pull and [this time] I dropped the hurley down a bit – he went over the ball. I did that about three times and every time he pulled he missed the ball – I got a kick out of that. Club hurling was tough for the inter-county player at the time, every fella wanted a go at you.

But I wasn't really into tricks, pulling the jersey or anything like that. A guy who was good at catching, I might get the hurley across his face, cover his eyes, little things like that, especially if he was a big lad – once he lost the vision he wasn't going to make the catch!

Primary advice to a promising youngster, above all else, to master the left-half-back position

Concentration. That's a thing that's often neglected, but it's crucial, watching everything around you, knowing what was happening at all times. No matter where the ball was, keep your eye on it. If the ball goes wide or in for a score, watch the keeper. He might give a glance down the field, now you have an idea where the ball is going to go, even before he has it in his hand. I'm assuming you have all the skills, so now you have to make best use of them – concentrate. You see a back with the ball, about to open the shoulders to clear – reverse a bit, get into position for the long ball. Be aware at all times, reading the game – concentrate.

Elegance, that was Cork's Denis Coughlan. A dual player, member of Cork's All-Ireland-winning senior football team of 1973, Coughlan was a wing-back of superb athleticism. He could leap like a stag, had an outstanding catching hand, sweet striker off left and right – made-to-measure, really, for left-half-back.

DENIS COUGHLAN
(b. 1945, Glen Rovers and Cork 1965–80)

AWARDS & MEDALS WON
1 Hurler of the year (1977)
5 All-Ireland senior (4 hurling, 1 football)
4 All-Star awards (all hurling)
4 National Hurling League
2 Railway Cup (1 hurling, 1 football)
1 All-Ireland U-21 (hurling)
3 Oireachtas
1 All-Ireland junior (football)
2 All-Ireland senior club (both hurling, 1 as captain)
7 Cork county senior (5 hurling, 2 football)

First position
I started off at centre-back, played there for most of my young career. Even as a young senior player with the Glen, against the Barrs in 1967, I was there. Then from 1968 to 1974, I was centre-field, nowhere else. I retired from inter-county in 1974, came back, and played left-half-back, and that then became my favourite position.

The transition
I always felt – even as a youngster, without knowing anything about the game – that left-half-back would have been my most natural position. In 1975 I was still retired from inter-county hurling, Blackrock beat us in the county final up in the 'Dyke. A month later the National League was starting, Cork were to play Tipperary, again up in the 'Dyke, with Páirc Uí Chaoimh being renovated. Christy Ring had just been appointed a selector with Cork. Without even being asked, I was told

that I was playing centre-back against Tipperary, and I did, played probably my best ever game in that position. Afterwards I met Ring and he said to me, 'You won't be playing centre-back anymore, you'll be playing left-half-back'. He told me they had Johnny Crowley in mind for centre-back. I don't think he even knew Johnny at that stage, but already he had his backline set in his mind.

What's the difference between left wing and right wing?

There is a difference in the half-back-line, but there's an enormous difference between the two corner positions. I don't know if you need to be a great hurler to play right corner, but you do need to be a particular type of hurler, a spoiler. The ball doesn't naturally go to the right side of the field, I think it falls more often on the left and you need to be a good hurler to play on that side, in the left corner, left half – and I'm not trying to say here that I was a superior-type hurler! But you need to be able to read the play there, that's very important.

Did you ever play right-half?

I did. I played my last two years with Cork at right-half-back. They switched myself and Dermot McCurtin, 1980 and '81. It is different. When you're a right-handed hurler playing at left-half-back and the ball falls between the centre-back and the centre-forward, it's very easy to come in behind, pick it up on your right side and clear it. Even for a good two-handed hurler it's more difficult to come in from the other side.

The qualities needed to be a top left-half-back

You need to be able to read the game. Of all the positions in the field that is most critical here. You've got to be able to anticipate what's going to happen fifteen or twenty seconds before it happens. I always maintained that if you know how to play your position, you know how to win, and that goes for every position. The ball can only ever come to you two ways, it can come high, it can come low. At left-half-back if it comes high, you must be behind your man, not beside or in front. If you anticipate it coming in low, be in front. And if you were reading the game properly, if a goalkeeper for example was about to clear, you should know even as he hits it where it's going to go and what type of ball it will be. And I think that was one of my strengths, I found it easy to read the ball.

Finnerty had his square marked out, bossed that area. Did you?

I did, absolutely, I played the position. There was no point in being over in the right-half-back position unless you absolutely had to be there.

Did you see your primary job as keeping your man scoreless or being the linkman to the forwards?

Oh, to keep my man scoreless, always.

What was your best trait? Your catching ability?

Maybe, but I'd say my anticipation, that was my forte.

Was football an advantage? Ray Cummins [another Cork dual star of the period] said yes.

Funny enough, I didn't find that at all. I played midfield for both hurling and football for Cork for about seven years, in the late '60s/early '70s. During that period the Munster finals would alternate, the hurling first one year, with the football on the following Sunday, the football final first the next year, the hurling on the following Sunday. What I found was that if the football final was first, I was training with the footballers up to that final, and you'd take up a certain position on the field in anticipation of where the kickouts would land. The following Sunday then you're playing hurling, but it would take me a long time to adjust to the puck-outs, where they were landing. That was the hardest adjustment.

Where to stand in relation to your opponent

The coaching manual will tell you that you always keep the forward outside you – I always, always, kept him inside. And the forward didn't like that, he naturally expected you to keep him on the outside. I always felt if you could keep him inside you, you had half the game won. Most of the clearances came down the line and I always had half a yard at least on him then, and if the ball did go inside me, the centre-back and centre-forward were there already, that slowed everything down.

Tricks

I discovered very early in my career that I had no tricks. I couldn't hit anyone. If someone hit me, I didn't have the knack of hitting them back, I just suffered it. I didn't get hit a lot though, I'd have to say. I don't think I ever missed a match through injury.

Martin Coleman clears against Kilkenny, watched by teammates (from left) Martin Doherty, Brian Murphy and Denis Coughlan with Matt Ruth of Kilkenny in the background in the All-Ireland final in 1978.

Tricks seen

Before the 1969 Munster final, on St Patrick's Day, the Glen went to Carrick-on-Suir to play Carrick Davins. Mick Roche was with the Davins, centre-forward, I was centre-back with the Glen. A ball was coming down off the air and I don't know how he did this, but he ended up with the two hurleys – my hurley and his – in one hand, caught the ball with the other. I couldn't figure out how he did that, but I made sure it didn't happen when we met again in that Munster final. I'd come in a fraction of a second late with my hurley, so he didn't get that opportunity again! But that was a good one.

Primary advice to a promising youngster, above all else, to master the left-half-back position

Know your position, know how to play your position. If you don't know how to play, you don't know how to win, and that applies to any sport, any position.

If you don't know where you're going, how do you know when you've arrived?

Exactly. Watch videos of games, study your position, the great players there. I studied Tom Cashman when he was only a minor, and I was thirty then. I'd watch Pat Horgan in the Glen at the same age, because you can learn from anyone. When you go to a match, study the play in your position, study the players, and learn.

What was the best advice you ever got?

Know in your mind before you go out how to play your position. All I had on my mind were three or four things, advice given to me by Ring. 'Messages' he called them, you needed to have only three or four messages in your mind. That was all.

Like golf, don't confuse yourself with too many thoughts when you're standing over the ball, just trust your knowledge?

Yes. I came up with the Glen, one of the best clubs in the country, but for the most part you were left to your own devices growing up, you learned as you went along. It wasn't 'til the autumn of my career that I started to get these little gems of advice, from Ring. Know your position, know how to play your position, know how to deal with the different kinds of ball that come to you, know when to go, know when to stay.

You gotta know when to hold 'em, know when to fold 'em?

Exactly!

'No longer the whipping boys of Munster hurling!' That was Anthony Daly's memorable proclamation after Clare had beaten Tipperary in a tumultuous Munster hurling final of 1997. It was their second title in three years but only their third in sixty-five; many decades of frustration ended. Crucial to that success was the confident leadership provided by Anthony Daly, confidence that was best encapsulated in the final tense minutes of the 1995 All-Ireland final. With the game still in the balance, Daly came forward to take a 65, overruling the claims of the regular long-range free-taker, Seánie McMahon. He speared the ball between the posts and secured Clare's first All-Ireland senior title since 1914. In its way, a far bigger statement than that of 1997.

ANTHONY DALY
(b. 1969, Clarecastle and Clare 1990–2000)

AWARDS & MEDALS WON
2 All-Ireland senior (both as captain)
3 All-Star awards
2 Railway Cup (1 as captain)
1 Munster senior club
5 Clare senior hurling

First position
I started in the corner, grew up there. I won a Harty with Flannan's in the corner, won about three championships with Clarecastle there [also won an All-Star with Clare], but after 1994, I suppose your man [Ger Loughnane, Clare manager] felt they needed changes in the half-back-line.

The transition
Myself and [Liam] Doyle were the corner-backs in the 1994 Munster final, but Loughnane moved the two of us out to the two wings for 1995. It's funny how it happened. Doyle started in the right corner against Cork, I was outside him on the right wing but I was getting a bit of a roasting in the air from Mickey Mullins [Cork wing-forward] – five

catches I think he had. John Chaplin was on the left wing and he was in trouble as well, so we were switched. At half-time John was taken off, Doyle was brought out to the right wing. I think Frank Lohan came in at corner-back and that was the six that was there for the next few years – O'Halloran/Lohan/Lohan, Doyle/McMahon/myself.

I wasn't that happy about it at first. After winning an All-Star in 1994 at right-corner-back I was bulling about the move, to be honest. I was saying to meself: 'What's he doing to me at all?' I had a few very bad games there, was bad in the league final, was poor enough against Cork in that Munster semi-final, I was getting really frustrated with it. Wasn't I grand and happy at number two – why wasn't I left there? I had a good enough Munster final then, and it's funny how one game can change your mindset, give you a bit of confidence. I got to like it then, always preferred it after that.

Was it your favourite position?
It was, for a finish. You didn't have the same responsibility there that you had in the corner, as I got older I came to realise that, and appreciate it! When you grew up in the corner you didn't mind it, but when I was out on the wing, Frank Lohan behind me, Ollie Baker in front of me, Seánie McMahon to my right – there was a bit more comfort in it!

The qualities needed to be a top left-half-back
A few good lads around you! It's very different to the corner in that you feel you have more responsibility to set up things up front, you're sort of the launch-pad for attacks, whereas in the corner you're almost totally negative, your primary goal is to stop the corner-forward. At wing-forward you must get on the ball a lot more.

You needed to be able to handle the opposition puck-out, which I wasn't good at in the beginning. It was a real culture shock to me to be under puck-outs! A corner-back under puck-outs? I was more used to bursting onto the ball, me and my man. I learned to adapt. I never became a good catcher and in the beginning fellas used to make a lot of catches off me, that first year especially. Mullins against Cork – those five balls he caught off me. I was trying to break his fecking hand, but he was still catching it! I learned for a finish just to go up with the hurley, one hand, break it down to yourself – we were good on the ground then. But you did that, you adapted.

That was one of the qualities needed at wing-back, you needed to be able to read the game a bit better on the wing. Mind you, that's changing now, the corner is a different position to when I played there. It's all about being first to the ball now, whereas in my day it was all about keeping your man outside you. You need vision out there too. What was such a great help for me was that there was such stability around us. It was always Baker and Lynch in midfield, Seánie and Doyle across the line, Frank and Brian Lohan behind. The only change really was Brian Quinn for Mikey O'Halloran in the corner, but he was on the panel anyway.

Right wing against left, corner against wing – is there a difference? I didn't find it. I'd have played any side – left, right, corner, wing. I was just happy to be playing, but Johnny Callinan [outstanding Clare half-back of the 1970s, double All-Star winner] always said to me that number seven was the easiest position on the field – you could see the game, and if you were a right-handed hurler, which I was, you were coming onto your strong side down the middle. But I was comfortable on my left as well.

Reach for it, get in the hook *– Anthony Daly on the trail of Liam McGrath, Tipperary, in the All-Ireland final in Croke Park, Dublin, on 14 September 1997.*

Where to stand in relation to your opponent

Half a yard in front, if I could. If the ball was at the other end I'd be having war with my man, trying to get in front. If he went too far out then I'd just drop back, ten or fifteen yards behind him, get him wondering – always mind games.

Tricks

Sure, if I could put a fella off his game I would, but despite what people say, I never got involved in verbals with anyone unless they started it. I never started a bollicking match, though I've met people over the years who gave me a hard time over that. People talk about a match against Cork and Seánie McGrath in the 1998 championship. I had a fella come up to me on holidays one time and accuse me of having said things about Seánie's mother – I never did. In fact, Seánie McGrath invited me to his wedding! But I had marked him twice earlier that year, in the early rounds of the league and then again in the league semi-final, and he had beaten me both times.

'Right,' I said to him at the start of that one, 'what's the game today? I'll give you two points, and any point you get more than that I'll buy you ten pints for it during the course of the year, but if I get one, it counts for two of yours!'

'Right, game on boy!' he said. After he got his second point I said, 'You're getting close kid!'

'There's definitely three or four in me, mate!' he said, but there wasn't. We took over the game after that. I remember then I got a massive point, from about 95 yards, a launcher, could have gone any-where, and I turned to him: 'Oh boy, that has to be worth five points!'

'Ah, you prick you,' he said, under his breath. That's how it ended up, and maybe I did put him off that day, but the rest of them – ask [Johnny] Dooley, ask [Tommy] Dunne, did I ever get onto them – I didn't. Now Johnny Leahy …

But I didn't go in much for tricks, tipping the hurley, the push, the pull. [Liam] Doyle was king of that, but he'd get away with it. [Brian] Lohan was deadly at it, where I'd probably be caught, and all you're doing then is giving away frees and I hated that. There was an uncle of mine and that was always his advice to me – don't give away frees! Let them hit it and they might hit it wide, but if they have any kind of free-taker at all, all you're doing is giving away an easy point. I always agreed with that as a player and it's something I carried into management, I keep saying it to the lads. I always counted a free given away and scored as a point conceded, while some eejits don't see it like that at all. If they give away six frees but they're not marking the free-taker, even if he converts all those frees they still think they're holding their man scoreless. Stupid! They prefer to give away a definite point from a free, don't want to be seen to concede a point from play, when they should be just trying to defend, maybe put a fella off his shot.

Primary advice to a promising youngster, above all else, to master the left-half-back position

Depends on the type of player he is. My successor at left-half-back with Clare was Gerry Quinn, a super player, but very different in style to me. Gerry is an athlete, very strong, very fast, an animal in the air. A fella like him I'd be telling to forget about doing anything fancy, to just beat his man, and you're almost guaranteed then that he'll do that, and he'll get in his clearances. Either way, you must mark your man first, that's the number one priority. Don't give away frees. Even inter-county forwards can miss from the wing, especially under pressure. Learn how to frustrate, learn how to dispossess. Above all, don't let the ball past you in the half-back-line. Puck-outs – if you can't catch it, kill it, keep it in front for the midfielders to win. Break up the play on that line.

Autographs of the players – *The Wexford team that defeated Cork in the All-Ireland hurling final by 2-14 to 2-8 at Croke Park on 23 September 1956.*
Front row (left to right): Tomas Ó Riain, Mick Morrissey, Jim English, Art Foley,
Tim Flood, Tom Dixon, Seamus Hearne.
Back (left to right): Billy Rackard, Mick O'Donnell, Ned Wheeler, Jim Morrissey,
Martin Codd, Nicky Rackard, Padge Kehoe, Bobbie Rackard.

Midfield
The Athletes

Ned Wheeler (Wexford)
Richie Bennis (Limerick)
Gerald McCarthy (Cork)
Patjoe Whelahan (Offaly)
Pat Critchley (Laois)
John Fenton (Cork)
Johnny Pilkington (Offaly)

By all accounts, the Wexford team of the 1950s/early 1960s that won three All-Ireland titles were mountains of men, freakishly big and strong in an age when people generally weren't as big as they are now. That was a time when 6 foot, 15 stone and seventy years of age were benchmarks for great height, great weight and great age. Well, they weren't nearly seventy, but many of that Wexford team met the other two criteria, and some exceeded it. On the matter of height, Ned Wheeler certainly did, and still does. He now also meets and exceeds the third benchmark, a healthy seventy-six. As for the 15 stone, if it's still there it's all solid muscle, honed by thrice-weekly trips to the gym.

NED WHEELER
(b. 1932 Faythe Harriers and Wexford, 1949–65)

AWARDS & MEDALS WON
3 All-Ireland senior
3 National Hurling League
4 Railway Cup
4 Oireachtas
3 Wexford senior hurling
2 Wexford senior football
1 Wexford junior hurling

First position
Middle of the field, club and county, although I played centre-back as well as I got older. You didn't have as much running to do.

The qualities needed to be a top midfielder
In my day the main job was to keep the ball flowing into the forwards, the first-time pull in the air and on the ground – keep that ball moving. The idea was to catch the backs unawares, leaving the forwards to do their work. I played midfield with Jim Morrissey and we never caught a ball. We pulled overhead, we pulled on the ground – didn't always connect, but the ball was kept moving and the forwards were delighted with that type of ball. What turned me off catching the ball was an incident against Tipperary in the 1951 All-Ireland final. We were going fairly well, then a few minutes before half-time, a ball hopped about 8 inches off the ground in front of me. I put down my hand, caught it, the referee blew me up, gave a free against me. He thought I picked the ball off the ground. It was only two minutes before half-time. Pat Stakelum came up and took the free, they scored a goal inside, and that score destroyed us. I swore after that I'd never catch a ball in my hand again.

Sideline pucks are very important for a midfielder, but that too seems to have almost disappeared, although you still see one or two who are good at it. But Jim Morrissey could cut a ball over the bar from 80 yards, and I'm talking about the old ball. I'm totally against all that lifting now, in midfield and everywhere else. When you see the referee having to continually stop the play to throw in the ball, you know there's something awful wrong with hurling. And that's happening, there's too much bunching, several players rooting at the ball. Rucks, that's what they are, and why? Because the ball is being held up. Isn't it a lot easier on the system to keep it going, let the ball do the work? Getting rid of it first time is so much easier on the body. You're not running with it, you're not poking at it, pushing at it, caught in a ruck. The minute it landed in your area it was gone, and you had a breather.

Then you see all these fellas nowadays falling on the ball, for a throw-in. You wouldn't see that thirty or forty years ago, far from it. If you threw yourself on the ball you were taking your life in your hands.

The throw-in, you see a fella sticking in his leg and going down to catch the ball, getting a belt across the legs for his trouble, but also getting a free – why? Isn't it supposed to be a clash ball? Why is the guy who goes for the clash and pulls, penalised? Then you see the fella who goes up to catch a ball and again, the fella who pulls is penalised. Those frees that aren't frees at all are discouraging first-time pulling. The minor final of a couple of years ago, 2006, Galway against Tipperary, the Galway half-back put his hand up to catch a high ball, the Tipperary half-forward pulled on the ball – free for the Galway-man. That's disgraceful. The referees and the system are penalising the overhead stroke. You see lads now, even at inter-county level, going up for a ball without even protecting the hand.

I remember Nick O'Donnell [Wexford full-back], playing against Galway around the early 1950s. He cleared the ball, Nicky Rackard got it at the other end and put it in the back of the net – wasn't that speed? How many pucks did that take, how many seconds to work the ball from one end of the field to the other? In 1954, three of us from Wexford were picked on the Leinster team. Tim Flood, Mick Hanlon and myself, we played the cream of Munster, and that ball never saw grass for the hour. We won by four points, nine points to five was the final score and Jim Langton – lovely man, wonderful hurler – was corner-forward that day. He had won his previous Railway Cup medal in 1941, thirteen years earlier. That was the Ring era, Munster had won every Railway Cup in the intervening years, with the exception of 1947 when Connacht won.

Where to stand in relation to your opponent

I always tried to be in front. I was mostly left-handed, but a strange thing – I'd take a sideline puck with the left hand, but I could not take a free with my left side! I'd take it but it could go anywhere.

Tricks

I wasn't into that at all. Maybe I didn't have the intelligence.

Tricks seen

Billy Rackard was a bag of tricks. I'd play on him in training, he'd lie on you, he'd fall on you, he had all the tricks that the ref couldn't see. Ring was another. I don't think he ever did the same thing twice in a row.

Primary advice to a promising youngster, above all else, to master the midfield position

I'd tell him to keep his eye on the ball at all times, keep his concentration; and I'd tell him to use the hurl and spare the body. The solo run is very taxing on the body – years ago you earned your solo! The likes of John Doyle and those fellas waiting for you? It took a brave man to put the ball on his hurl.

Jack Lynch used to tell the one about the Tipperary keeper with the stammer, Tony Reddin, a Galway-man. Jack was newly elected to the Dáil, was coming to the end of his career, playing corner-forward. You start [your career] at midfield, into the half-forward-line, then full-forward, and now there's only one line left to cross! Jack was on the Rattler [Mickey Byrne, Tipperary corner-back] and Reddin was inside, having an outstanding match, catching everything and clearing it the length of the field. Cork were going badly. Willie John Daly was at centre-forward and at half-time Lynch said to him, 'Send in a few low balls and I'll test Reddin.'

Now that wouldn't be Jack's style, but he was probably getting desperate. A low ball came in anyway, Jack side-stepped the Rattler – which wasn't an easy thing to do – and just as Reddin cleared the ball, Jack hit him, hard. Reddin turned around – 'Ly-Ly-Lynch,' he said, 'If-if-if you try that again there'll be a by-election in Cork next week!'

I thought that was brilliant, to come out with that in the heat of the moment.

It will be argued forever: 1973, dying moments of another torrid Munster final. Favourites Tipperary and Limerick had gone at it hammer and tongs for two exhausting halves of top-class hurling and it all came down to one 70. Up stepped Limerick midfielder Richie Bennis, rose, struck. To this day, there are people – and not all of them from Tipp either – who are adamant that the ball went wide. Marginally wide, but wide. The umpire, however, raised the white flag. A point for Limerick, and victory. That year they went on to win the All-Ireland, their first since 1940, their last to date. It was a seminal year for Limerick and for Richie Bennis, currently manager of the Limerick senior hurling team.

RICHIE BENNIS
(b. 1945, Patrickswell and Limerick, 1964–78)

AWARDS & MEDALS WON
1 All-Ireland senior hurling
1 All-Star award
1 National Hurling League
2 Railway Cup
10 Limerick county senior

First position
I played every position for Patrickswell in championship, including goal. We were in fourteen county finals and won ten. I played in the forwards for the county, but ended up in midfield. I played minor for Patrickswell in the minor city final in 1958 when I was only thirteen, corner-forward. In 1962/'63, when I was still a minor, I was put in corner-forward against Tipperary in a senior match in Bruff – on Kieran Carey! He nearly killed me! I can still visualise it!

The qualities needed to be a top midfielder
Positional sense was very important then. In my time the puck-out landed around midfield and you had to be there to contest it. Now, midfield tends to be bypassed. The main thing for the midfielder then was: on their puck-out you stopped the ball from going through; on your

own puck-out you kept it going. That was the basic. Overhead play was very important. Some fellas loved to catch the ball, but I loved to pull, especially on the dropping ball from our own puck-out. On their puck-out, I'd bat it. You don't see a lot of that now, although in 1996, when Limerick beat Cork down in Cork – beat them well too – there was a fella midfield on Mike Houlihan, Seán McCarthy. Houlihan broke more hurleys belonging to McCarthy that day! McCarthy was no angel either. They were standing back and full length they were pulling on the dropping ball! I don't know how many times McCarthy was left with just the handle of his hurley. Houlihan had a very fast pull, though he never got the credit he deserved either for his skill. He was a fine midfielder.

The modern midfielder, it's all about work-rate, work-rate. It's important in every position now but it's critical in midfield, and they must still be able to read the play. Work-rate, stamina. It was just coming in in my day, but I was slow. Eamonn Grimes was the fast man, he did the running. I held my position, which allowed Eamonn a bit of freedom to roam.

Free-taking was important to me. It was a great way of building up your confidence when things weren't going well for you.

Where to stand in relation to your opponent

I stood off him, would then come in, maybe give him a slight bit of a nudge. I was 6 foot, 12-and-a-half stone in 1973, though I was a bit heavier in 1975, my last championship, at corner-forward. I copped myself on then, trained like a devil, got down below 12 stone. I was very disappointed when I never regained my position with the county.

Tricks

I had a share of them! When I was centre-forward I wouldn't be pulling on the dropping ball at all, I'd be pulling a few inches below it, letting it through.

Soloing with the ball, I'd pretend to handpass, wouldn't, dummied it, though I was blown for that a few times. Mick Slattery blew me up in the Munster final in 1973 when I had the goal at my mercy. I cursed him to the pits of hell! Only for he knowing me so well, I'd have been gone. I wasn't playing well, but I got through this one time, about 40 yards out,

Limerick manager Richie Bennis giving instructions during the All-Ireland Senior hurling final against Kilkenny at Croke Park in 2007.

drew Mick Roche [Tipp centre-back] then caught him with the dummy handpass. In past him, nothing between me and the goals – Slattery blew for a free. The dummy handpass fooled everyone, including the referee – the Tipp crowd roared, and I think that's what triggered his whistle.

I could catch the ball with either hand, which was a great advantage – sometimes I'd catch with my right, sometimes with my left, so your man didn't know which side to stand on [Richie's nephew, Gary Kirby, had the same trick]. I'd always coach a half-back – stand on his catching-hand side. He can't push you off, and if the ball drops, you're on the right side for the break.

At the throw-in I'd never pull. I'd stick my leg out, go for the catch. Often, when the other fella pulled across your leg, you'd get the free. In that Munster final of 1973, for the winning point, there was a throw-in ball and Liam O'Donoghue was going in for it with Len Gaynor – a young fella on an ould fox. I told Liam to go away and I went in. Whoever won that throw-in was going to have a huge advantage, be in a position to set up the winning score. I stepped across the ball and, lucky enough, I caught the ball, soloed, passed to Frankie Nolan, he took a shot and it was blocked out for a 70, the winning 70.

Was it a point?
Definitely, it was at least a foot inside the post, and I'm not just saying that.

Tricks seen

Mick Roche and Gerald McCarthy were very good at this: they'd stand behind you, then at the last second they'd come around you, to the front. You'd be all set but they'd come in, take the ball. Gerald was a gifted hurler, good strong man.

Primary advice to a promising youngster, above all else, to master the midfield position

Do as little soloing as possible, use the ball intelligently but keep it moving. Don't ever lose concentration. I was listening to Christy Ring giving a half-time talk to Glen Rovers in a tournament game in Charleville in the early 1960s – he was playing corner-forward himself that night. I sneaked over and listened, and he was laying into them: 'Never lose concentration, never take your eyes off the ball, even if it's gone 40 yards wide. Keep your eyes on the ball at all times. If you're after taking a shot, whether it's gone over the bar or waved wide, don't stand there admiring it or giving out about it – watch for the puck-out, straight away.'

That left a big impression. It drives me mad when I see fellas turning their back to the ball, walking away. Watch the ball, get straight to your position.

Those who grew up in Cork in the late 1950s/early '60s endured some very lean times. In 1954, Cork completed their third three-in-a-row and were considered to be, along with Tipperary, the dominant hurling force. Then came the second longest drought in Cork hurling history.

From 1954 to 1966, no All-Ireland title came to Cork. Even in Munster, they suffered defeat after defeat. One title was won in 1956, but Cork were then beaten by Wexford in one of the most famous All-Ireland finals of all – Art Foley's save from Christy Ring and all that. For the remainder of the period, however, humiliation on humiliation, most of it inflicted by Tipperary. Then came 1966. A band of kids, nearly half the U-21 team, not a legend in sight. Ring had retired in 1964, aged forty-four. He was still one of the top forwards in Cork in 1966, but turned down a place on the bench. Game by game, the kids started to build.

A shock defeat by Limerick put paid to Tipperary, but Cork struggled to get past Clare in the first round and played two games before prevailing. They then met Limerick in the Munster semi-final in Killarney, Limerick the favourites, but there was another surprise. Two goals inside a minute – one from Charlie McCarthy and one from Seánie Barry – inspired Cork to a two-point win: 2-6 to 1-7. Against Waterford then in the Munster final, it was a two-goal win – Croke Park beckoned. Again, against a strong Kilkenny team, Cork were the underdogs, again they defied the odds, and a whole generation of young Cork hurling supporters won a reprieve and could begin to believe. Captain of that Cork team? One of the youngsters, a precocious Barrsman, Gerald McCarthy, who later that year would also captain the U-21s to All-Ireland success, is now the Cork senior hurling team manager.

GERALD MCCARTHY
(b. 1945, St Finbarr's and Cork, 1964–79)

AWARDS & MEDALS WON
5 All-Ireland senior hurling (1 as captain)
1 All-Star
4 National Hurling League
5 Railway Cup (1 as captain)
3 Oireachtas
2 All-Ireland senior club
4 Cork county senior hurling
1 Cork county senior football

First position

I played most of my hurling as a midfielder, with the Barrs in particular, but also with Cork. I won two All-Irelands in midfield, two at centre-forward, one at wing-forward, and the two All-Irelands we lost, I was at midfield and wing-back.

I started in the forwards with the Barrs when I was sixteen – wing-forward, centre-forward – but within a year or two I was in midfield, played most of the rest of my career there. It was so much a different game then, a much tougher game. The rule changes have been superb, they have speeded up the game and put the emphasis on skill. The days of just dogging it are gone.

Tough Barry [legendary Cork hurling trainer, Jim Barry] told us this one in London one year, when we were there for the Wembley tournament. He had transferred to Blackrock from a junior club, was playing his first senior game for them. He was a bit of a speedster, so they put him in corner-forward. First ball came in, he was getting ready to go, when he felt a hurley pressed across his neck from behind, bent him forward, almost into the ground. He was still trying to get to the ball but no use, it flashed out wide. Next ball, same again – hurley across the neck, forced forward and downwards, helpless again as the ball went wide. This went on for the whole game, he told us, neither himself nor the corner-back ever touching the ball. When it was all over, the corner-back walked over to him, hand out: 'Shake hands there, Jim boy. This is a great game – when you learn how to play it!'

The third-man tackle was a major cause of fights
Yeah, the main job for the full-backs was to keep out the forwards at all costs. Don't let them near the goalkeeper.

The qualities needed to be a top midfielder
Your main job is to connect with the back-line and send good ball to the forwards, fast ball. I was always a firm believer in fast ball, particularly for corner-forwards. The high dropping ball – no good, corner-forwards hated it. Even Ray Cummins, for all his height, didn't like it, he always preferred the ball out in front of him. Move it quickly for the forwards, that's what I tried to do. I think I mastered that, put a huge amount of practice into it. Even a ball in the air coming against me, I perfected the art of deadening it with the hurley, hitting it then as it dropped, not taking it into the hand or even putting it on the stick. That was very effective, I loved doing that. Doubling in the air as well, I enjoyed that. Quality ball, that's what you were trying to deliver.

Did you see yourself as an auxiliary back or an auxiliary forward?
A bit of both, really, but probably more so a forward, maybe because I played there so often.

Who played midfield with you?
Justin [McCarthy], Roger Touhy, quite a lot of fellas.

Roger, the small fella, the acrobat?
That's right. He used to do a handstand on the hurley before a game, put the hurley in the ground, put his head on the hurley and straighten up, legs in the air, balancing on his head on the hurley. I'd say a lot of fellas were quare worried when they saw that for the first time! I played a lot of minor hurling against Roger.

Where to stand in relation to your opponent
For our own puck-out, I'd try to lose my man. I'd try to get an advantage, arrange a signal with the goalkeeper, know where the ball was going to go and be on the move. Jim Power was good at that, so was Paddy Barry, and both of us in midfield would know what was happening. For their puck-outs, I'd stand in front of our half-back-line, be coming onto the ball, while keeping an eye on my man in case he had his own signalling system with his goalkeeper! But I'd try to stand behind him in that situation.

Thinking time for Cork coach Gerald McCarthy in the Guinness All-Ireland Hurling Championships in Thurles, County Tipperary, in 2007.

Tricks

None really, I was pretty straightforward. There were things you'd practise in training, not tricks really, just specific skills, like the one I spoke of earlier, deadening the high ball on the stick then striking it before it dropped, without catching, without putting it on the hurley again. That surprised a lot of fellas, gave them less time to block you or hook you – early ball into the forwards, one move.

I was much stronger on my right side, but I could use both. I practised off a gable-end wall on the street, Bandon Road, two fine gable ends at the top of our lane. We used to play in between those when I was a nipper. You needed an understanding neighbour though, sometimes you'd be shifted, all the thudding off the wall!

Tricks seen

You'd come across a few quare ones alright. We played in a National League final in Gaelic Park, against New York, and one of the Hennesseys from Kerry – I think it was Brendan – had this great knack of heading in towards goal, his back to the referee so that his hurley couldn't be seen. He looked like he was soloing, but the ball was actually in his hand. He was a demon at it, got away with it quite a lot.

Fan Larkin's hatchet: he often did bring it down! It wasn't always a dummy!

Primary advice to a promising youngster, above all else, to master the midfield position

Work on that fast ball to the forwards, the first-time pull on the ground and in the air, the ability to bring down a high ball and hit it before it hits the ground. Work on those skills, on moving the ball.

A lot of people would say that the classic midfield, as in Lyng and Fitzpatrick with Kilkenny, is still the best, that Jerry O'Connor and Tom Kenny, the two Cork midfielders, are freaks of nature?

In today's game almost the whole team has to have that kind of stamina, that kind of fitness. When I started playing hurling, the typical full-back-line would be big, strong men, tough men, didn't move too much from their own area. It's very different today. Your full-back might have to be one of your best hurlers, likewise your corner-backs; they're all very proficient hurlers now and fitness levels have gone through the ceiling.

The primary job in midfield remains the same, to link, to supply the forwards, help out the defence. But look at the number of really vital scores those two have got over the last few years for Cork by joining in the attack, very often linking up with each other, and at blinding speed. But that's something that only comes off a couple of times in a game. The primary job is still the same, to provide that link. They still do that, but when you have their kind of athletic ability, it's a huge advantage to be able to penetrate a defence with these runs.

How do they compare athletically today?

They're far fitter today, which is not to say that we weren't fit back then. Training was hard then too, but today it's far more scientific, far more specific to the different positions – really good.

You played in games where you were really fit, yet came off exhausted. Look at those games on TV now and they look pedestrian. Why?

I reckon we were so good that television just couldn't capture it! My kids heard so much about the 1966 All-Ireland, when I was captain, but there was a twenty-fifth anniversary 'do' down in Midleton, and we all got a presentation of a video of the match. The kids stuck it on and that ruined everything! They all thought we were supermen but now I got – 'Dad, ye couldn't puck the ball 30 yards!'

But the ball was so much heavier, the game was so much tougher, the cameras were so much different, not close to the action like they are today. Today they're pucking the ball to the half-back-line and beyond, regularly. That time it would take two pucks to get it that far, and that alone makes a huge difference.

The name Whelahan is synonymous now with hurling, with Offaly hurling especially, but long before Brian was winning hurler of the year (twice, in 1994 and 1998, the first player to do so), before he was named on the GAA hurling Team of the Millennium in 2000, long before his brothers Simon and Barry joined him on the Offaly team and on several Birr club All-Ireland-winning sides, there was Patjoe, a midfield star with St Rynagh's, Offaly and Leinster in the 1960s and '70s. Had Offaly managed to do what they threatened to do on several occasions during his playing years, what they finally managed to do just as he hung up his spurs, there is no doubt that people would have heard of the Whelahan name decades before Brian began to make waves. Since then, with eleven senior county titles with various teams in various counties under his belt, seven Leinster titles and four All-Irelands with Birr, Patjoe has established himself as the most successful club coach of all time. He also coached Offaly to their three minor All-Ireland titles, and several Leinster senior crowns.

PATJOE WHELAHAN
(b. 1945, St Rynagh's and Offaly, 1965–80)

AWARDS & MEDALS WON
1 National Hurling League (Division 2)
2 Leinster senior
10 county senior club
1 All-Ireland inter-firm

First position
I played mostly midfield with Rynagh's, centre-forward and midfield for Offaly. I preferred centre-forward.

The qualities needed to be a top midfielder
Two things we had back in our day were overhead hurling – the ball couldn't touch the ground – and ground hurling. Ground hurling was very important in midfield that time. That has changed completely now. There's no longer any ground hurling, and overhead striking is gone

from midfield.

A relationship with the goalie, you had to be able to read what he was going to do, for puck-outs and clearances. A good partnership is important. With Birr now we have Rory Hanniffy, great motor on him, he's absolutely fabulous, and we have Barry [Patjoe's son] alongside him, a great workhorse. That's a great midfield partnership, very balanced. You need that in midfield, one fella always staying back, and I'm always on to the lads about that. If one goes forward, the other always stays back. You never want to see yourself too exposed in midfield.

Where to stand in relation to your opponent
Well back, then come into it.

Tricks
We were playing Tipp one day in the 1960s, I was middle of the field on Mick Roche and coming near the end, we were winning by two points. I was hurling great the same day, delighted with myself. A high ball came down out of the clouds, we both went up, I came down with the ball in my hand. Bould yoke that I was, I turned around and showed him the ball. It was the wrong thing to do! Vexed he was, and in the next couple of minutes he scored two points from over 80 yards. That was telling me – you cheeky little bastard from Offaly!

The one-handed overhead flick, I did that, never let the ball hit the ground. Another one, we met a very good Kilkenny team here one year and beat them. I ran at Eddie Keher, flicked the ball over his head and ran onto it again, caught it, cleared it. I did the same to Pat Henderson another day – cheeky hurling, you'd get killed for it, like nutmegging in soccer. You'd do it the league, but not in the championship. Ah, I used to drive Pat Henderson mad, tipping.

Tricks seen
Fan [Larkin] was the best for tricks. I went in on him one day below in Kilkenny, next thing I knew he had my jersey rolled up on the handle of his hurl. I hit him with the handle of the hurl into the guts and it was like hitting the wall, he only laughed at me. 'Now Whelahan,' he said. 'Anywhere you go I go!'

I saw Keher one day, I played with him in Ballinasloe [probably

Patjoe Whelehan in action for St Rynaghs in the Offaly senior county final in 1964.

Railway Cup for Leinster against Connacht]. He was wing-forward, the ball was coming low up his wing, he turned and ran with it, caught it behind him with his hand turned backwards, so he was already heading for the goal.

Primary advice to a promising youngster, above all else, to master the midfield position

There's a chap I brought onto midfield in Limerick from an inter-mediate club, Donal O'Grady, and he was nominated for an All-Star last year. He came in to us raw, a left-handed hurler, but we improved him, made a midfielder of him. It's all about fitness now, positioning, about fast delivery to your forwards. You get a ball in the middle of the field and it has to go in, immediately. Look at Waterford, that never happens. If you're full-forward you might as well be out in the next field and that's why they haven't won an All-Ireland.

All of those featured so far in this book are from what would be recognised as the established hurling counties – Kilkenny, Cork, Tipperary, Limerick, Wexford, Galway, Offaly, Clare and Waterford. But what of the others? In many other counties, notably in the midlands but also up along the western seaboard, almost lost among their stronger football brethren there are strong hurling pockets. Laois is one such county.

One All-Ireland title, back in 1915 and two Leinsters – 1914 (beaten by Clare in the All-Ireland final) and 1949 (beaten by Tipp) – tell a story of little success, but also a story of little successes. There are others. In 1976 and again in 1996, Camross won the Leinster club senior hurling title; in 1979, 1986 and 1990, the same club reached the Leinster final and performed admirably before losing narrowly. In 1986 and 1996, it was the turn of Portlaoise to reach the Leinster final, although they were beaten in both; Castletown suffered the same fate in 1997. In other counties that would be a catalogue of failure; in Laois it's encouragement, a sign that at club level at least, they can still compete with the big boys.

On a smaller scale again, there is more encouragement. Over the years there have been many individual hurlers in Laois who have caught the eye of the All-Star selectors and earned nominations – James Young is the latest in that line. In 1985 it was the turn of midfielder Pat Critchley, and Pat went on to claim that award, the only All-Star, so far, from Laois.

PAT CRITCHLEY
(b. 1960, Portlaoise and Laois, 1980–91)

AWARDS & MEDALS WON
1 All-Star award
1 All-Ireland senior club football
3 Leinster senior club football
7 Laois county senior football
7 Laois county senior hurling
1 Limerick county senior football

First position

I started at corner-forward with the club at U-12, very young, and held the same position when I started with the county. My second year with the club I was outfield. I played every position from midfield forward; never played in the backs, though I've often wondered what it would have been like. I think midfield suited me. I wasn't a prolific scorer, got a few scores at crunch times with the club maybe, but my bigger contribution was work rate. I played a lot of sports – hurling, football and basketball especially – and that enabled me to reach a very high level of fitness that I was able to maintain throughout the year.

What was the major difference between the three?

I was in a good position in that as well as playing, I coached all three games. Basketball is probably the best game to coach, you have more control, it's all very tactical. Hurling can be over-coached. It's a very spontaneous game, free flowing, a free spirit to it. Football then is somewhere in between.

D. J. Carey played handball as a court game, reckons it is really beneficial to his hurling. Is basketball the same for football?

I think it's a great game to combine with all Gaelic games, even the hurling. Watching D. J. playing hurling you could see the handball influence, but I found basketball gave me very good peripheral vision and in a tight situation that's a great advantage, especially for the handpass, and that applies in hurling and football. It also helps you to read the play, but there are so many other elements. Blocking out in basketball is very physical, rebounding likewise, and again that can help you to stop a player from getting possession or spoil a player on the puck-out. I developed the technique in hurling, from basketball, of denying a midfielder possession, and once the ball hit the ground John Taylor would come in and sweep up. He was the half-back behind me with both club and county, probably the best player in the county at the time to take that kind of ball out. When you have a player like that around you, you don't need to win possession yourself, you just break it out for him.

I also played on John Taylor, my first league game with Cork, 1981 in Páirc Uí Chaoimh I scored 2-1!

I remember that game, Páirc Uí Chaoimh wasn't long opened. We actually beat Cork in the league a couple of years later, 1983, one of the best results ever for Laois hurling. It was played in Borris-in-Ossory because O'Moore Park [Laois county ground in Portlaoise] was being done up. We came from behind to win, I think that was our first competitive win over Cork since the 1915 All-Ireland final. My first year with Laois we beat Tipperary, came from a good bit down at half-time to do that, I think it was the 1981 league quarter-final. The emotion of that win, from the older people especially, was something else. Laois had got a big hammering from Tipperary in the 1949 All-Ireland final, we hadn't beaten Tipp since long before then, so again, that was a huge memory. For small counties like Laois these are milestones.

You were good in the 1970s and 1980s?

Yeah, we got to the 1985 Leinster final, but just at a time when Kilkenny were weak, Offaly became the bane of our lives. We ran them close several times after they had made the breakthrough, but we couldn't make that breakthrough ourselves. In the end we didn't even win a Leinster, which was a pity.

You played with Leinster?

I did, but the years I played with them, we never won the Railway Cup. I ended my inter-county career without a medal, a blank! A few tournaments maybe, the opening of pitches.

Which was your own favourite sport?

Hurling. I played National League basketball with Portlaoise, the Panthers, a very strong team coming up from juvenile. Brother Somers from Kilkenny started it off, something to keep us ticking over during the winter. We didn't have too many tall fellas, so we all had to be very versatile. Sometimes I played point guard, sometimes I was a forward, sometimes you'd have to post up. I found changing from one game to another brought a freshness, a new challenge, especially come the autumn when you were starting back to the basketball – you always had something to look forward to.

One thing I loved about hurling was the characters. The other club here in the parish, Clonad, had some great characters in the 1960s. There was a Conroy family, a cluster of brothers that formed the backbone of the team. Red Din was their father, he was over the team and they had great success around that time – Billy Bohane would have played before that. There was very bad blood between Clonad and Kyle, a few skirmishes. Red Din was riling the team up before they went out anyway, D'Unbelievables style: 'Now boys, Kyle are going to come out slashing. They're going to be slashing and they're going to expect us to retaliate. DON'T …' and he paused, the lads couldn't believe their ears, then he continued, 'DISAPPOINT THEM!'

The qualities needed to be a top midfielder

You have to have a big engine, that's number one. You need to be versatile, you need to be able to play as an extra back or as an extra forward, but you need to be able to read the game to decide when you need to drop back or when it's safe to go forward. You're the linkman, you must be able to read the game. You must know your own players, know what kind of ball the different forwards need.

Where to stand in relation to your opponent

I'd usually look to have my right shoulder on his left shoulder, which put me in the stronger position, able to push him off line and make the catch with my left hand.

Which side of midfield?

It depended on who you were picking up, but I didn't mind which side. If our goalie was pucking-out, I liked to leave a little bit of space between me and the sideline, and use that if I won possession.

Tricks

At club level Goggie Delaney was our goalkeeper. If my direct opponent was taking a long-range free, I'd go over to the other side of the field for the fast puck-out from Goggie and a good few times we'd get a point back immediately using that ruse. Even if it didn't work, that player would have to sprint across the field to get to me and as soon as that play was over I'd sprint back across to the other side again, keep him running, wear him down. That mental battle was there always.

I also used Chunky O'Brien's fake handpass a lot. I remember going to Boston for the first time in 1980. I went over from college for the summer, playing with Fr Tom's against Galway. I had only used that trick in training, hadn't had the right opportunity really to use it in a game. There was a lad with Galway, Big Jack was his name, he was kind of hospitalising lads he was so physical. I got a run through midfield, spotted him out of the corner of my eye coming hard for me.

I went as if to give a handpass, he came twice as hard but I caught it myself and burst on, just got out of the way. I heard the crash behind me as Big Jack ploughed into his own man. I kept going, got a goal as well, but that poor fella was taken off on a stretcher – it wasn't a good moment for Big Jack! That was the first time I used the fake handpass.

Another trick I had, and I kind of developed it unknown to myself, was the reverse pivot, from basketball. I'd win the ball and spin around the opponent. Sometimes it was to get in a strike, but mostly it was to beat them on a solo run. I started coaching hurling when I was very young and it was actually a couple of young lads who pointed out to me what I was doing – I wasn't even aware of it.

Tricks seen

There was talk that big Seán Cuddihy, who used to take the penalties for Camross, used to switch in a juvenile ball for those but we have no evidence of that! But that was a common one, the changing of the ball, Goggie would have a towel in the back of the net, he'd go down injured, change the ball. I remember when the Cummins ball came in at first, they created a bit of a stir – smaller rim, could travel huge distances. Goggie was fierce anxious to get his hands on one, so he could drive his puck-out further – and he had a good puck-out. The club couldn't really afford them, they were expensive enough, but my father got half a dozen. We were playing Seir Kieran [Offaly] in a practice match – we used to play them every year – and the ground was like concrete, very dry. The regular ball went over the bar and my father threw in a Cummins ball. 'Here Goggie, you're always talking about this Cummins ball, let's see what you can do with it!'

He landed it down on the other 21, was well pleased with himself, grinned over at my father. A few minutes later the ball was back up at our end, one of the Dooleys took a shot, a blinder, over Goggie's shoulder and into the net – nearly took the head off him. Bombed it out again anyway, came back up again, another blistering shot from one of the Dooleys, bang, back of the net again. My father was umpire, this ball had gone through the net. He went back, picked it up, threw in an O'Neill's ball – 'Here you are Goggie. Those All-Star balls are great to puck-out, but they're fierce hard to stop!'

When Nuri started first they came out with an experimental

all-weather ball. We got a few prototypes, had them down at the field trying them out in training and giving Nuri the feedback. In the early experiments they had fierce trouble trying to keep the speed of the ball down. After I finished playing with the county I was playing in San Francisco for the summer, and you'd always have to bring over hurls and sliotars with you when you were flying out. I went out to the back shed and there I found some of those prototypes, brought them over with me. They were dangerously fast, especially in the American conditions. I remember we played in one North American Board final and Ger Tynan, one of our mentors, switched the ball in for a penalty. It went through the net!

Primary advice to a promising youngster, above all else, to master the midfield position:

For the modern midfielder, if you look at Cha [Fitzpatrick, Kilkenny] for example, it's the ability to hit that long-range point, I think that's a crucial aspect now. Puck-out, catch, point – two strikes and you have a point, that's a big psychological blow to the opposition.

Pat Critchley (second from left) in action against Tipp in that historic National Hurling League quarter-final win in 1981. On the ground is Tadhg O'Connor (Tipp). Behind Tadhg is Michael Doyle (left) and P. J. Cuddy with a watching brief.

John Fenton is one of the few players to win five All-Stars in a row, a feat he achieved from 1983 to 1987. An elegant stylist, one of the purest strikers of a ball on the ground or in the air, John ended his career with a bang, captaining Cork to win the centenary All-Ireland in 1984. He was a winner again in 1986, before enjoying one of the greatest moments in any GAA player's career, winning an All-Ireland title with his club, Midleton, in 1988. One year earlier, in his last championship with Cork, John Fenton scored what is generally accepted as one of the most spectacular goals of all time; against Limerick in the Munster championship, he connected with such force, such sweetness, on a ground ball that the brilliant Limerick keeper Tommy Quaid was left rooted to the spot as the ball screamed into the net.

JOHN FENTON
(b. 1955, Midleton and Cork, 1975–87)

AWARDS & MEDALS WON
1 Texaco hurler of the year (1984)
3 All-Ireland senior
5 All-Star awards
1 All-Ireland U-21
2 National Hurling League
2 Railway Cup (1 as captain)
1 All-Ireland senior club
2 Munster senior club
4 Cork county senior
1 Cork county intermediate

Before we start, can you talk about that goal?
The first thing that comes to mind when I think of that goal is Tommy Quaid, how he died – tragic [fell from a ladder on a construction site, still in his prime]. Tommy was one of nature's gentlemen, one of hurling's gentlemen, a hurler to the core. The goal just happened, one of those things. It was the 1987 Munster championship, in Thurles, against Limerick. Limerick got a point just before half-time and I

remember saying to myself, we have to get a point now ourselves before half-time to equalise that.

Ger Cunningham pucked-out the ball, it landed roughly just in their half. For some reason Tomás Mulcahy [Cork forward] was out there. There was a schemozzle of players, he pushed the ball out to the wing. I ran on, pushed it past another couple of players, ran after it. Out of the corner of my eye I saw a red jersey in front of the Limerick goals – John Fitzgibbon, it turned out to be – and my intention was to get the ball into him. I knew there was a Limerick guy behind me so the chances were if I lifted the ball I'd get hooked, so I just let whip – it was about 45 yards out, right of centre. I've had fellas tell me since that it was 90 yards, but no, about 45.

A rocket?

It was, but in saying that, it was ground hurling and that was what I was used to. I probably hit more balls on the ground than most fellas at the time. It was dry weather, dry ground, dry ball, and I caught it on the sweet spot. Years later, when Cork played Wexford in the National League trilogy – I think it was the second game, up in Thurles – I was going into the stand during the curtain-raiser, a football game, and Tommy was standing down near the wire at the players' entrance. I said to him, 'Jaysus Tommy don't tell me you're taking up this game!' He turned to me, 'At least I'd see that ball!'

That was one of the things I loved about hurling, the craic, the camaraderie. On one occasion in Thailand, a GAA celebrity golf tour was organised by Seán Skehan. Joe Hayes from Tipperary was there and he was going out with Ann Downey at the time, the former Kilkenny camogie player. We were at a meal, everyone sitting down, when Joe and Ann came in, the last two. Someone tapped their glass and said, 'Would you all please welcome the bride and groom?' So everyone stood, clapped them to their table, and that was that – or so we thought.

Everyone had their meal and next thing someone else stood up – I think it was Nicky English – and tapped his glass again, started off. 'I'm delighted to welcome ye all here today to the wedding of Joe and Ann,' and it really took off from there, the wedding speeches.

The first fella he called on was Eoin Liston from Kerry, the Bomber, and as it transpired Eoin had a black shirt on him, a black trousers – he was the priest, and he said a few words. Next up was Babs

Keating, as the father of the groom. Poor Seánie Walsh from Kerry, who happened to be sitting beside Joe and Ann, became the best man, had to give the best man speech. Ann stood up and spoke on behalf of the bride's family, and so it went on, for over half an hour. Some poor woman from the north had to stand up and give a speech and she was absolutely fabulous. In fact everyone who spoke was fantastic – this was D'Unbelievables, live, at its best. Finally Joe stood up and what he didn't say about Babs, his 'father'!

I retired from club hurling in 1992, retired from Cork in 1987 – it was like a death in the family. I missed all that. I'd go training, come home in absolutely great humour – the craic we had, and it was all so simple, boyish if you like.

First position

I started in goals but I'd say I played in every position on the field in championship matches over the years, except centre-forward and full-forward. I was in goals for the Midleton minor team at thirteen, played corner-back for Imokilly, centre-back and centre-field for the school, played in all the forward positions except those down the centre.

The transition

I suppose you'd say that wing-back, midfield, were my two most natural positions. I played centre-field for the Cork minors, wing-back on the U-21 team. From there on midfield became my main position for both club and county. I'd play anywhere, I just loved to hurl, but midfield was probably my favourite position, there and wing-back, wing-forward. I played corner-forward a few times, played championship hurling there with Midleton, but I don't think I was a success. I remember one evening going into Páirc Uí Chaoimh and Mick McCarthy from the Glen called me aside and said, 'Would you ever go back out to centre-field. You have to be born inside in the corner! You're not suited to it, go back out to midfield.' At the time in Midleton we were struggling to find a team, you were making fish of fowl, but eventually we were all settled back into our most suitable positions.

The qualities needed to be a top midfielder

I'm taking it as read that you already have the basic skills, the lifting, the striking, the ground-hurling ability, which – to me anyway – is an essential part of playing midfield. You've got to be able to read the game, you've got to know what's going to happen before it happens. You've got to be versatile; you've got to be able to do everything a back can do and you've got to be able to do what a forward can do, because you're the link between the two. There are times when you're an auxiliary back, helping out in defence, there are times when you're an auxiliary forward, when you've got to take a score. Eye/ball/hand coordination is vital, you must have it; speed off the mark also, and quick reactions.

An exercise I'd do to improve reaction was during the break in the league in December [several league games were played pre-Christmas in those years], I'd put the hurley away for a few weeks, wouldn't touch it, but I'd start getting ready again on Christmas Eve, that was my start point. I'd get a rugby ball, train with that. There are so many things you can do with a rugby ball. I'd kick it in the air, about 10 yards, then go after it so that it would land at my toes – the test then was to trap the ball before it bounced a second time, kill it, and that was a real test of your reactions. The ball could bounce in any direction, you had to be alert, move fast – that helped to speed up your reactions. Another routine was to kick the ball about 30 yards ahead of you, move after it at pace, then try and pick and go, without breaking stride. Again, this improved your reactions.

Theo English, the great Tipperary midfielder, was the guy from whom I learned most about playing in that position. He told me: 'Your place is between the two 50 yard lines. There's no point in you being back around the goals and clearing the ball out to where you should be yourself. If you clean up between the two 50 yard lines, that's your job done.'

Did you speak to him personally?
Oh yeah, I was in the oil distribution business, he was in the oil distribution business, so we'd meet occasionally. But I'd talk to anyone about hurling, no matter what their code, and I'd learn from anyone. That was his advice to me, and that was the advice on which I based my midfield play. If you're there when the ball breaks around that area and you send it up to your forwards, that's your job done.

Mine – no, it's mine! *John Fenton keeps a firm grip on the McCarthy Cup as the Cork team leave Kent Station for their victory parade after the win over Offaly in the Centenary Senior Hurling Championship Final at Thurles, County Tipperary, on 3 September 1984.*

Would you be a proponent of the running game?

Absolutely not. If I wanted to see a guy running with a ball, I'd give it to Eamonn Coghlan and let him off with it. There are certain times you have to run with it, but not as a matter of course. There's an exercise I do when I'm coaching young fellas; I ask them to pick out the fastest runner among them, I take him out near the middle of the field, give him the ball, tell him to sprint 30 yards with it then hit it over the bar. When he's gone about 20 yards, I'll throw a sliotar to someone else and tell him to hit it over the bar from where he's standing. He'll have that done before the other fella has even finished his run, and that guy must then turn and come back out to midfield again. No, I'm absolutely not in favour of this running game. Then again, it's horses for courses, that's how we were taught.

I read a brilliant interview with Pat O'Shea, the Kerry football coach, in which he stated that he would never change the basic Kerry football tradition. He'll tweak it but he won't change it, because there's no need to change it – look at how many All-Irelands they've won, playing their own traditional game. I would be a traditionalist in hurling.

Newtown perfected the running game, because it was the game most suited to the players they had, and they won county titles with it, an All-Ireland title. But I've seen so many teams in Cork now trying to play the same game and they can't. They haven't got the players for it, they don't know how to do it, and it's destroying the game, particularly at club level. At county level the Cork players are more in tune with it; they're fitter, faster, they're more in the athlete mould, which is what I was talking about – give the ball to Eamonn Coghlan and let him off.

Where to stand in relation to your opponent

I'd anticipate where the ball was going to land, then stand about 10 yards behind that so I had a run at it.

Would you man-mark in midfield?

They have a term in basketball, zonal defence – that was how I approached it, in the beginning especially. After I'd built up my confidence at county level I focused a lot more on just playing the ball, but when I first started with Cork I was a lot more conscious of the reputations of those around me, in awe of some of them, the likes of Frank Cummins, Mossie Walsh, and I worried about how much ball they were hitting. As I got more used to the pace of the game though, I was less concerned about that – let them worry about you. There's a saying, a good player goes to where the ball is, a great player goes to where the ball is going to be – anticipation. That's what I aimed for, to be able to read the game, anticipate where the ball was going to land and be there before anyone else.

Did you have an understanding with Ger Cunningham on puck-outs?

No, with Ger, nearly every ball went over your head, into the half-forward-line, so what I was getting were the leftovers, whatever came back. We weren't disciples of the short puck-out, we weren't interested in it.

Might have worked in 1983, the day of the big wind?

Might have; we played against the wind in the first half and at half-time, I was sitting beside Ger Cunningham. He asked Johnny Clifford, 'Johnny, what will I do with the puck-outs in the second half?' Johnny said, 'Hang on a while, I'll come back to you.' He went away, discussed it with the other selectors, came back to Ger and told him, 'Hit every ball as long and as far as you can, down the middle.' Now, possibly Ger should have seen it wasn't working and changed, but Ger was a young fella coming onto the team, he was going to do what he was told.

Tricks

I used to do a pile of training on my own, but I found that tricks in hurling, particularly at a higher level, rarely come off. I remember a game in Cork, an intermediate match, a forward soloed in, flicked the ball over the Tipperary fella's head, gathered it again on the other side and I said to myself, he won't get away with that again. But he did, it looked great, the crowd loving it of course. He came in a third time and tried it again, and the Tipperary fella buried him, absolutely buried him, and I said to myself – he deserved that.

I didn't really use tricks in a game – brown bread and milk, that was my game, simple stuff. There were things I did in training alright, like practising line balls from my knees. I'd start around the 21-yard line and work my way out. The main reason was to strengthen the wrists. Another drill I had was to run out to a ball with my back to the goals, flick it up with my heels, turn and put it over the bar in one movement.

I got as far the 70-yard line where I was able to do that, but I never did it in a match, never got the opportunity really.

When I was playing corner-forward for Midleton, Seánie Brien [Midleton half-back] and myself had a tactic worked out for the long-range frees. He knew where I was going to be, I knew where he was going to put the ball. We practised this in training, up in the school field in Midleton. The minute he went to take the free I'd turn my back and go, in towards goal – no looking back – and he'd put the ball down in front of me, in over my head.

I was right-half-forward one evening against Na Piarsaigh, Dave Boylan [Midleton] was in the corner and we got a free like that, back in our half-back-line. I told Dave to go for a run, take the corner-back with him, clear that area; Seáno took the free, I turned and ran, the ball landed just in front of me. I was going full tilt, hit it first time on the bounce and it cracked off the outside of the post, wide. If that had gone over the bar, it would have been a fantastic point! Another night we played the Glen, up near Kilbarry when they were developing their new grounds. I was corner-forward on Teddy O'Brien, we got a free in our half-back-line. I always knew what side of the field Seáno was going for, he'd touch the side of his head with his right hand if it was going right, his left if it was going left. I bent down as if to tie my lace, Seáno touched left side – my corner. Teddy took his eye off me, thinking I was gone out of the play, Seáno took the free, I was gone, out to meet the ball. I was actually on my way back in after scoring the point when I met Teddy coming out! These were the kind of things you tried in training but they rarely came off in matches.

Primary advice to a promising youngster, above all else, to master the midfield position

Have the hurley in your hand for up to twenty minutes every day of the week, and practise your striking, your ball control. Even ten minutes a day is better than a two-hour session once a week. I would always have a hurley and a ball; even if I was only sent to the shop I'd bring the hurley and ball.

Silky Pilky he could have been called, wrists to die for as they might say in another jurisdiction. Johnny Pilkington graced centre-field on the Offaly team from 1989 to 2003, and graced is the operative word. Like Cork's John Fenton he was a true artiste, a stick-man foremost; he played the game as he saw it, kept it simple. This is not to say that Johnny didn't appreciate the subtleties of the game, the complexities; few were better at reading the breaks, at spotting the opening, at reading the opposition. But Johnny had a very old-style attitude to the game, and to his position. Direct, keep it direct.

JOHNNY PILKINGTON
(b. 1970, Birr and Offaly, 1989–2001)

AWARDS & MEDALS WON
2 All-Ireland senior
1 All-Star award
1 National Hurling League
4 All-Ireland senior club
8 Offaly county senior

First position
I started off at corner-forward, U-14, probably around eleven years of age. Myself and Brian Whelahan, the two of us were very, very small so we were shoved in corner-forward. We got a phone call one evening before a county final, 'Come on out.' I think we won, but I'm not sure. I don't know how I ended up in midfield, or why, but I played midfield in the Community Games so I was there early. In hindsight it was probably the legs, the stamina, the running, the ability to keep the ball running. That was in the beginning, but one of the key things at the end of my career was to be there first when the ball broke.

The qualities needed to be a top midfielder
Everyone thinks you have to be super fit nowadays, all this running up and down, but I'd say just the ability to read the breaks. You don't need huge strength, you don't need great pace, you don't need to be a great catcher of the ball – it's just being there, reading the game properly,

getting onto the breaks. After that it's support play, forward and back, but most especially support for the half-back-line. Your half-forward-line is going to do exactly the same thing as you're going to do, just keep the ball moving along to the inside line. Your half-backs will be under more pressure, they'll be in trouble occasionally, getting blocked down, that sort of thing. You have to be there to help them, get the breaks.

Move the ball or carry it?

Move it, always move it. Like every other young fella starting off, I loved to solo with it but more often than not you were soloing into a dead end, into corners, rather than running with purpose, with meaning. Then you lose the ball. Eamonn Cregan [coached Offaly to an All-Ireland title in 1994] was the man who did most to change me. He pulled me back.

I think Offaly were unique in the way we played. We didn't need as much possession as other teams did in order to win, simply because we got rid of the ball so fast, up to the forwards. There you had the likes of Johnny Dooley – one touch, turn, over the bar. Puck-out comes out, Dáithí Regan catches, handpass to John Troy – turn, over the bar. A lot of our scores were that simple. Our half-back got the ball, moved it on; midfield, same thing. There was none of this possession game, trying to hold onto the ball, trying to get around a man, short passing sideways and backwards. We used to love seeing teams doing that. They'd win the ball, try to get around the man. Offaly would block, hook, flick the ball away, take it off you, go down the other end and get a point. Another team might get four balls, five balls, up to the forwards and they might get a point out of it, whereas we'd expect a much higher rate of return, that if our forwards got three balls we'd get two points from it. It was gone there for a while but it's coming back again now.

Storey spoke of that, said Kilkenny did the same thing, take the ball off you then relish getting a point – heart-breaker?

Yeah, even with Birr and Ballyhale in the Leinster club in 2007 you saw it – the last ten minutes, we never fouled [Birr held on to pip the Kilkenny champions]. Teams like Wexford, Galway, the Munster teams, they'll come out with the big huge shoulder, knock a fella down, and what happens? Nine times out of ten, they give away the free. With Offaly we just tracked back, shadowed them, waited for the ball to show, flicked it away. Simple.

Johnny Pilkington about to post another Pilkington special in the AIB All-Ireland Club Hurling Championship semi-final between Birr and Athenry in Cusack Park, Ennis, County Clare, on 16 February 2003.

Where to stand in relation to your opponent

I would never stand behind the half-back-line, always in front. You'd pick up ball occasionally if you're behind, but who's out in midfield? If the ball breaks out, your man is on his own, most likely, in great position to score. You must be in position to pick up the breaks.

Did you calculate that break, gauging the strength and weakness of your own players under the ball, the opposition likewise?

No, I didn't. You didn't have time for all that calculation anyway – while you were thinking the ball would be gone. Maybe it just came naturally. You'd see early that one was going to pull, maybe the other would try to catch it – it's your reaction time after that. A lot of it is just positioning. Midfield is probably unique in that you don't really have to worry about your man; the wing-back has to worry about his man, so does the centre-back – we don't. That's not to say there isn't any contest in midfield, there is. In the 1994 All-Ireland final Limerick did a strange thing. I started off on Ciarán Carey, Dáithí [Regan] on Mike Houlihan, and we were really losing that midfield battle. And then, for some reason best known to themselves, after about twenty minutes Limerick switched Carey and Houlihan. That switch suited us, brought us back into the game. That was a strange one. I don't think I ever roasted anyone in my time, but I was being dominated by Carey in that game. Regan was able to dominate him though, because of his physical strength, and Houlihan suited my game better.

It all comes back to reaction, in midfield, working on that. And you can work on it: an alley, a wall, a ball. It's important also to be using your head – how far does your own goalkeeper hit it, in these conditions? How far does their goalkeeper hit it? You have to try and read what he's doing. Then you have to know where to be, where to go; if one of your own defenders gets the ball – if Brian Whelahan caught it, for example, I'd be laying off him, in case he got caught up.

On our own puck-out, the beauty of it is that it will land on your own half-forward-line. Your wing-forward or centre-forward could catch that ball, what you do then is break in alongside him, be ready to take the handpass. That's very important for a midfielder, support play. But you had to know your half-forwards too – Gary Hanniffy could catch, a little pop-pass and you're gone through the centre; John Troy wouldn't catch it at centre-forward, he'd break the ball, but you're still up there, getting onto the break. And then move it, just move it. I'd always wait off three or four yards, try to react to the break.

Tricks

I don't think I had any. I wouldn't have been very strong under a high ball, probably the weakest part of my game, so I tended not to stand there. There was one alright I used a lot, flicking a ball back over my shoulder to a teammate, blind. You'd know they were running with you. I did that with Brian [Whelahan] a lot. We were playing Meath one time, well ahead, I ran onto a ball, picked it and handpassed it behind me to Brian. Into the tackles, a little flick backwards, but that was it – no more tricks.

Primary advice to a promising youngster, above all else, to master the midfield position

It's really just reading the breaks. A puck-out is coming down your half-back-line, or on the half-forward-line, it's going to do one of three things – break through, break in front, or break to the side. It's just to be there for that break and move the ball on immediately. The opponent never concerned me, where he stood, it was the ball all the time. You kept an eye on him, especially at puck-out time, but you kept a sharper eye on the goalkeeper, try to read what he was going to do.

Right-Half-Forward
The Sniper

Jimmy Doyle (Tipperary)
Liam Griffin (Wexford and Clare)
Johnny Dooley (Offaly)
Tommy Dunne (Tipperary)
Dan Shanahan (Waterford)

He was deadly, this man, ice in the veins when the game was on the line. Almost anyone you speak to, of his own era especially, will say that he was the best right-half-forward of all time. Tipperary's Jimmy Doyle, the prototype, the perfect example. From his position out on the wing, he could make teams, he could break teams. He knew when to run, when to hide, how to appear, how to disappear; he knew when to part with the ball, he knew when to go; he knew when to take his point, he knew when the goal was on, when the goal was necessary. Deadly alright.

***Getting to know you** – Tipperary captain Jimmy Doyle, right, and Wexford captain Tom Neville pose for the shot before the All-Ireland Senior Hurling Championship Final in Croke Park, Dublin, on 5 September 1965.*

JIMMY DOYLE
(b. 1939, Thurles Sarsfields and Tipperary, 1957–73)

AWARDS & MEDALS WON
1 Team of the Millennium (right-corner-forward)
1 Team of the Century (left-corner-forward)
1 Hurler of the Year (1965)
6 All-Ireland senior (2 as captain)
6 National Hurling League
8 Railway Cup (Tipperary record; two as captain)
5 Oireachtas
11 Tipperary county senior hurling
1 Tipperary county senior football

First position
I played in goals in the beginning. I played there in the minor championship in 1954, we were beaten by Dublin in the final.

The transition
I didn't like the goalkeeping position and coming home from that final,
I said to Brother Dooley, who was over the minors: 'I don't like the
goals, I want to get out of it.'

'God,' he says. 'That's a pity, you're a great goalkeeper. Why do you
want to leave it?'

'You can block twenty or thirty great balls then drop the one – the
public will talk about the one. I'm not for that. I'd rather be out right-
half-forward or left-half-forward, I'd rather be doing the scoring than
the blocking.'

'We have a match coming up shortly in the Dean Ryan, we'll put
you out wing-forward in that.' In that game, with Thurles CBS against
Limerick CBS, I scored 1-8 – I never again played in the goals! Well
I did – I started in goals with Tipperary, I finished in goals with
Tipperary. It was 1973, Tadhg Murphy [regular goalkeeper] went to
England, couldn't get work at home. My father was with the senior
team, they were training, he came home one evening and said to me,
'Jimmy, you'd better be ready. The selectors are going to be coming to
you soon.'

'For what?'

'With Tadhg Murphy gone they have no goalkeeper. They want you to play in goals against Waterford on Sunday week. You'd better start making your mind up.' So they came anyway and I said I would, first round of the Munster championship. We beat Waterford, I let in two goals, then we played Cork in the semi-final. Tadhg Murphy was back at that stage and I didn't wait for the selectors to come to me – I went to them. There was a match on with the U-21s.

'Put me in the goals for that one,' I said, 'And put Tadhg back in the goals against Cork. I want to retire.' And that's what happened, we beat Cork in the semi-final, but lost to Limerick in the Munster final that year. So I played my first game with Tipperary in goals, for the minors, and I played my last game for Tipp in goals, for the U-21s – nineteen years later!

The qualities needed to be a top wing-forward

The most important – you couldn't take your eye off the ball, ever. You had to be elusive, you had to be able to lose your man. Martin Coogan was one of the best left-half-backs of all time and he told me he could never keep an eye on me. In one All-Ireland final, he told me that Bob Aylward said to him, 'You're on Jimmy Doyle on Sunday – I want you to stay within an arm's reach of him at all times. Anywhere he goes you're to go with him – keep him within an arm's reach.'

'But Jimmy,' he said to me, 'any time I turned around, even for a split second, you were gone!' At right-half-forward you have a huge area to cover. You can go out the field, back in towards the corner, into the centre, even across to the other side. Donie Nealon was usually on the left when I was on the right and he was a great wing-forward, but got hardly any recognition at all. If you were fit, if you were right, you could cover the whole area and that's what we did, we went wherever we felt like going, but – and this is important – you always came back to your own position.

Find his blind spot, get away from him. Judge where the ball was going to drop and go. While he's looking for you, you have the ball in your hand. 'Jimmy,' Martin said to me, 'you had four points got in that All-Ireland and I still couldn't find you!' But that's what the game was all about.

What was the difference between right-half-forward and left-half-forward?

Well you see, I'm a *ciotóg,* as was my father, a pure *ciotóg.* I caught the hurley with my left hand, caught the ball with my right. If I were left-half-forward I'd have been out on the line when I was taking the shot off my stronger side, where on the right I was cutting into the centre. I did play left-half-forward in a couple of All-Irelands and I could strike off my right, got a lot of scores that way, but I always preferred the right. You had to strengthen your weaker side, people very quickly got to know the side you preferred to strike from and would try to force you away from that, so you had to be able to score off either side.

Where to stand in relation to your opponent

I always liked to be facing the ball, coming onto the ball, out in front. I'd often stand around the halfway line and work my way in.

Tricks

I didn't have anything, really. The dummy hit, go to hit the ball but take it back on the stick. There was one year alright, a Railway Cup final against Leinster, I got two goals with the same trick. Ollie Walsh was in goal for Leinster, the ball came to me from Frankie Walsh of Waterford and I ran straight into a gap, faced with Ollie. I was still running, threw the ball up, swung hard with the left but swung under the ball. Ollie went one way, I shifted position and swung back then with the right, put the ball in the net on the other side. I did that again, identically, in the same game, caught him twice with the same trick. 'Oh Jaysus, Doyle!' he says. But that was control and you learned that from practising on your own, and I did a lot of that.

I love to see a player banging a ball off a wall then controlling it. I could make the ball talk. I could bend it, put top-spin on it, anything I wanted. That was from training on my own. I'd finish school in the evening, go home, throw my schoolbag into the corner and get my hurley and ball, and the dog, and we'd come up to Semple Stadium, hurl 'til six o'clock in the evening. My mother would come to the gate: 'Come down Jimmy for your supper.'

'I'll be down in a minute.' But a minute would be an hour. I'd go down then and have my supper, get the hurley and ball again and back up, stay at it 'til dark, ten or eleven o'clock at night. The dog would stay with me all that time, fetching; a great dog he was, a sheepdog – everywhere I went he was behind me.

Tricks seen

A lot, by the backmen especially. Holding, there was a lot of that. The dummy clearance by the wing-back, pretending he was going for the long shot then holding onto it, turning onto his other side and gone. We did that as well, as forwards, but it meant they were doing their own practicing off their own wall.

I hurled with Christy Ring with Munster and that was a dream of mine. When he won his first All-Ireland I don't think I was even born [Jimmy was born in 1939, the year Ring won a minor All-Ireland with Cork]. Hard to believe then that I got to play with him for years afterwards, in the Railway Cup. But when I was a young fella, no matter what hurley I picked up, I was Christy Ring. Up there against that wall [we were in the Thurles Sarsfields clubhouse], hours and hours, and I was Christy Ring.

'Christy Ring grabs the ball, turns, and it's over the bar. Christy Ring shoots, and it's a goal!' It was all Christy, Christy, Christy. And then I hurled with him, a legend. He was as good as everyone says he was, he was brilliant. He had it upstairs; we read the break of the ball but Christy read everything, he read the whole field.

I saw him doing something in Croke Park one day that no one else would do, and he even said it to me himself. We were playing Connacht, the full-back was after giving him a belt across the head and he was lying on his back on the ground, being attended to by the two Knights of Malta men. We were playing into a gale, into the Hill 16 end. I was after moving out to the halfway line, when Philly Grimes of Waterford got the ball and drove it into the Connacht goal. Ring was still on the ground at this stage, panned out. He never took his eye off the ball though, and all the while he was following the play. He jumped up, grabbed the ball, turned, stuck it in the net, and fell back down on his back again. I was after following up and he looked up at me. 'Doyle,' he said, 'you never did that!'

I was in Barry's Hotel on the eve of a Railway Cup final, sharing a room with Ring and Paddy Barry. Christy was in the middle bed, lying down on the flat of his back, I was in the bed on his left, Barry on his right, and he was hitting the ball off the wall above us – left, right, the two of us ducking! 'What are you doing Christy?' I said; 'Ah Jimmy, you mightn't do it, but I like to keep me eye in!' Brilliance. Lying on the flat of his back, a hurley and a ball, hitting it, snapping it, hitting it, snapping it, first the right, then the left.

We were going to Belfast one day, hurling Ulster in the Railway Cup again, and I was with Ring. The two of us got out and next thing he was fumbling in his pocket. 'What are you doing Christy?' I said. 'I'm looking for me cap,' he said, 'I don't want to be recognised up here!' I laughed, couldn't help it. Christy Ring! Sure, he was recognised all over Ireland. Ah, he was brilliant. I can't say he was the best ever, because I never saw Mackey, and I heard he was good, but he was the best I saw.

Primary advice to a promising youngster, above all else, to master the wing-forward position

It's nice to be nice, that's number one. You must have discipline, don't go out to damage anyone. If you want to make the big-time, live with the hurley, use it every opportunity you get. I still have my hurley. I have two in fact, one beside the bed and one in the boot of the car. I'm looking at the hurley, always; I could still go out there [Semple Stadium pitch] and stick a ball over the bar from 40 or 50 yards, out on the wing, but I won't do it. When your day is up your day is up. I went to Croke Park with the Millennium team, six of us alive, and they gave us hurleys, had us out on the pitch. I wouldn't go, just sat down. I finished with the club in 1975, I suppose I was thirty-six or thirty-seven.

Far more famous for his management skills than for his actual playing career, Liam Griffin had a brief inter-county stint before work intervened. Regrets? Like many of us, he has a few.

LIAM GRIFFIN
(b. 1946; Wexford and Clare, 1967–68)

AWARDS & MEDALS WON
As player
1 All-Ireland U-21 (1965 with Wexford)
1 Leinster intermediate
2 Clare county senior (with Newmarket-on-Fergus)
1 Munster senior club (didn't play in the final, emigrated to
   Switzerland)
2 Munster senior club championship football (with De La Salle of
   Waterford)
As manager
1 All-Ireland senior (Wexford 1996)

Primary position
I played in the half-forward-line, right-half-forward mostly.

The qualities needed to be a top wing-forward
You had to be a really good reader of the play, both from puck-outs and from clearances. You had to be reading the ball to put yourself in best position to win possession. Scoring is vitally important, you have to be a good striker of the ball off left and right, a confident striker, and you must be capable of scoring from long distance, on the run if necessary. You must also be accurate, able to score from difficult angles, all of that is very important.

It's a huge advantage if you can win clean possession from the puck-out in the air, win the dropping ball cleanly and if you're a good striker of the ball, bang, that's a score. My own best asset was pace. I think that's important at wing-forward. You're in a scoring area – if you win possession, get away and you're a good ball-striker, you're in a good position to score, whereas if you're slow, even if you win possession,

Liam Griffin leads the De La Salle College Waterford team around the pitch in their first ever appearance in a Harty Cup final in 1965.

Liam Griffin in his 'work uniform' in May 2008.

you can still be hooked or blocked. When you're blocked down, the ball becomes available then to the half-back, who will most likely clear it, put your own backs under pressure. A good first touch is paramount if you want to make it to the top level.

Tricks

Because I was very fast, the dummy run out the field to take the wing-back out of position, create the space for the ball to be delivered in behind, then get back before him. I was skinny, depended on speed. Pull him out of position, then good first touch, get the ball into the hand, no messing.

Primary advice to a promising youngster, above all else, to master the wing-forward position

Develop both sides to the extent that you can strike with equal ability off left and right.

Best advice you ever got

Develop your hurling on your own. I don't know who gave it to me, but that was it. Always have the hurley in your hand, become so used to it that it's just an extension of your arm. People are fascinated by drills at the moment, in every sport – the most important drill you'll ever do in hurling is the ball off the wall, back and forward, first touch, and the beauty of it is that you can do it by yourself, on your own.

A ghost, D. J. Carey called him, one of those forwards with the ability to appear out of nowhere, usually in the open, unmarked, in perfect position to take a pass, to take the score. Johnny Dooley was one of three outstanding hurling brothers with Offaly, the baby brother of Joe and Billy. Brilliant stick-man, superb free-taker, Johnny was another who made this position his own.

JOHNNY DOOLEY
(b. 1971, Seir Kieran and Offaly, 1989–2002)

AWARDS & MEDALS WON
2 All-Ireland senior
3 All-Star awards
2 All-Ireland minor
1 National Hurling League
4 Offaly county senior

First position
Midfield with the U-8s and U-10s in national school, but I played a lot in the forwards, centre-forward. We were a very small national school so the stronger players would be played up the middle, expected to steer the thing. What it meant too was that you'd be playing for the school from about third class on, you'd be lining out against guys who'd be six or eight inches taller than you; a few years older than you, bigger and stronger. They wouldn't spare you, wouldn't want to be seen to be shown up by fellas who were younger and smaller. I suppose, in hindsight, it didn't do us any harm, you were getting good competition from an early age.

The transition
I would have played right-half-forward with the minors, over time I just seemed to be slotted in there. I played there with the county minors, with the U-21s, and then I started playing there with the club, and that's where I stayed. I did end up back in midfield again with the club, but I never played centre-forward, never played full-forward, never played left-half-forward.

Is there a difference between the wings?
There is. Playing on the left would be like asking me to control the hurl
with the other hand – it would just feel strange. It suited me coming into
the ball on the right wing, I used the hurl hand to protect myself. Most
wing-backs would stay inside you, which suited me as a right-handed
hurler. If a fella stood on my other shoulder, he'd have me caught. One
of my stronger points was being able to catch the ball out of the air, I
was able to shield the catching hand with the hurl on the inside; if the
defender stood on my outside I couldn't do that – now my hand was exposed. Joe [his brother] played on the opposite wing but that suited him
because he was left-handed, controlled the hurl with the left hand. You
had to be able to strike the ball back-handed. Any good wing-forward
should be able to do that.

**Some backs made it a tactic to play on the catching-hand side for
the opposition puck-out?**
Yes, but it was a dangerous game for them to play, because now, if
you do get control, they've put themselves on the outside and that's not
good for them. One way or the other you were on a winner, but I always
found I had better protection for my hand on that side. But if someone
did stand on my left, I always found that very awkward, it threw me off
my usual game. If I just pulled, the chances were it was going to go out
over the line.

The qualities needed to be a top wing-forward

You had to be strong under the high ball. You're going to be under a
share of puck-outs and you have to be able to win your share. Then,
move the ball in. I think Eamonn Cregan was one of the first guys to
drill us to move the ball in quickly, first and foremost. Most half-back-
lines try to dominate their opponents – you have to resist that, try to
win the ball, move it in, then follow it up. Even if you're staying out
wide – which we'd have insisted on – there's a lot of running involved
at wing-forward. Keep it wide and then when the ball comes down the
centre, sprint across, get onto the breaks. It's a constant struggle with
your wing-back, you're trying to pull him out, yet you want to get back
in, so there's a lot of running involved. Most wing-forwards now play
far out, around the 70-yard line, so they can pack their own defence,
then run at the opposition in attack. Quick ball in, that was our game.

Cork brought in the running game – we couldn't do that, I couldn't do that. I wasn't a runner, I wouldn't try to take on any man and beat him in a solo run. I played to my strength and that was winning the ball, throwing a bit of a shimmy, playing it in front of the full-forward and then chasing it in at about three-quarter pace, hope to pick up the break coming out.

Two chances on the wing, instead of one in the corner?

Yes, but you must work hard for that second chance. Wing-forward is a hard-working position. Put the ball in and chase, try to beat your defender in. If the corner-back gets it, be ready to close him down coming out, if your corner-forward gets it, make yourself available for the pass. You're talking about runs of about 40 yards – in, out, in, out.

Ghosting, D. J. says you were the best he ever saw at it. Were you aware you were doing it?

I wasn't, to be honest with you. You have to be able to drift away from your man. We played Tipperary in the league in 1997, in Nenagh, a lot of hype about the league at the time. It was a good game of hurling, but four times in the first twenty minutes I just drifted across to the other wing, Brian Whelahan picked four balls and put them straight into my hand – four points. Another wing-back might have put the ball down my wing, made me look stupid, out of position, but Brian had the vision, just had the look up, sent me the pass.

As Jimmy Doyle said, find the defender's blind side

Yeah, defenders can get sucked into the intensity of a game, can start ball-watching, and you can go on a little trot. Sometimes it works, sometimes it doesn't. A forward can't be one-dimensional. He has to grab the ball, turn, either create a chance or score, and all with the back breathing down his neck.

Tricks

I was always accused of 'tripping' the hurl, that was a habit I developed as a young fella training at home in the yard. I'd go up for the ball and you have to be cute, you make it look as if you're only protecting your hand but you use your hurl to push his out of the way. I got away with it most times – a Kilkenny trick but I used it all the time. You wouldn't give his hurl a belt, you'd make it look like it was just incidental, all one move. I got away with it more often at county level than at club level, I got caught more often there.

I wasn't much into the dummy handpass, but I was good at the shimmy, pretending to go one way but going the other. You can create a lot of space like that; a lot of guys today are like robots, run in straight lines, no shimmy. I didn't have speed, so I had to have another way. Be flexible enough to be able to go either way, keep the defender guessing. Another one was to pretend to be going to catch but then stand back and pull – keep him guessing. You have to be able to vary your game; become predictable and you're gone.

Tricks seen

I think the Kilkenny lads have an awful lot of tricks, tipping and hooking and blocking, pushing everything to the limit. I think that's a gift in itself, a skill, being able to push the game to its limits without getting caught. You have to admire them for that. Even if you win the ball, they know exactly what to do to put you off your strike. We had a fella, Paddy Connors, we were playing Birr one day in the county final and he was on Simon Whelahan. He had him by the jersey, the crowd could see it because of the stretch but the ref couldn't, and the crowd were going mad. He got away with it too, no cameras at those games!

Primary advice to a promising youngster, above all else, to master the wing-forward position

Work rate, that's a huge part of wing-forward. It's one thing having all the skills but work rate, doing a lot of extra stuff on your own – working on your speed, your stamina, your sideline cuts, your frees, sharpening up on the shooting off both sides. Work on your work-rate, if you like; the one way you'll put it in during a match is if you put it in in training.

After a game against Kilkenny in Croke Park, I remember something my father said to me – 'You didn't work hard enough today.' I actually checked that out on the replay and he was right; a few balls I didn't contest, a few balls I left go too easily and it suddenly clicked with me – why didn't I work harder? It's too late when the game is over, you must work during the game. Look at all the best players, look at all the best teams – the one thing they'll all have in common is work- rate. A forward must score, every forward; if you can pick up three or four points in every game, you're doing your job, but if you're not even shooting at the target, what's it all about?

The best advice ever received

I got lots of advice from my father, never anything huge, just little tips, but one thing he'd always say to me, even before a big game in Croke Park: 'Get in you now today and pull your hurl!' He'd have the hairs standing on the back of my neck, going out.

The free that broke the heart of a whole county – Johnny Dooley takes the free which resulted in the goal that kick-started the Offaly comeback in the All-Ireland Hurling final against Limerick in Croke Park, Dublin, on 4 September 1994. On their marks for the rebound that never came are Limerick players Joe O'Connor (left) and Declan Nash. Billy Dooley (Johnny's brother, in the black helmet) scored a succession of points after Johnny's goal to increase Offaly's lead over Limerick.

Another Tipperary-man, another with all the skills. Tommy Dunne was a bit of a jack of all trades with Tipperary during the course of a long career. He made a big impression in midfield especially, but, by his own admission, wing-forward was his position.

TOMMY DUNNE
(b. 1974, Toomevara and Tipperary, 1993–2005)

AWARDS & MEDALS WON
1 Hurler of the Year (2001: GPA, Texaco and Vodafone)
1 All-Ireland senior (as captain)
3 All-Star awards
1 All-Ireland U-21
3 National Hurling League
2 Railway Cup
3 Munster senior club
10 Tipperary county senior

First position

I started off at corner-forward, U-12, nine years of age, brought on and off. There was myself and a friend of mine, James McGrath, he was a year older. One day he'd start, I'd come on, the next day I'd start and he'd come on. Early on in my career with Tipp, I was at corner-forward, played the 1996 Munster final there against Limerick; then wing-forward in 1997 and '98, number ten, before being moved to mid-field that year. In 1999, I played at 10 for the league and championship. In 2000, I was between midfield and the forward line. I first played mid-field against Down in 1997, the first year of the backdoor, played there in the All-Ireland final then against Clare, myself and Conor Gleeson up against Baker and Lynch. We lost by a point, a game we could have won. Colin Lynch and myself got All-Stars in midfield that year. I got another one there in 1999, though I think I was actually nominated in the forwards.

What was your favourite position?

I really enjoyed wing-forward, particularly in 1999, I was playing fairly well at that stage. Wing-forward is a lovely position, my most natural position, I'd say. I played all my minor hurling there with Tipp, all my U-21, and I was always in the forwards with the club. Over the years I've probably said otherwise – when you're playing well you're enjoying it no matter where you are, though I must say I never enjoyed corner-forward. Full-forward yes, anywhere in the half-forward-line or midfield; there you had room to do your own thing, you were able to dictate things, as opposed to corner-forward, waiting for things to happen before something could happen for you. The real carrot at full-forward is that if you win possession you're really close to the goals, in position to score a goal – every forward loves scoring goals!

John Fenton says you have to be born in the corner

I agree, I even see that with young fellas. The corner positions are really hard to play, whether you're in the backs or forwards. You have to be a natural to play there. It's very hard to manufacture a corner-forward or a corner-back, though there are exceptions, always – look at Pat Fox. Then again, he started as a corner-back, so maybe it wasn't such a huge change. He was always a corner-man!

The qualities needed to be a top wing-forward

I think you have to be a good all-round player. In the modern game, you have to be a good ball-winner number one, that's probably the primary thing, supersedes everything else nowadays with most of the puck-outs landing in this area, midfield being bypassed. You have to have a real physical presence. Look at all the great teams of the past, the one thing they had in common was a half-back-line that was the base for launching most of their attacks. If you have a half-forward-line that can counter that, break it up, even win the contest sixty–forty, you're in good shape. You have to be a scoring threat. Catch the puck-out and put it straight over the bar, that's probably the ideal. You need pace, which will allow you to punish the defender once you get inside. And you need accuracy, which is what I meant when I spoke of scoring threat.

Where to stand in relation to your opponent

In front, always in front if I could. Often I'd come in off the wing to the space on the inside, rather than turning out to the stand all the time. There was so much more you could do with the ball coming in off the wing.

Did you have any signals with the keeper?

Not really. We might have an understanding that the first ball was going to Declan [Ryan] or to Mark [O'Leary] or to myself, but after that no, no real system. That was probably something we could have worked on. But I'd always know the way it was coming from the way Brendan Cummins was shaping up to hit it; even before it left his hurley I'd know where it was going to go. That was one thing I'd say, we were very seldom caught off guard with our own puck-outs, and that's important. When Nicky [English] came in 1999 we changed things a bit alright, we worked on that scenario where Brendan wouldn't take as long about his puck-out if the game was going our way. We started hitting free men much more often – corner-backs, wing-backs, midfield, whoever was available. That's important too, getting the tempo of the puck-outs right – faster if you're going well, slow down if you're not, but that takes work, training. And guys turning their backs to a ball – that's just a no no.

Were you good to catch?

Only average, I wouldn't have been a Teddy McCarthy or anything, but I could hold my own. You had to be able to do it; at half-forward it's an integral part of the game.

Tricks

I didn't have any real tricks, it was all simple enough really. I was probably too honest for my own good. Maybe I should have developed a few things. I had little things, but it was skills more than tricks – I loved to steal the ball off a fella between rising it and catching it, that fraction of a second when the ball was in the air; a flick, knock it away. I got lots of scores doing that sort of thing. The best one I think I pulled was the first goal against Cork in 2000, in the Munster final. I remember going through, thinking of a point but the whole thing just opened up in front of me. I was going to strike off the right shoulder but I caught Sherlock [Wayne, Cork corner-back] out of the corner of my eye. He was tracking me, ready to hook, and I knew I was in trouble on that side. I just dipped the left shoulder, shifted to that side and the ball flew into the top corner. I still wonder about that one, how I pulled that off, but I suppose it's just years and years of practice. I've seen fellas going to hit off their right, about to be blocked down, then just flicking the ball onto their left – Johnny Leahy was deadly at that – but I've never seen fellas making the switch when they were going to be caught from behind, on the run. Looking back now, I'd be very happy with that.

Tricks seen

Ah you'd see little pushes, little touches of the hurley, that sort of thing but the game was too fast really for tricks, you didn't have time enough on the ball.

Primary advice to a promising youngster, above all else, to master the wing-forward position

A couple of things: you have to be strong on the ball, so work on the physique; you have to be prepared to suffer, to take a lot of punishment under puck-outs and things like that; and you have to be accurate – when you get your chance you have to be able to take it.

Tommy Dunne, Tipperary, in action against Kilkenny's Henry Shefflin in the Guinness All-Ireland Senior Hurling Championship semi-final in Croke Park, Dublin, on 17 August 2003.

Dan the Man, they call him, not just a hurler anymore but a folk hero, one of those rare breed whose identity comes down to just one name. Big Dan, Dan the Man, Waterford's latest sporting titan, Dan Shanahan. He's a different hurler to the others in this position, tweed rather than silk, but a lot less rough-cut than many would judge. He can hit and with that massive gym-hewn frame he can hurt, but he can hurl also. He has become renowned over the past few years for his goals, many of them scored as he drifted in from the wing to the edge of the square, but many of his points have been right out of the top drawer.

DAN SHANAHAN
(b. 1977, Lismore and Waterford, 1996–present)

AWARDS & MEDALS WON
1 Hurler of the Year (2007: GPA, Texaco and Vodafone)
3 All-Star awards
1 National Hurling League
1 Railway Cup
3 Munster senior championship
1 Waterford county senior hurling
1 Waterford county intermediate football
1 Waterford county junior football

First position
I started at full-forward. I was big at underage, a targetman more than anything else. Since then I've come into it a bit, they started moving me out the field. Underage I wasn't great; I played Tony Forrestal [inter-county U-14] alright, but only for a year. I was on the age [fourteen], where a lot of fellas were there at thirteen. It was only from minor on that I started to blossom, it was then I was moved out to wing-forward, under the puck-outs, and I've been there since, with an odd spell at full-forward. My favourite position would be centre-forward but people would probably say now my best position is right-half-forward, coming in off the wing onto the ball. I've got a lot of goals like that, in around the full-forward position, coming in off the wing. Centre-forward is

tougher because you're there with the centre-back, he's going to try to hold the middle, you have a big job to do, but you can lose your man more easily on the wing.

The qualities needed to be a top wing-forward

You have to be big to win the puck-out, that's important. Most wing-backs nowadays are big, you're not going to win ball unless you have a bit of size. You must have intelligence. It's not all about power and physique, it's also about timing your run, making space for yourself and for others, switching wings, getting onto the puck-out. You need pace, you need to be able to get away from your man after you've won the ball, or to get onto the break. You're going to be marking some of the biggest names in the game, guys like Seán Óg Ó hAilpín, J. J. Delaney, Tommy Walsh – all phenomenal hurlers. Trying to win ball off them is always a challenge, you need to be able to get away from them, take up different positions. And you need accuracy, you need to be able to score from 40, 50, 60 yards, out on the wing. It's a great advantage too to be able to catch a ball, but that's going to be made very difficult for you on some of the lads I mentioned earlier, they have the advantage there; what you must do then is to plan for the breaking ball, how to deal with that.

Is there a difference with the other wing?

I think so, definitely, if I was played over there I wouldn't be as strong. I like coming in from the right wing. Maybe if I caught the hurley left hand on top I'd be more comfortable on the left wing, but I prefer the right. Also, when you strike off your right, the ball is going to curl back, you can shape the ball over the bar. I can do the same thing off my left, from the left wing, and that's important, to be good off both sides.

Ghosting? Your goals against Limerick in the 2007 Munster final?

Yes, I couldn't believe the amount of space I got, but I suppose for the last one they were chasing the game, pushing forward, and when I see that I let my man push on, let him have the shot for a point even, because I know we now have an extra man up front and all it takes is one clearance and I'm free, in the clear. That's what happened against Limerick for the last goal. Tony Browne gets the ball, he doesn't even have to look, he knows where I am, and that's from playing together over the years.

And another one bites the dust *– Dan Shanahan scores a vital second-half goal against Limerick despite the best efforts of midfielder Donal O'Grady in the Guinness Munster Senior Hurling Championship final at Thurles, County Tipperary, in 2007.*

Where to stand in relation to your opponent

I like to keep my opponent guessing. Stand this side of him for one ball, the other side for another ball, move in, move out, move across; keep him off balance, keep working.

Tricks

People say I played the hurley a lot in the early days. If you time it wrong, you're caught, but if you time it right, it's a great way of winning good possession. It's much harder now, a lot easier for a back to do it than a forward, he can sweep your hurley and your hand in one movement and make it look like he's just protecting his hand. One I have is when I'm in on goal, to go as if I'm going to blast the shot then hit it softly, that throws the goalkeeper off balance.

Goals have been scored accidentally like that?

Exactly, the keeper is expecting a rocket, sets himself. I've seen [Paul] Flynn in training doing all kinds of things with the ball, dipping it, swerving it, all kinds of stuff. The goal he got against Cork [a dipper from 35m in the 2004 Munster final], that was deliberate. When he's setting up to take a free like that, I'll always stand in front of the goalie with my hurley up – have him guessing all the time, he doesn't know if you're going to get a tip on the ball at the last second. He's trying to concentrate on the man taking the free – don't let him settle, put him off.

Primary advice to a promising youngster, above all else, to master the wing-forward position

The biggest thing now at wing-forward is the puck-out; don't allow yourself to be pushed around here. Build yourself up, get stronger. And one thing, if you're going for it, go for it with everything you have. Develop an understanding with your goalkeeper, know what's going to happen, get your timing right. Get someone to hit long ball after ball at you, get to know how to cope with all the different kinds of ball that are likely to come your way. Know how to stand under the ball, know how to time your run, know how to time your jump.

Best advice you ever got?

To hell with the begrudgers. People are always waiting to knock you – to hell with them. I have a tattoo – 'If you don't know me, don't judge me.' A lot of the supporters know nothing about you, nothing about hurling, are only waiting to criticise you – ignore them. Work on your game, work for yourself, for your team. I have a regular job, I'll go to the gym now, two hours, go training tomorrow evening, a match at the weekend, and I have a young kid at home. We're all doing that, all the county players; no one sees it but everyone expects it.

And where d'you think you're going? *Joe Cooney, Galway, is 'tackled' by Noel Hickey, Kilkenny, in the All-Ireland Senior Hurling Championship semi-final at Croke Park, Dublin, on 13 August 2000. Peter Barry is in the background.*

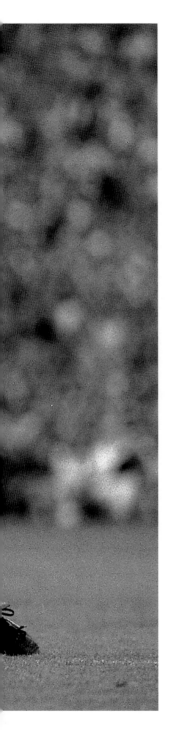

Centre-Forward
The Gamebreaker

Joe Cooney (Galway)
John Power (Kilkenny)
Gary Kirby (Limerick)
Martin Storey (Wexford)
Henry Shefflin (Kilkenny)

Goalkeeper apart, centre-back is the pivotal position on the hurling field. At least that was the majority opinion of those who were interviewed for this book. The centre-back is the glue that holds it all together, the man most expected to break up the opposition attack, the primary launch pad for his own attack. So where does that leave the centre-forward? He is the guy charged with the responsibility of taking on that centre-back; break through here, goes the logic, and a vital path is opened to the opposition's soft-spot. So, what tactic to use? What kind of player?

Here, we meet five players, four different styles. Joe Cooney and Gary Kirby were very much alike, two big, strong men, unorthodox hurling grip which even the best centre-backs found awkward to deal with, intelligent users of the ball, deadly accurate. John Power was simply an animal; not particularly tall, not particularly big, but with phenomenal drive, reckless courage, would give and take buckets of punishment, all with a singular aim – break that centre-back, open that gate for those around him to burst through. Then you had Martin Storey, and he was a different story. He had Power's briary combative attitude, but he also had ferocious pace, was a lethal marksman, a different challenge entirely for any centre-back. Finally, there's the man who has a little of them all, hurling's current marquee name, Henry Shefflin. Big, strong, athletic, good hand, fierce competitor, absolutely lethal with ball in hand. So, which style was most effective? As with every other position, different players with different physiques and different styles can slot in and do a job. What doesn't change, in any of the positions, are the basics.

JOE COONEY
(b. 1965, Sarsfields and Galway, 1984–2000)

AWARDS & MEDALS WON
1 Hurler of the Year (1987)
2 All-Ireland senior
5 All-Star awards
1 All-Ireland U-21
1 All-Ireland minor
3 National Hurling League
4 Railway Cup
4 Oireachtas
2 All-Ireland senior club
5 Galway county senior

First position

My primary position was probably centre-forward, but I preferred mid-field, the freedom you got there. You go forward, come back. In later years, as you slow up, it's a better position. You still have to cover ground, but you don't have to move as fast. If you can read the game it's a lovely place to finish up; you're never caught, you can see what's happening at both sides of the field.

The qualities needed to be a top centre-forward

You have to be good at ball-winning, that's very important for a centre-forward. Being a good man to catch is a major advantage, but if you can't do that, be able to hold it up there at least. Part of your job is to bring those around you into play, so you also need awareness, you have to know what's happening around you. You need to give the right type of ball, at the right time. There's no point in giving a high ball into someone who can't play the high ball, or an angled ball into the corner to a corner-forward who can't run. You have to know your forwards, know the kind of ball to give them to their advantage. Use what you get and use who you have.

The timing of the pass was very important, and [Brendan] Lynskey [former Galway great] was brilliant at that, a great head on him. He'd always give the ball at the right time. You know the fella who always gives it only when he has to, gives it at the last minute when the backs are after closing in on him, and on you – no good, you couldn't bear a lad like that. But the man who gives it at the right time – that was Lynskey. When I started, I was at wing-forward and he was brilliant at bringing you into the play. He could win the ball in the air, he could hold it, he could carry it when he had to, and he could pass. It was great to play beside him. You knew when to make the move, you knew when you were going to get the ball. You had to learn from a player like that.

Tricks

I suppose you'd have a few. There was one I had that I never tried at the top level: make the catch, shove the ball under your armpit, stand around for a few seconds as if you're looking for the ball, then when everyone is distracted, take it out again and hit it. I did it in a match against London once, in Athenry. A puck-out came and I caught it, in the middle of a bunch of players, stuck it under my arm. The lads were looking around the place, couldn't see the ball anywhere. I moved away a couple of paces, took out the ball, hit it over the bar. You'd be surprised what you'd get away with!

Tricks seen

Tony Kilkenny, who used to play midfield for Galway, was a devil for playing the hurley. He'd break your heart when you were on him. You'd have the hurl up to block the ball, next thing a full belt on your hurl, ball gone through. Most referees never spotted it, he got away with it most of the time.

Sylvie [Linnane, ferocious Galway corner-back], if he lost his hurl and the ball was still in his area, would take yours, he'd pull it out of your hands. I saw him doing that a few times.

Primary advice to a promising youngster, above all else, to master the centre-forward position

Hold your place, don't hold the ball. Don't go too far, don't crowd the midfield, don't crowd the full-forward. Get rid of the ball as fast as you can once you've won it, don't delay. It doesn't matter if you score yourself or not; keep the ball moving, keep the supply going into those inside, break it for the two wings.

Power by name, Power by nature, that was John. Due respect to all others, but this guy best epitomises the attitude needed for the centre-forward position.

JOHN POWER
(b. 1966, John Lockes, Callan and Kilkenny, 1986–2002)

AWARDS & MEDALS WON
1 Kilkenny Team of the Century (2000: centre-forward)
4 All-Ireland senior
1 All-Ireland junior
2 All-Star awards
3 National Hurling League
3 Railway Cup
2 Kilkenny county intermediate
1 Kilkenny county junior

First position

Initially I was wing-back, number five. Actually I played both centre-back and centre-forward for the centenary minor team in 1984. The best hurler I ever saw in Kilkenny was on that team, but he never made it afterwards as a senior – Tommy Lennon, our captain. With Kilkenny minors in 1984, I played centre-forward for the first couple of rounds, met Limerick in the All-Ireland final. With twenty minutes to go we were getting bet by eleven points and fellas on the line were saying we weren't worth feeding in Langtons [where Kilkenny teams traditionally get their meals after training], that this was a terrible display.

They brought Tommy up centre-forward and I went back to centre-back on [Gary] Kirby. I'd safely say I never hurled as good a twenty minutes, and Tommy Lennon got as good a goal as I've ever seen in hurling, put us a point ahead. It was from about 30 yards out, two lads went to challenge him, but he was very strong – broad shoulders, big chest, a pair of wrists that he'd shave you [with the hurley], left side or right. He was poor on his feet – a lorry rolled over his feet when he was a young lad – but other than that he had everything. He struck that goal off his left, roofed it, the top left corner, and now we were a point ahead, a total change around. The next puck-out, there was a chap called Stapleton with them, a huge fella, a man among chaps, and he caught it, let fly, over the black spot – a draw. We played them in the replay on the following Sunday and they beat us by a point, another great game. I saw something in that game though that I never saw before or since, in games or training, with club or county: Billy Ayers from James Stephens was midfield for us, he hit a ball, and it hopped on top of the post, the very tip of it, hopped the wrong side, and was waved wide, and we lost by a point.

The first game I played with the seniors was against Laois, 1985, at wing-back on Eugene Fennelly. I was only nineteen, just off the minors, Eddie Keher in charge, Walsh Cup in Durrow. That was in February. The talk then was that I was the coming man at wing-back. For the club I was midfield, centre-back, and if things were going bad I might be shoved up to the forwards.

The transition

That's a painful story. I went on playing wing-back, held down the position all through the league of 1986, met Westmeath in the quarter-final when they had a good team – the Kilcoynes, Mick and David. I broke my arm in that game, was in plaster up to the elbow, missed the semi-final and the final, against Galway, a dirty game up in Thurles, very physical, that set things up for the All-Ireland final in 1987 when there was no love lost. I got the cast off, came back. Seán Fennelly had taken my position at that stage and the Fennellys had kind of the upper hand, the Shamrocks going so well [seven Fennelly brothers on the team that won the county in 1988, four of whom played with Kilkenny at senior level]. I knew it was going to take a hell of a shove for me to get back for the championship and I never managed it – on the panel but never made the team.

In 1987, I was wing-back again, played the league there. I was head to head with Liam Walsh from Glenmore for the position, with Tommy Lennon also on the panel. I played in the Leinster final, didn't play in that All-Ireland semi-final against Antrim – injured again. Tommy got on in the final alright, but I didn't [Kilkenny lost to Galway].

The following year, I made my first real championship start, midfield with Ger Fennelly, scored 1-2. Wexford beat us but I got a goal in the last five minutes, that was a big thrill. I won a Railway Cup at wing-back in 1988, played there again in 1989 and got man of the match in Casement Park in one of them.

Pat Dwyer, Willie O'Connor and all those came through in 1989. I was a year or two ahead of them in experience, but we were the same age. We beat Wexford in the first round, I got man of the match in one of the papers – I was brilliant the same day, never hurled as well at wing-back. We were up against Offaly in the Leinster final and on the Wednesday, Thursday and Friday of that week I got a dose of the runs. Dr Bill Cuddihy came out to the house and gave me a load of tablets, rehydration drinks, the whole lot. I was adamant I'd play, but he was advising me against it.

'Don't play,' he said, 'you'll think you're fine but your muscles won't be right.' That was it anyway, I played, was on Mark Corrigan, their free-taker. He ended up with 3-6, but I'd say I was responsible for only 1-1, played reasonable enough. He got no point from play off me, one goal, but Jaysus I was hounded after that, suffered torture that summer. I was hearing it on the radio – 'John Power is not good enough for Kilkenny, can't take the pressure of the big day, will never make it.' That's why I treasure the All-Ireland medals I won afterwards so much – people have no idea of the hardship I suffered.

Dermot Healy took over in 1989 and '90, and I was very determined to make my point. I'm not sure what he thought of me though. In the run-up to the league in 1990, we had a game in John Locke Park in Callan, Healy in charge. I was the only Callan man on the team and I wasn't played, not even as a sub. We were having a bit of grub afterwards and Healy was passing me. 'I didn't like your attitude today,' he said.

'To be quite honest, Dermot,' I said, 'my father is eighty-five years of age; he's not able to go Croke Park, he's not able to go to Nowlan Park, but he was able to come to John Locke Park today, the only chance he'd have to see me play with the county. I'm that disappointed with you, as a person,' I said – I didn't hold back; 'If you had one man in Conahy [Healy's home club] who was on the county panel and there was a league match being played there for the first time in the history of the club, wouldn't you like to see him playing? In that situation I'd put you on, so I hope you understand the working of my head on this one. And we'll leave it at that.' I didn't raise my voice, didn't curse at him,

John Power, Denis Walsh, the ball. Everything else is a blur. As it should be. The All-Ireland Hurling final between Cork and Kilkenny in Croke Park, Dublin, on 6 September 1992

Five Kilkenny farmers. Five All-Ireland winners in 2002. From left: Charlie Carter, Richard Mullally, John Power, Noel Hickey and Walter Burke.

but I made my point.

Through the league in 1990 I'd say I was brilliant in every match – tunnel vision, I was so scalded by the criticism on papers and radio. I remember a fella, Prionsias Ó Duinn, from Kerry originally, on the radio one day said I shouldn't be on the team, I wasn't able for it – I was listening to it on the tractor and Jaysus I could have dived into the radio, I was so mad.

We won the league in 1990, Eamonn Morrissey was brilliant in the final. I was on John O'Connor [Wexford], played well again, I'd say it was a toss-up between myself and Eamonn for man of the match but he got it. We played the away final in New York, I was on Harry Ryan, a Kilkenny-man. The two of us were going for the ball, he was coming like a train for me, and whatever way I caught him with the elbow, into the ribcage, I nearly folded him – down he went. 'Jaysus' he said, 'for a light man, you pack some belt. I don't know what you hit me with!' He didn't complain though, in fairness to him. [Ray] Sampson from Limerick came over on me then, a big bulky lad. We won handy enough eventually.

Reigning league champions, we played Offaly in the Leinster final. I was still at wing-back, and it was supposed to be a foregone conclusion, we were going to beat them by twenty points. They beat us by eighteen instead. The World Cup was on in Italy and Kilkenny people left early to go away and watch the games, we were that bad. After eight minutes we were three points down and a few minutes later, myself and D. J. [Carey] found ourselves back in the dugout, taken off. The funny thing was, neither D. J. nor myself ever took a drink and I wondered if that was a factor, that we didn't join in with everyone else in the celebrations in New York after the league win, that maybe our faces didn't fit. Back on the farm again anyway, out of the championship in early July.

My mother died then on 19 July, after a week's holidays in Tramore; just dropped dead at the table, a young woman, and sure that was it, we buried her. I don't know what happened club-wise that year, but we didn't go great either. After what had happened the year before also [1989], I was cannon fodder now, over and done with, could never be put back out again for Kilkenny. That October, Ollie Walsh took over.

I was after winning a junior All-Ireland with Ollie back in 1986, at wing-back, up in Thurles, got man of the match. First thing Ollie did anyway was draw up a panel and we were all to go into Kilkenny in October to a players' meeting. With all the criticism I was after getting, all the disappointment, and with my mother after dying, I was in no humour for that, completely devastated. All I was doing was working, six in the morning 'til midnight. I didn't show for the meeting. We played Waterford in the park [Nowlan Park] and my name was still on the panel, but I didn't go in for that either. About three weeks before Christmas, a bang came on the door – Ollie. 'What's the matter?' he said, 'Aren't you coming in?'

'No, Ollie,' I said, 'I have no interest in hurling, I'm so disappointed, I'm giving the whole thing up.'

'Don't do that,' he said, 'Have a think on it. I have a jersey here for you. It's not number five, it's not midfield, it's not twenty-five either – it's number eleven. I have that jersey for you, I want you to do a job for me there. The next league game,' he said, 'that's where you'll be.'

'Why is that?' I said.

'I've been looking at you since you were a chap,' he said. 'You're the best man in the county to carry a ball and that's what I want you do to. When you get the ball, take them on, carry the ball. I'm putting it to you this evening,' he said. 'If you want a jersey, it's there for you. We're back training on Wednesday night, you're welcome to come. I understand only too well what you're after suffering with the loss of your mother; if you want another month to think about it it's there for you, but two months isn't there.'

The following Wednesday night I was there, in the gym with Mick O'Flynn – he was after taking over the training – and I spoke to no player, I was still that down, still devastated. I was coming out of the shower and Ollie came up to me. 'Are you coming down to Langton's?'

'Ah I won't, Ollie, I'm going home.'

'Into the car with me now,' he said. 'There's no more going home.' I got into the car, he had a brown paper bag, handed it to me. 'There's your jersey now for next year,' he said. 'Number eleven. Get yourself in order for it. I told you the other night what you have to do, and you don't have to do anything else.'

We were playing Wexford a few weeks later in the park. I was marking Liam Dunne and absolutely tore him to shreds. I ran myself into the ground, scored about 1-5, and I'd say that was probably the best

I ever played in that jersey. Dunne leathered me, he did all he could to me, but I just walked in over him. After that, with Ollie, I just went from strength to strength, my confidence kept growing. And that's how I ended up at centre-forward – desperate hardship. But, I'd be very grateful to Ollie, always, for what he did for me.

What was your favourite position?
I loved wing-back, but it has to be centre-forward now. There was that buzz; no matter what way the ball came to me it made no difference, you just went for it, took it on. Wing-back was a lovely position to play in. I've always said, if you're a hurler, wing-back is magical. You have your sidestep, your striking off left and right. If you're a hurler and can't play wing-back, you're a non-runner.

The qualities needed to be a top centre-forward

No fear, no fear under the flight of the ball, no matter what way it's coming. It's a fearless position, the ball is coming from any direction, there are bodies coming to meet you, you have to be ready to take the hits. I don't think being good in the air is critical. Being able to gain possession and stride towards goal at the same time, that's critical – break the line. The man who can do that is the most dangerous man of all. He has possession and he's already a half-step ahead, going towards goal. Distribution is important, intelligence. A lot of people think John Power had no hurling brain at all, a bull-in-a-china-shop kind of fella. I disagree. I had the skill, I had the brainpower – you can't play at that level if you don't. Crashing into fellas is fine, but you need a lot more than that; giving the pass, having the cop-on to know when to do it, to be aware of who's moving with you, that's very important, and I think I had that.

At wing-back, I think the side-step is the thing; lose the wing-forward with one step then deliver good ball to the forwards, that's what you want. Good on your feet, good hurler, good ball control – go back the generations, those are the guys.

Where to stand in relation to your opponent

I'd never stand in front of him before the throw-in, I'd always stand behind him, force him to come back. Under puck-outs I'd stand shoulder to shoulder, if I could.

Tricks

I often tripped a fella on the run back towards the goal after the ball breaks in past you. I'd stick the hurley between his legs and in the mad rush back no one would see it, or take any notice – the referee is following the ball. You'd end up on your own when you get the ball and maybe get a score, but you'd almost certainly get a belt on your way back out. But sure you wouldn't mind at that stage, damage done.

I saw Pat Delaney one very dry day scooping a heap of dust around the square with the nose of the hurley and scattering it, no one could see what was going on.

A favourite of mine was the dummy handpass. Adrian Ronan was giving me a hard time about that one day. 'But sure Adrian,' I said, 'I'm playing with so many dummies what else can I do?!' I even did it last year, in a special junior game, and it still works.

Primary advice to a promising youngster, above all else, to master the centre-forward position

The high ball – if you're going for it you're going for it, full on, and if you're going to let it off, let it off, but make up your mind early. Go with the hand or go with the 36 inches [the hurley], and in either case, don't spare the body, yours or his.

The vast majority of those who feature here have at least one All-Ireland senior hurling medal. Gary Kirby could have had two, probably should have had two, but in 1994 Limerick lost a late six-point lead to Offaly, were stunned and eventually lost by six. Then in 1996, just two years later, they let another great opportunity slip when and playing fourteen-man Wexford. It's not by medals alone that hurlers are measured, however; without question, Kirby was up there with the best.

GARY KIRBY
(b. 1967, Patrickswell and Limerick, 1986–99)

AWARDS & MEDALS WON
4 All-Star awards
1 All-Ireland U-21
1 All-Ireland minor
2 National Hurling League
3 Railway Cup
2 Munster senior club
10 Limerick county senior

The qualities needed to be a top centre-forward

I don't care what position you're talking about in the forwards, you must be able to score. A half-forward must also be strong under the high ball, he must be able to contest the high ball – he needn't necessarily win it, but he must be able to hold his ground, stop the half-back from making a clean catch, a good clearance. He must also be a half-back, and by that I mean he must be half a defender, half an attacker. He must be able to defend, must be able to spoil. I would never claim to have been a good hurler, but I was awkward, I got in the way of the centre-back, made it difficult for him. Communication is important, you've got to talk to the other forwards, let them know what's happening.

I've often heard you compared to Joe Cooney from Galway

I don't think I was as good as Joe, but we had similar styles. We were both okay in the air, both worked hard for the team. A lot of centre-forwards think they have to win every ball. You don't. I remember a

This is easy – I can do it with my eyes closed! *Limerick's Pat Heffernan, Gary Kirby and Damien Quigley with Offaly's Kevin Kinahan and Martin Hanamy, sleeping on the job in the All-Ireland senior hurling final on 4 September 1994.*

club match against Adare, I was on Shane Fitzgibbon, he pulled like a madman on every ball and the Adare crowd were going wild, loving it. I didn't even bother going for the ball at all. All I was trying to do was let it in behind, I'd lunge across him as if I was trying to catch it, throwing him slightly off his stroke. I don't think I hit a ball, but Barry Foley scored four points in the first twenty minutes because of that. The crowd can be very critical at times, but they don't see these things. At half-forward especially, a player can be doing a lot of unseen work but the ball must go through – this is a critical area.

We put Ollie [Moran] up to centre-forward because we wanted a strong man up there [Gary is a selector with Limerick for the past two seasons]. We felt he wasn't a man-marker at wing-back. Go back a few years, Neil Ronan [Cork] got four points off him in twenty minutes. Ollie likes to hurl too much, not good for a back. He had played there before but wasn't consistent, probably because he wasn't persisted with enough. We told him at the start of 2007, 'This is your position, get used to it because you're not going back.' A few times in the league, people were saying we should move him back but we wouldn't. Against Galway in 2007, he scored three points in the first twenty minutes, then disappeared. I talked to him, pointed out to him what he was doing wrong – back around the half-back-line, in midfield, everywhere but where he should be, the pattern ruined. And he listened; that's the thing about him – even at this stage he's willing to listen, to learn. We stuck with him and by the end of the year, I don't think he had any real rivals for the All-Star centre-forward position.

Where to stand in relation to your opponent

As a centre-forward I never liked to stand in front of the centre-back. Either shoulder-to-shoulder or slightly behind, that suited me. That way I was just able to touch his stick, catch the ball. It's a foul but you'd get away with it, in inter-county matches more so than in club matches – with big crowds, the ref wouldn't hear the little touch on the hurley, but in club matches he would. And that little touch would make all the difference.

Centre-backs hated it, even though they did it all the time as well. In training one night, myself and Ciarán Carey had war. We had brought in a referee for a match, the first two balls I went up, touched Ciarán's hurley, caught the two balls, two points – he cursed the referee out of it. The next ball that came down I did the same thing, the referee blew a free. 'You wouldn't have done that,' I said, 'only he roared at you. I'm entitled to protect my hand going up for the ball, aren't I?' At that stage it was getting serious; next ball we both stood back, let fly. I hit him right across the forehead, ten stitches. And this was in training! They still talk about it here [in Patrickswell]. That was the last time we ever marked each other in training!

At centre-forward also, you had to try to open the gap down the middle, pull the centre-back out of position, and that actually worked very well for us when I played with Ciarán at centre-back. He knew my form, I'd always be trying to pull my man away from the middle. For Ciarán's point against Clare in 1996, that's what happened [Munster semi-final winner, one of hurling's best ever]. Ciarán came through with the ball, on the solo, Seanie McMahon knew if he didn't go with me Ciarán had the option of passing the ball to me, so he came with me, over to the left. That was an understanding I developed with Ciarán over the years with Patrickswell – move out of the way of the man coming through.

John Power, former centre-back/wing-back, on Martin Storey, centre-forward/wing-forward – now that's a clash a lot of people would have paid good money to see! This interview took place in the company of Liam Dunne.

MARTIN STOREY
(b. 1964, Oulart-the-Ballagh and Wexford, 1985–2001)

AWARDS & MEDALS WON
1 All-Ireland senior (as captain)
3 All-Star awards
1 All-Ireland junior
2 Railway Cup
2 Oireachtas
5 Wexford county senior
1 Wexford county intermediate
1 Wexford county junior football

Favourite position

Centre-forward, because you're so involved. You can go out to midfield, to the two wings, into full-forward, the corners – you're touching on eight positions at centre-forward. It's part of your job to be involved, to chase everything, and I loved that.

The transition

I don't know how I ended up there to be honest – I was always on the wing with Wexford, but I seemed to have a different centre-forward beside me every year! Griffin [Liam, Wexford manager in 1996, when they won their first All-Ireland since 1968] took me as his consistent centre-forward, put me there and left me there. 'I don't know how to play here,' I told him, 'I'm used to the wing, doing things out there that won't work in here.'

'We'll show you,' he said, and I had to totally change my game in six months. On the wing I was able to turn inside or outside my man, use my pace to get away and make the room for the shot. All of a sudden I'm in the middle and I have to stand my ground, start creating things for the lads around me, take on the defence the odd time, but don't let the centre-back dominate. If you break the centre-back, you break 60 per cent of the setup for their forwards.

Did you train on Liam Dunne?
No, never – Griffin said we'd only take it in turn to hit the ball. We didn't train on each other with the club either. I loved being involved at centre-forward, I'd chase the ball all day. And I didn't care who I was marking – the bigger the name, the better I liked it, the more I loved to lower their colours. Brian Whelahan, Hubert Rigney, Pat O'Neill, Gerry McInerney, Peter Finnerty – I'd be rubbing the hands.

The qualities needed to be a top centre-forward

First-phase possession: puck-out, catch, turn and gone. Take them on, down the barrel of the gun. Your man is behind you now, you have to pull another defender out of position, create the scoring opportunity. Cause bedlam, that's what our neighbours in Kilkenny do. Down the middle, make sure you have the overlap. I've heard it said of a couple of young lads here in Wexford that they were lacking [ability]. I won't name names, but to me, they were the best wing-forwards I ever played with, for one reason; they always went with you on those runs and every time they called for the ball they were free – over the bar. They never called for the ball unless they were in position to take it. Make space, take the pass, and you were guaranteed they'd score.

Where to stand in relation to your opponent

It never bothered me – front, behind, the side, it was all the same. For their puck-outs I'd move out towards midfield and hope that man [Liam Dunne] would break the ball out to me. Even at club level I'd do the same, get to within about ten or fifteen yards of him. For our puck-outs I liked to stand behind if I could, then paw and maul all over him. If you can catch it or break it, you're now inside, he has to turn and try and catch you and that's very difficult for him, almost impossible unless he's lightning fast altogether. Maul him to death.

Tricks

Tipping the hurl at the last minute when I was catching the ball from behind, pushing the hurl out of the way. Holding a fella's hand, the hurl

Ye think ye have me, don't ye? Martin Storey finds his path blocked by Tipperary's David Kennedy and Thomas Costello (2), Eamonn Corcoran in support behind, during their All-Ireland Senior Hurling Championship semi-final at Croke Park, Dublin.

hand. We're running out to the ball, I'm on your hurl side, holding the hand, then let go at the last second and pick up the ball – fellas used to go mad. Walking on a fella's toes at the last second, putting him off balance. Running from about ten yards back and jumping up to catch the ball with your two knees up, burying yourself into the back of someone, with the referee seeing nothing.

Primary advice to a promising youngster, above all else, to master the centre-forward position

If he couldn't stand and catch first-phase ball I'd send him home!

King Henry he's being called in some quarters, much to his embar-rassment, but sometimes you get a nickname that just fits. This guy is indeed regal, a supreme hurler. If he stays healthy, he's going to break a lot of records, starting with D. J.'s All-Star awards total of nine.

HENRY SHEFFLIN
(b. 1979, Ballyhale Shamrocks and Kilkenny, 1998–present, all-time All-Ireland championship top scorer)

AWARDS & MEDALS WON
2 x 3 Hurler-of-the-Year (Texaco, Vodafone, GPA, 2002 and 2006)
7 All-Ireland senior (one as captain)
9 All-Star awards (joint top with football's Pat Spillane)
2 All-Ireland senior club (one as captain)
4 Kilkenny county senior
RTÉ Sports Person of the Year 2006
5 National Hurling League
3 Railway Cup

First position
When I was very young on the club team I was corner-forward, two girls in sixth class and myself were vying for the same position. Ann Moloney and Frances Houlihan, two very good camogie players, while I was only a young fella. From there on, centre-forward would have been the thing. We were a Roinn B club, short of numbers, myself and Aidan Cummins were two of the bigger, stronger lads so he played centre-back, I played centre-forward.

The transition
When I was in primary school my teacher, Joe Dunphy, was probably a bit ahead of the posse in his thinking; he wouldn't play me at centre-forward at all, he'd play me on the wing. His logic was that their centre-back would be their best player, so he'd play me somewhere else. With the club team, U-14, U-16, minor, I was always centre-forward.

What was your favourite position?

Anywhere on the half-forward-line. I was never mad about corner-forward, or even at full-forward you can be starved of possession. Out on the wing the puck-outs are coming down on you, a lot more action. And you have a bit more freedom there, you can end up in the full-forward line, out around the middle of the field, in the centre. It's the same at centre-forward, you have a bit more scope.

The qualities needed to be a top centre-forward

You need a biggish man, someone who is physically strong. Puck-outs are very important now, winning primary possession. Look back through the years, there haven't been too many small centre-forwards. If you have handy hurlers on the wings you need a fella who can mix it up, win the ball and throw it out, a ball-winner, where if you have a good ball-winner on the wing you can play off him. It's a real mix-and-match position, depending on the kind of players around you.

Ghosting ability?

I don't know where that comes from. Some lads would say you're just hiding, not getting stuck in in your own position. I feel that if one of our wing-backs or one of our midfielders gets the ball, there's no point in me holding my position because nine times out of ten, the ball is going to go in over our heads in the half-forward-line. In Kilkenny or in Ballyhale, where I grew up, when the ball is won on one side of the field, more than likely it's going to end up diagonally on the other side very shortly. If a wing-back or a wing-forward got the ball, more than likely he was going to hit a diagonal ball, criss-crossing, that was always the way we played. That meant that if you were centre-forward and the right-half-forward got the ball, you'd head for the left corner, and very often you'd end up with a free shot.

It can look spectacular when it comes off

It can, if you're in there and your man is still outside. I don't know if you'd call that ghosting but that is something I like to do, to drift, but you need the other lads to spot you, you need them to see what's happening, give you the ball, otherwise if the ball is hit straight to your position you can look very stupid.

Johnny Dooley said exactly the same thing?

Yeah, the other lads have to know where you are. And you need the ball-winners too in every game, the likes of John Power, John Hoyne, always there, doing the hard work for those around them. It's not something I think about, to go ghosting; wherever they play on the field most players like to be on the ball, though corner-backs might be a bit different. Corner-backs are more tidy, but wing-backs like to do a bit of hurling.

John Power was a very different type of centre-forward to yourself, but you can play direct too?

I suppose, yes, sometimes you need to be direct, but it depends on a lot of things. Early in the year the conditions are heavier, you're not going to be able to drift as much as you would in the summer, the ball isn't flying around the place. It also takes a lot more out of your legs to be drifting all over the place, so you conserve energy. Once the summer comes the ball is flying, lads are fitter, you can mix and match it a bit more, but you're still depending on those around you to spot your moves. If you're caught out of position a few times and the centre-back is clearing easy ball, you'll hear it from Brian [Cody, manager] soon enough – stay in your position. But some days it will work out great, everywhere you go, the ball follows. Some days though you'll come off the field thinking you played well, you got your scores, but when you look at the video you see that your man hit an amount of ball, so you have to get the balance right.

Do you play differently for club and county?

I don't think so, but I suppose with the club you'd be taking on more responsibility, you'd try to be more of a primary ball-winner. There aren't too many massive big lads in the forwards with the club, they'd be more hurlers. With the county there's a bit more size, more ball-winners, which would encourage you to drift a bit more. When you have the likes of J. J. Delaney, Tommy Walsh, Michael Kavanagh, Jackie Tyrrell on the wings, coming out with the ball, they're very cute on where they put it. They don't waste too many balls, which gives me a bit more leeway in the way I play. But I think I'm lucky with both club and county to have so many good hurlers around me.

Did you model yourself on anyone?

Not really, no, I never looked at anyone and thought, 'I want to play like him.' When I was growing up I liked watching Gary Kirby at centre-forward, I thought, 'Wouldn't it be great to be going out and scoring fifteen or sixteen points in every game?' Joe Cooney was another, he was brilliant. Galway were brilliant for a few years, then you move on,

Limerick were there, then Jamsie O'Connor, John Leahy, John Power, but I don't think I went out to model myself on anyone. You have your own strengths, your own weaknesses, you play accordingly.
Jimmy Doyle was Christy Ring growing up, you weren't Ring or Keher or Doyle?
No. I'd love to have been all those, but unfortunately I wasn't.

Where to stand in relation to your opponent

I was always kind of stood beside him, but that has changed. When I started you might be half a yard in front, but he'd be on your back and then it was a tussle for position. He was trying to get in front of you, you were trying to get in front of him, depending on the ball that was coming in. Now, where I stand varies, I might be at the side, come in at the last second.

Tricks seen

There was a lad with Graigue-Ballycallan, against us, a high ball coming down and next thing the helmet was knocked over the eyes. We had a great centre-forward, Jimmy Lawlor, he was the best man I ever saw to double on a ball in the air, did it so many times under a puck-out. I'd see him in training, bang, bang, bang, every time – that was something I couldn't do. That's a great skill, one I'd love to have in my armoury. Another one, the day John Troy bounced the ball back up into his hand, an amazing bit of skill, against Antrim in an All-Ireland semi-final.

Primary advice to a promising youngster, above all else, to master the centre-forward position

If he has all the tools, then I'd say use that toolbox, put in the hard work. There are plenty of lads out there who have all the skills, but they don't have the work ethic. If you're going to be playing centre-forward you're going to be involved a lot, in the middle of things. Get out there and use those tools. Work off the field, work on the field. I remember hearing this story from the parents of a young lad at home: there was a local school match the following day and he was picked, his first game ever. That evening his mother was giving him his dinner and he says, 'Mammy, I don't want dinner tonight.'

'Why not?'

'I have a match tomorrow, I want to be hungry for it...' But that's what you need to be – hungry.

The best advice you ever got

I'm after getting so much advice, and still getting it – you never stop learning. I can't remember anything that ever stuck out for me. I remember my father said to me one day, a little league match in the school, I was on my brother Paul, smaller than me, not as good as me, small field; we lost to Aidan Cummins' team, but I scored four goals, was pleased enough with myself. Two of those goals were from 65s which would actually have been a 15-yard free – it was only a 30-yard field. Going home, however, my father was giving out to me; 'You were hiding,' he said. I didn't like to hear that, but he was right, and that stuck with me – I had been hiding. Because of that I realised early you can't hide; even if you're scoring well you must keep working, and if things aren't working out for you, you concentrate on stopping your own man from hurling anyway, from doing any damage. Don't rest on your laurels if you're after getting a few scores, but don't give up either if things aren't going right for you.

Catch me if you can *– Henry Shefflin hits the turbo, chased by Pat Sheehan of Limerick on the evening the refurbished Gaelic Grounds reopened its doors.*

Left-Half-Forward
The Wing-man

Frankie Walsh (Waterford)
Mick Ryan (Dublin and Cork)
Eddie Keher (Kilkenny)
Gerard McGrattan (Down)

The current Waterford team has earned a reputation for itself as one of the most entertaining teams of recent years, as one of the most talented, as one of the most mercurial. Long before this side, however, there was another Waterford team with all the talents, another Waterford team that entertained the whole nation. They managed to win the big one, All-Ireland champions of 1959, but, like their modern counterparts, they were good enough to have won more. Captain of that 1959 side, right-half-forward, was Frankie Walsh.

Frankie Walsh (right) and Larry Guinan with the All-Ireland Liam McCarthy Cup, won in 1959.

FRANKIE WALSH
(b. 1936, Mount Sion and Waterford, 1955–1971)

AWARDS & MEDALS WON
1 All-Ireland senior hurling (captain)
1 National Hurling League
5 Railway Cup (1 as captain)
3 Munster championship
13 Waterford county senior

First position
I started at right-corner-forward.

The transition
In 1956, against Cork in Fermoy, in the championship [his first championship game], I got my skull fractured. I was advised afterwards never to play hurling again. I was a month in hospital, two weeks without visitors.

At that time, they didn't have team doctors as we have today, we were going around Fermoy after the match looking for a doctor. We couldn't find one and eventually I had to go to hospital. There was a lady surgeon there, she put me on the table. I thought it was only going to be for a few stitches, but she said to me, 'Young man, you're going nowhere tonight.' I was only just nineteen at the time. Pat Fanning [former GAA president, long-time Waterford official] was with me, and he said, 'What do you want to do Frankie?' I looked up at him. 'I want to go home Pat.' So Pat signed me out, off we went. I got sick on the way home, I had concussion and everything else.

Took me a while to recover, but when I got back I was moved out to the half-forward-line in challenges and so on with the club, and I have to say, I found left-half-forward a lovely position to play. You can move in, move out, move across, you're not as confined as you are inside, at least that was the situation in those days – I know it's changed a bit now. You're very dependent in the corner on the supply of the ball, on the kind of ball you're getting.

The qualities needed to be a top wing-forward

You had to be very alert and very accurate. You had to be able to go into the 21-yard line and take your score, but you had to be prepared to cover your man as well, that was very important as far as I was concerned. You don't see that enough nowadays – a half-forward should think like a half-back at times; when you're attacking you're attacking, but when your opponent has the ball you do the covering, the harrying, whatever is needed to win back that ball, or to slow down the clearance anyway. Give a hand in centre-field as well, when it's needed.

What was difference between the wings?

I was an unorthodox left-handed hurler. I had the right hand on top and it suited me to play on the left hand side. I was usually hitting into the strong side of my opponent also, but that was okay. I wasn't very strong off my right, but I was able to get out of trouble. I was strong on the ground, which was very important for a small man.

How small were you?

We were going up to the All-Ireland final in 1957, stopped the car in Carlow. Seamus Power [another star of that Waterford team] and myself said we'd stretch our legs. Cheasty [Tom, ironman at centre-forward] was with us – what he was doing in a Mount Sion car I don't know – and he said he had a pain in his head, went into a greengrocer's for an orange. Power went into a bookies to back a few horses. There was an ironmongery shop there, I was looking at the window display. Headed back to the car and there was a chemist shop with a weighing scales outside. Cheasty got up on it, over 13 stone, Power got up, over 12 stone or whatever it was, and they turned to me – 'Come on, get up.'

'Ah no,' I said, 'I know what I am, it's alright.'

'Too mean to spend the penny!' said Cheasty, 'Get up on the scales!' I got up anyway – 9 stone 7 pounds. 'A fecking jockey you should have been!' says Power. 'And I'm going to play an All-Ireland final with you tomorrow!'

Size wasn't that important though, not if you were pretty quick, which I was. I was able to get out of trouble. The tendency now is for big half-forwards under the puck-outs, but in my day the ball would usually only reach to centre-field anyway. I was able to double on the ball – most times, but not all the time; that was a big help also. At my size, you can't really contest the ball in the air, but you can keep it moving on the ground and the breaks will come. Throw it up the wing, the corner-forward might get it, keep going and you might get the return pass. That was our forte, in those days.

Was your first instinct to go for the score or just let the ball in?

It all depended on how much time you had, but if you were under pressure, if there was someone on your back, you just let the ball in. By all means, though, if you were in the clear, have a go.

The balls were very different back then?

They were; we used the McAuliffe ball in the Munster championship, made in Limerick. A week or two before the championship we'd get them. The Munster Council used those – it was a very big ball, a big rim, with a different flight to it. In training we used a Lawlor number one and number two.

What was the difference between those two?

I'm not sure, I think it was the ridge size. Later then, if we got to the All-Ireland series, we were playing with an O'Neills ball, which was different again, almost oval-shaped, and a very hard ball. After training with the Lawlor ball I found it difficult to adapt to the other balls. All the balls that time would lose their shape very easily. Another problem we had too was that if the ball was hit into the crowd, very often it didn't come back, the game would be held up for a while. I found the Lawlor balls best, maybe because we were more used to them. Kilkenny used them too, to my recollection. The modern ball is more like a tennis ball with a leather cover – I cut one of them open one day with a hacksaw, it was like a sponge ball.

What happened in that famous 1959 Munster championship semi-final against Tipp, reigning All-Ireland champions, but trailing Waterford at half-time by 8-2 to 0-0? They weren't exactly a Mickey Mouse team, and certainly it wasn't a Mickey Mouse defence, the men of Hell's Kitchen all intact?

No, it was the full Tipp team. We had played them in the league final, lost by fifteen points to seven, but we learned from it. We knew we had the beating of them after that, if we could keep the ball moving. And that's what we did, we kept the ball flying and they had no answer to us. There was a strong wind with us in the first half. We finished up with nine goals – I got two, Larry Guinan got three, Charlie Ware got three and Duck Whelan got one. I was the only one who scored for Waterford in the second half, I think it finished 9-4 to 3-4.

Where to stand in relation to your opponent

I didn't stand, I'd bring him on a little journey. Wherever the ball was I'd be moving, be ready for the break. I wouldn't be lying up against him anyway, put it that way. I'd do the running, let him do the chasing. But always, you have to be looking at the ball.

In the All-Ireland of 1959 we had a system where we'd interchange, which was unheard of at the time. John Kiely to full-forward, Duck Whelan moving out, Philly Grimes, Larry Guinan, Seamus Power, myself – if the inside forwards wanted to move out the field a bit, we might move out to midfield, under the puck-out. People were wondering what was happening but we knew. And always, you covered. No good having a midfielder in corner-forward and the ball being pucked out, no one on the opposition midfielder. Even if someone was down injured, someone would drop back to fill the gap – wing-back to corner-back, midfielder to wing-back, wing-forward to midfield, corner-forward to wing-forward; fill in the gap back along, leave it up in the full-forward line.

That was a revolutionary approach?

It was. If the centre-back comes out on a solo run, fill in behind him in case he loses the ball.

Tricks

No tricks, only one thing to do and that's get out in front at all times, if possible. Do your best, that's all.

Tricks seen

They say Mick Mackey, in a league final in Croke Park, took off on a solo run with his back to the referee, pretending he had the ball on his stick, but all the time it was in his hand! But tricks were rare, really. I saw Philly Grimes alright, used to catch the ball behind his back. Philly was a plasterer and when he was trowelling, he was able to toss the trowel over his shoulder and catch it behind his back, without looking. In the league final in 1963, he was left-corner-forward, I was left-half-forward, I drove a ball up along the wing and Phil took off, running with it, caught it on the run behind his back with his hand turned backwards, then over the bar – magnificent. He had a great pair of hands, he'd have made it in any sport, including boxing.

Port Láirge: Laistiar: S. Ó Catáin, D. Mac Ionnractaig, M. Ó Concubair, L. Ó Dubsoai, S. de Barún, M. de Lása, A. Ó Floinn, P. Ó Foglú, T. Ó Siosta, É. de Paor, L. Ó Dunpaí, S. Guid.
Cun Tosaig: T. Ó Cuinneagáin, S. Ó Cavla, L. Ó Guineáin, R. de Róiste, P. Ó Gréacáin (Capt), M. Ó Flanngáile, M. Ó Muirgeasea, P. Breatnac, S. de Paor, D. Ó Faoláin, S. Ó hÁirne.

In every hurling parish in the nation there are those who know their hurling inside out, real scholars of the game. They are not household names, never were, never will be, but their opinions are as valid as any multiple All-Star, as any multiple All-Ireland winner. To represent those thousands I've chosen a man from my own parish of Ballyhea, County Cork, a man from a magnificent hurling family. Had the breaks fallen a little more kindly for Mick Ryan, he would have made it at the very top. Mick is the grandfather of Dublin's Wayne Brogan, granduncle of Cork's Neil Ronan and granduncle also of promising Cork inter-county referee David Copps.

MICK RYAN
(b. 1929, Ballyhea, New Irelands, Cork, 1956–58, and Dublin, 1951–55)

AWARDS & MEDALS WON
1 All-Ireland junior hurling (Dublin)
2 Dublin county senior (New Irelands)
1 North Cork junior (Ballyhea)

First position
I started with Ballyhea school team at right-corner-forward, against Newtown of all teams [Newtownshandrum, Ballyhea's fiercest rivals]! I was probably about ten or eleven then.

What position did you play with Cork?
I started off in my first game, against Dublin, at left-half-forward, then they moved me at half-time to where I was playing with the club at the time, right-corner-forward, and that's where I stayed. In the first round of the Munster championship in 1956, against Waterford, I was on John Barron, scored 2-3 from play. I played against Tipperary then in the semi-final, in Limerick. I didn't score, but it was an awful day, we played against a storm in the first-half, hardly scored at all. None of the forwards got that much service, a very bad supply of the ball. I was dropped after that. Con Murphy, the great full-back, always said to me afterwards that I got a very raw deal. If he had had his way, I'd have been on the selection anyway. The team got a trip to America

afterwards, after losing the All-Ireland final, but he always said, 'Only for your 2-3 we wouldn't have beaten Waterford in the first round.' We beat Tipp in the finish and I did win a few frees off John Doyle.

Was he as tough as they say?
I played on John Doyle on a few occasions, in club matches as well, and I never found him dirty. I could never say that he pulled on me dirty, and that was saying something for the time. He'd hit you a good belt of a shoulder, try to drive you through the wire – in fact the best thing to do if you saw him coming was to get out of the way, because if he did hit you, you knew all about it! He was a big man, and a strong man.

Was he a good hurler?
I would have to say I didn't consider him a good hurler, not like Jimmy Finn anyway. I would rate Jimmy Finn and Seán Herbert as the two best wing-backs I ever came across, a Tipperary man and a Limerick man.

How did you lose your place for the Munster final?
I was newly married, living in Dublin, and I went to London a fortnight before the final for the weekend, on holidays – I should never have done that. I should have gone down to Cork training, made the wrong decision. I was running around the strand in Scarborough, when I should have been running around the Mardyke. It was stupidity, that's what it was, because I didn't even really want to go, I wanted to be in Cork. I still regret that. But, that's the way things go. I played again in 1957 and 1958, a couple of smaller matches, but I never played in the championship again. The last match was against Dublin in Croke Park, the finish up of the league.

I played for Dublin for three years, 1950, '51 and '52, but mostly junior. I never played much senior for them, never in the championship. I was picked for two matches alright, but didn't travel – once I had the flu. For the 1952 All-Ireland junior final, there was a bit of trouble with the county board. We were told we wouldn't be getting the jerseys if we won; we eventually got them because we simply refused to give them back.

Dublin club hurling was very strong that time. You had Faughs, Vincents, Young Irelands, all full of inter-county men. We had inter-county men as subs on our team that won the Dublin championship. P. J. Walsh from Offaly and Dublin, Seán Quinlivan of Clare, they were subs. We had Willie Jackson and Christy Hayes from Dublin on the team, the rest were outsiders. We won it twice, 1958 and 1959. We beat Vincents in the 1959 final, all the great Dublin players they had at that time.

Could you have played on the opposite wing?

I could, and did, but a place I found very hard to play was left-corner-forward. If I were in the right corner I was coming on to my left, which was my best side, but in the left corner – never liked it. The advantage of playing at wing-forward was that very often you got two chances from the same ball. You can play the ball in and go for the score, or if that isn't on, you can play the ball into the inside line and follow it up, and you have a fair chance of getting the ball again on the way out. That made it much easier to play on the wing than in the corner.

The major qualities needed to be a top wing-forward

First and foremost, speed and accuracy, and you must be able to read a game. What you need too is good service from your half-back-line.

Where to stand in relation to your opponent

I always stood between him and the sideline and that was for the overhead pull. The funny thing was that even though I was left-handed, I was better at the overhead pull with my right; break it through, follow up and I had a good chance then of taking it on my left. Ring always used that trick on the wing. On the left, he'd pull with the right, but break after it immediately, pick it the instant it hit the ground and he was gone. The greatest thing about Ring, when he arrived at the ball, when he went to pick it, most people slow down but he did the opposite, he accelerated through the ball and he was gone, like a greyhound. And you wouldn't catch him, he had a good burst of speed.

What was he like in training?

He took it deadly seriously and he expected everyone else to do the same, and he was the same in a match. My first game with Cork, against Dublin, I hit a ball in, stopped for a second where I was and watched it, and it went over the bar. Next thing Ring was beside me, looked me straight in the eye: 'Are you tired?' he asked. 'No,' I said, a bit puzzled by the question. 'Then go out and mark your man!' He came up to me then at half-time: 'Do you know Mick, if that ball had been pucked out quickly to your man, with you still standing there admiring your shot, the ball would have been down in our square and that score could

1956 Cork Senior Hurling Team. *Front row (left to right): Jack Barrett, Jimmy Brohan, Paddy Philpott, Mick Cashman, Christy Ring, Josie Hartnett, Christy O'Shea, Mick Ryan. Back row (left to right): Jim Rodgers, Willie John Daly, Gerard Murphy, Paddy Barry, Terry Kelly, Vincie Twomey, John Lyons, Jim Barry.*

have been cancelled out. What you do is done, no point in star-gazing. Move on.'

He had the biggest hands of any man I saw hurling. When he caught the ball, it almost disappeared in his fist. Against Waterford, the ball came up my side, I pulled left-handed across the square, Ring got it. He was on a fella called Johnny Cusack, and Cusack hit the ball in Ring's hand, just as he caught it – Ring held onto it. Cusack pulled again on his hand and again Ring held onto it, that was twice;. He slipped the hurley about six inches in his hand, shortened the grip, swung, put the ball in the roof of the net. And his hurley! The weight of it was fierce, and more tapes on it! No wonder he was able to drive the ball, with that weight, that power in his hand.

Tricks

I don't know if this was a trick but whenever I broke through and I was going to shoot for a score, I'd always dummy to shoot with the opposite side first, then bring the hurley across my body and take the shot. I found that very effective – get him to try and hook you on one side, change to the other and he wouldn't be able to follow as quickly, or shouldn't be!

Tricks seen

Mick Roche of Tipp, a class hurler, was very good at holding a man off while he was catching a ball. I saw Bobby Rackard at his best, at centre-back, doing the same thing with Wexford, and his brother Billy used it afterwards. With his right hand on the hurley, Bobby would force you forward, under the ball, so that you were helpless, and he was then able to make the catch. But Bobby Rackard was a lot stronger than he looked, I'd say he was the best hurler of the Rackards.

Did that Wexford team introduce the catch to hurling?

Yeah, the Rackards especially, Bobby and Billy, Nicky also to a certain extent, but more so the other two. Martin Codd won the All-Ireland for them in 1956, catching the ball over Willie John Daly – Willie John had no hope, far too small; I don't think he even saw the ball in that All-Ireland final, never mind the match!

Primary advice to a promising youngster, above all else, to master the wing-forward position

Whatever weakness he had, whatever he most lacked for the position, work on that, over and over again. If you're mainly one-sided, work on the weaker side. I was left-sided, but I developed a very good right, to the point where I could take frees with my right. Work on your weaknesses because in top class hurling you'll very quickly be found out.

You finished up with Ballyhea?

I did, back where I started, won a north Cork junior with them in 1965. We had some great characters around that time. Mick Doherty was a very witty man. Ballyhea were playing a match one day, I think it was against Doneraile in a tournament. Doneraile weren't expected to beat Ballyhea, but they did. Mick was asked what happened: 'I'll tell you the truth, I counted thirteen combs out before the match. Hub Pickett didn't need one, because he's bald, and I don't use a comb. And that was our problem.' Vanity, you see, fellas were more concerned about how they looked than about the match.

Just as there will be eternal debate in Kilkenny about who was the better goalkeeper, Ollie Walsh or Noel Skehan, the question will be posed – who was the better forward, Eddie Keher or D. J. Carey? Both operated on the left flank of attack, on the wing and in the corner, D. J. also spent a few good years at full-forward; both were brilliant.

EDDIE KEHER
(b. 1941, The Rower-Inistioge and Kilkenny, 1959–77)

AWARDS & MEDALS WON
1 Team of the Millennium (right-corner-forward)
1 Team of the Century (left-half-forward)
1 Hurler of the Year 1972
6 All-Ireland senior hurling (1 as captain)
5 All-Star awards (2 at left-half-forward,
   3 at left-corner-forward)
4 Cuchulainn awards (pre All-Star)
3 National Hurling League
9 Railway Cup
3 Oireachtas
1 Kilkenny county senior
1 Kilkenny county junior

First position

Wing-forward, number twelve, that was my most comfortable position. You had freedom out there and in my younger days I had speed, enough to be able to run onto a ball. That was my primary position starting off, but I finished off at left-corner-forward. The rule changes that came in in 1970 changed the role of the full-forward line. Before that, it was very physical, a lot of pushing and shoving, physical strength against physical strength. That was how the full-back-line played the full-forward line, but I had more room out in the half-forward-line. When the rule changed it made things easier inside. That gave me a new lease of life, in the corner. I was fortunate at the time to be playing with an exceptional Kilkenny team, backs, midfield and forwards. We got a great supply from out the field, we learned to read what was likely to happen – every forward sort of knew what was coming.

You could look after yourself though. Pat Henderson said you had a few interesting tussles?

We had, but Pat was very strong. I was strong enough I suppose, and fast, and if I hit someone I hit him; if I ran into someone or if someone went to take me on, I generally didn't come out second-best.

I felt my primary role as a forward was to win the ball and score, or set up a score. In the 1960s, I had a better chance of expressing that in the half-forward-line than I had in the full-forward line. After the rule changes in the 1970s, all six forwards now had to be hurlers, the thing was really opened up much more. It was still tough, and you didn't have all the precautions they take nowadays with doctors and ambulances on standby.

After I retired from hurling I was at a coaching seminar in Kildare, sitting beside Fan Larkin – he was over the Kilkenny minors at the time, I was managing the seniors. After the field-work there was a lecture on medical injuries, by an expert in the area. We sat at the back, side by side, listening to this. This kind of thing is mundane now but in the early 1970s, no. He was on about what you should do if a fella got an injury, that the manager had to run out, enquire if his neck was okay, if his back was okay, don't stir him if there was even a hint of risk. Check his neck, his stomach, call for a stretcher if he seemed to be in real trouble. I was listening to all this and I was looking at Fan beside me, out of the corner of my eye, wondering how he was reacting. Eventually he turned to me: 'Do you do all that?' he whispered.

'Oh God I do,' I said, to rise him. 'Don't you?'

'Oh God I don't,' he says.

'So what do you do if a fella is injured?'

'I run out,' says Fan, 'and I tell him – get up to hell, there's nothing wrong with you!'

The qualities needed to be a top wing-forward

In any half-forward position the first thing was to be able to win the ball in the air, either get it through and follow up, or win it outright. You also had to be able to read the game, see the gaps and go for them, either with the ball or for the ball. You had to be able to strike tidily, fluently, on the run, off the stick, off left side or right, whether you were going for a point or going for goal. In the full-forward line you needed to be able to open things up inside, create openings. Things have changed there since my time, now you have fellas playing all over the place. But in the traditional corner-forward role, your first touch needed to be at its peak. The ball generally came through the half-forward-line, from midfield or half-back – you needed to be able to run onto that ball at pace and control it first touch; you then needed to be able to hit it either on the run out, over your shoulder and over the bar, or be quick enough to make an angle for yourself to take a direct shot.

There was a difference between scoring from the half-forward-line and the full-forward line. Generally in the half-forward-line you were on your way towards the goal, whereas in the full-forward line you were going out from goal, you had to be able to hit backwards, over your shoulder or whatever. And patience, in the corner – you could be there for twenty minutes without getting a ball, depending on the way things were going. You had to be patient, and allied to that was concentration, you had to be able to hold your concentration during the valley period, then be off your mark before the back when the ball did come your way. Patience and concentration in the corner.

Where to stand in relation to your opponent

A step in front, in both positions, but obviously you'd be moving around, depending on what was happening down the field. But you wanted to be in front. I'd move, circle, try to have an advantage when the ball came, and I think I was fairly good at reading the play, generally got there first.

Tricks

I developed skills, as opposed to tricks, ways of getting the ball fast into the hand, that sort of thing. Everyone is using that now of course. The slice on the ball was something I used a lot; the dummy handpass the same, but more at club level than with the county.

Defence is an art form in Kilkenny. Was it tougher for you inside the county than outside?

It was, and this was true even in training. But Offaly developed the same style, even more so than Kilkenny for a while, though Kilkenny

45-degree angle to the ground and still perfectly balanced *– Eddie Keher in action against Cork during the All-Ireland Senior Hurling Championship final at Croke Park, Dublin, on 7 September 1969.*

are now gone ahead again. Kilkenny have the block, the hook, the flicks, the tap-away of the ball, but Offaly perfected that for a while in the late 1980s/early '90s. That's a great skill but some referees were blowing for that, which is wrong. I've always been a strong advocate of the skills in hurling, that should be the dominant feature, and it should also be uppermost in the minds of the referee. Skill should never be punished but some referees blow for stupid things, they don't recognise the skill involved.

Primary advice to a promising youngster, above all else, to master the wing-forward position

It's all about practising, developing your skill, your first touch, to the highest peak you can get it. Allied to that, concentration. There's no point in being able to dash out to a ball, being able to bring it into your hand with one touch, if you're being beaten out to every ball! You must concentrate, stay with the play.

I worked on my touch by hitting a ball against a wall, a soft ball, any wall. Left and right, pebble dash, move in and out, build up your skills, your reactions. We had a shop in the village at home and every so often I'd be asked to look after it. There was a little gap between the shop door and the hall door, a bit of wall, and between customers I'd be out there hitting the ball against that. After my move to corner-forward in later years, in the training pitch I'd have someone hit ball after ball at me, low and hard from about 30 yards, and practise running onto that from the end-line at full pace, controlling with one touch. I'd do that over and over again, a great exercise for corner-forward.

There have been many superb hurlers in Down over the generations, but lack of success at the top level means lack of exposure. It takes someone really special then, to win an All-Star award. That describes this man.

GERARD MCGRATTAN
(b. 1972, Portaferry and Down, 1992–2004)

AWARDS & MEDALS WON
1 All-Star award
1 National Hurling League (Division 2)
3 Ulster senior championship
1 Ulster minor
1 Ulster U-21
7 Down senior county (1 as captain)

First position
Corner-back! Gradually then I was moved up along the field – half-back, midfield, half-forward, and I stayed there. I won the All-Star on the right, but I played on both wings, right and left.

The qualities needed to be a top wing-forward
You need to be a ball-winner first and foremost. You need to have good catching ability, then you need speed to get away. You're the link player to the full-forward line, but you also need to be able to score, you need to be a good point-taker, off left and right. You must be able to score on the run, and you must be able to score from the angles.

Size is very important there. I was 6 foot 2, weighed in at around 14 stone, maybe a few pounds less, and that was an advantage.

You must be able to defend. Obviously their half-back-line is a major line, you must be able to break that down, stop them from playing, stop them from delivering good ball. The work-rate of the half-forwards can make a huge difference.

Difference between the wings?
It all depends on which side you're stronger on. I caught the hurl with my right hand on top, but I was a left-handed striker, so I always felt

Poise, balance, control. *Gerard McGrattan during the Ulster Hurling Championship semi-final in Casement Park, Belfast, on 21 June 1998.*

more comfortable coming into the centre off the right wing, onto my stronger side. But I don't think there's a big difference, certainly not if you're comfortable striking off both sides, which you should be at inter-county level.

After winning possession, did you tend to go up the wing or come into the centre?

I'd come up the middle, cut down the angle, and if you're two-sided then, you have more options.

Where to stand in relation to your opponent

If I was going to stand at all I'd prefer slightly in front, often on his catching-hand side, I'd use my body then to try and position myself to make the catch.

Tricks

Not many really. I was a very orthodox half-forward. My biggest asset was probably my speed and striking on the run. Maybe if you were on a smaller man you might throw the elbow in front, lean on his shoulder to keep him down, that sort of thing.

Primary advice to a promising youngster, above all else, to master the wing-forward position

Put in the hours, learn to strike equally well off both sides, work on all the other skills, work on your physique – you have to be strong in this position. Don't become predictable on the wing – move, don't be static. Learn how to move off either foot, how to change direction very quickly, move left and right, run at angles. Drop the left shoulder and come in on the right side, drop the right shoulder and come in on the left.

Best advice ever received

Have confidence in your own ability. Seán McGuinness, a clubmate of mine, told me that many years ago. Have confidence, but always believe you can improve, never think you're the finished article.

Right-Corner-Forward
The Cornerboys

Mick Bermingham (Dublin)
Charlie McCarthy (Cork)
Eoin Kelly (Tipperary)

It is absolutely, positively, the worst position in hurling. You wait and wait, hang around, hoping that any minute now the action will come your way. Like Gerard McGrattan, this guy didn't play for one of the leading counties, however, when a guy like Fan Larkin picks you as an awkward opponent, you definitely had something!

GAA president Nickey Brennan makes a presentation to Mick Bermingham to mark the thirty-fifth anniversary of the Vodafone GAA All-Star Awards scheme at a special celebration in Croke Park, Dublin, on 7 November 2006. Mick was an All-Star in 1971 and is one of only two Dublin players to win that award.

MICK BERMINGHAM

(b. 1942, Crokes, Kilmacud Crokes, and Dublin, 1960–78 at senior level, 1979–82 at intermediate level, Galway in New York and New York the county, 1965–70)

AWARDS & MEDALS WON

1 Team of the Century (1984: corner-forward on the non All-Ireland-winning team)
1 All-Star award (1971)
2 National Hurling League (Division 2)
6 Railway Cup
1 Leinster senior championship
1 Leinster intermediate championship
2 Dublin county senior (1 as captain)
2 Dublin county intermediate

First position

I started off in the forwards, half-forward, corner-forward. My father was from Ballinderry in Galway, a first cousin of Mick Gill. My mother was also from Galway, her brother was Paddy Forde from Oranmore, so there was a strong hurling tradition in the house.

The qualities needed to be a top corner-forward

Usually the corner-forward isn't a big man – I was about 5 foot 8 – so you don't stay static, you're always on the move, looking for the break. I don't know if I was fast, but I wasn't slow. Put it this way, I could get out of trouble. Those days too you had to be courageous, you had a very different setup in the backline, different mentality. You had the likes of John Doyle back there, he gave me a bit of a skelping in 1965 – I scored 2-3 off him, believe it or not. I got a few reminders from him, but in our house you never showed the white feather, that's not the way you were brought up. Doyle was hard, but he wasn't dirty. In fact I'd say I never met a dirty corner-back in my life. I met a few hard men though, I can tell you that, but then again no one ever forced me to hurl. You got a few stitches here and there, but you got on with it.

Did you score more goals or points?

I was always a goal man, goals, goals, goals. In around there, the chances are bound to come, but if you're any good you only need the half-chance.

Was there a difference between playing the two corners?

I don't know if there was that much difference. The thing about playing either of the corners, if you were good on your right side, you had to practise your left until you had that perfected, and vice versa. There was no use being one-sided at corner-forward, no matter what corner you were in, because you were too easily marked then. I was right-handed, but I had great confidence in my left also. And if you're corner-forward, you'll often have to go across goal to meet the ball. Don't ever be predictable; the corner-back loves to see you stay, he hates the man who moves around, especially the man who moves across the goal. They'd all love to be in their own little patch.

Where to stand in relation to your opponent

I'd let him see where I was, then as soon as he looked away I was gone. If he was ball-watching, I was gone. Over the years, when you were playing against the same guys for long enough, you got to know their tendencies and you could play to that.

What was it like as a forward against Kilkenny?

Honest answer, I don't think I ever failed to score against Kilkenny, I think I had a good percentage against them. Fan Larkin, Pat Henderson, Jim Treacy, I did alright against all of them. You got a few reminders, but you expected that.

Primary advice to a promising youngster, above all else, to master the corner-forward position

Concentrate; stay focused, and stay patient. That comes with the territory in there. Train hard in your off-time; the best training you'll ever do is on your own, you can't just rely on what you're doing with your club or county. Go away on your own with three or four hurling balls and perfect the skills, work on your weaknesses.

Best advice ever received

It was from my own father: 'Don't ever come home crying to me!' That was his attitude; play the game, look after yourself, and don't be complaining when the game is over. He had no time for the fellas who showed the white feather, ever.

He was Charlie, Charlie Mac, goal-scoring poster boy of Cork hurling in the days before hurling became the glamour game it is today, the guy with the pop star looks and the permanent tan. It wasn't for his looks he was most respected, however, it was for his lethal finishing.

CHARLIE MCCARTHY
(b.1946, St Finbarr's and Cork, 1965–80)

AWARDS & MEDALS WON
5 All-Ireland senior hurling (1 as captain)
3 All-Star awards
1 All-Ireland U-21
1 All-Ireland minor
5 National Hurling League
1 Railway Cup (as captain)
1 Oireachtas
2 All-Ireland senior club
6 Cork county senior

First position
Corner forward; I started there in primary school, the primary league U-14, Sullivan's Quay, under Brother Magill. I was nine, he came into class one day and asked if I'd go out training. My first time playing corner-forward would have been with that team, my first match against Greenmount NS. Previous to that I played in the Lough leagues, around midfield in that, but I wasn't strong enough for centre-forward with the school at U-14, too young, so I was shoved in corner-forward.

Did you have a go at the soccer?
I live around the corner from Turner's Cross now [home to Cork City soccer club], but I lived in Tower Street then, which is in further [towards the city]. Tower Rovers were very established around there as a soccer team. Most of my friends would have been playing soccer and I often trained with them, but my mother said no, had to be hurling and Gaelic football. Hard to believe now, I suppose, but she was a fierce GAA woman. I played with Redmond's for a few years before going to the Barrs.

What was your favourite position?

I'd have to say corner-forward, even though when I played I was only about 10½ stone, up against fellas who were 13 or 14 stone, 6 foot tall. Different rules then too – I was watching clips recently of Waterford and Kilkenny in the 1959 All-Ireland final and it just reminded me of what hurling was like back then. To my mind it wasn't hurling at all, a lot of the time; the ball would be 60 feet up in the air, going wide, but you were still getting a hurley across the back of the neck. No sense to it, but that was the way it was played that time. I wasn't able to go in and start pushing fellas around, not at my size, so my aim was to keep moving, get lost, don't let the corner-back nail you down because if he did, you mightn't get up for a while! I had to be faster than the man I was on.

Most players hated the corner. John Fenton says he was told you have to be born there

There's no doubt about that, yes; as a coach over the years you'd have lads at corner-forward and the one thing you have to impress on them over and over – you have to have patience. You could be there for the first fifteen minutes, there could be balls going wide 60 feet away from you, no hope of getting to them and you start wondering – are you ever going to get a ball at all? But there's always the chance of a break, there's always the chance of a goal, or maybe two; you mightn't get a puck for the rest of the game, but that's the way it was. That's the way I played it anyway.

It's a terrible position for sideline abuse. Your man goes out the field 30 yards and you go with him, the ball goes wide behind you and you're told – 'Get back into your position!' You go back, your man goes out again, clears a ball on his own, and the shout comes in – 'McCarthy, mark your man!' What did you do, go or stay?

As time went on I got better at judging every situation. Sometimes I went with him, sometimes I stayed back, took a chance that he might miss the ball. My thinking was that if the ball was being contested there was a better chance it would come through to me. Sometimes it did, but when it didn't, you could look like a right fool. But that was up to yourself, you had to make that decision. You poached a lot. A ball coming into the square, I'd never contest it in the air, I'd always step out, wait for the break. Seánie [O'Leary, other corner-forward] was another poacher.

Did you score more goals or points?

I'd say I scored more goals. You'd nearly always get a goal or two at corner-forward. There were days you wouldn't, you might get a few points and that was grand, but it was way better to get a goal – gives you confidence, knocks the confidence out of the corner-back.

Was there a difference between playing the two corners?

I played right corner, loved it; tried left corner a few times, but I preferred the right. I loved the low ball coming across the square from the left, a couple of inches off the ground. I scored a lot of goals just whipping on that ball.

But you were right-handed. Shouldn't the left corner have been more natural?

Maybe, but I had a very good left side, did a huge amount of practice on that side. The ball coming from the left corner, I loved coming onto that, I loved the first-time ground shot. There were times too you'd come around the other way, make an angle for yourself with your right side. Over the years I just got acclimatised to it, I suppose.

The qualities needed to be a top corner-forward

Patience, you certainly need that. A burst of speed was important also, a burst out to the ball, a burst across the goal – you needed that burst of speed. And concentration, staying alert at all times, that was critical. A high ball coming in, looks like it's going wide or over the bar, next thing it hits the upright – you have to be there for the rebound. How often do you see it happen that the ball comes back off the upright, nobody there?

First touch is important, getting fast control of the ball. The turn is important, after you win possession, and the swerve. I'm not boasting or anything like that, but I was fairly nifty over about 20 yards, and I could go off either side, which was a big plus. Quite a number of fellas would nearly always go to the same side, but I could go left or right. Anticipation is part of it. A ball is going between your half-forward and the half-back, you had to be going, reading what you think is going to happen. I know that the half-forward today is more likely to pick that ball, but in my time it was probably going to be hit on the ground, first time; you had to anticipate that, get out first

Courage is very important – you're codding yourself if you think you're not going to get knocks. You're not going to get anything easy in there. If you get possession and you want to get inside your man, you're not going to do it too easy, and if you manage it once he's going to be even more determined to take you the next time. That's a huge thing at corner-forward, you must be ready to take the knocks.

When Eddie O'Brien got his third goal in the All-Ireland final of 1970, Ned Colfer was after him, flaking him like you'd flake a horse – if that happened today, Ned would get twelve months but he wasn't even warned for it. That was the difference, to my mind that isn't hurling but it was par for the course that time. You're talking about courage – what Eddie had to suffer to get that goal!

I played on Jim Treacy, as tough as they come, but I never minded that. He wasn't the fastest, but he read the game very well, was able to hurl, knew when to give you the little touch to just knock you off stride, very strong too. You'd get the usual oul' belt but it was always with the ball around the area – if the ball was at the other end he wasn't 'dalking' you, poking you, like other fellas did.

Martin Hanamy spoke of corner-forwards who wouldn't take you on, who, even when they had the beating of you, would take the easy point rather than go for the jugular?

He made a very good point there. I've seen it so many times with Cork in the last ten or fifteen years – corner-forward gets the ball, wicked fast, heads for goal but never goes far enough, takes the point. That's taking the easy option. How many times have you seen Eddie Brennan or D. J. Carey [both Kilkenny] take on his man in the same situation, go for goal?

Ray Cummins, did he revolutionise the full-forward position?

Oh, he was a fantastic player, without doubt. The first time I played with him was the All-Ireland final of 1969, he had come on as a sub in the Munster final and he stayed full-forward then. He was the first I saw in that position who plucked the ball out of the air, which was a great advantage. If he was tied up, he was able to lay it off to Seánie [O'Leary] or myself, or whoever was there. He was fantastic like that, very unselfish, a great distributor of the ball with Blackrock and Cork – he definitely brought the game on. He had a brilliant way of catching the ball – he'd go up, make the catch, but before he hit the ground he was already turning, heading for goal. He wasn't the fastest, speed-wise, but he was good over ten or fifteen yards, and he'd always head for goal; nine times out of ten then it was either a goal or a free. A class player, superb.

Where to stand in relation to your opponent

I can honestly say, I never stood, I just kept moving, kept moving. My first senior championship match with the Barrs, I never forgot it. I was seventeen, we were playing the College, 1963, the semi-final of the county. I came on as a sub at half-time and Mick Ryan, who won three All-Irelands with Tipperary, a brilliant player, was full-forward with the Barrs – he must have been forty. He was watching me when the ball was up at the other end, I was standing in front of my opponent. He came over to me – I thought this was brilliant – he pulled me aside and said to me: 'Don't you ever stand in front of your opponent again when

Put it there, Ger *– supervised by referee Charlie Rankins, Charlie McCarthy shakes hands with Kilkenny captain Ger Henderson before the All-Ireland final of 1978.*

the ball is at the other end. He can see you, he can see the ball and he can see everything that's happening out the field. Take him out to the corner flag, take him out to the 21, come back to the endline – keep on the move, don't give him a chance to settle.' That stuck with me for the rest of my career and that's what I did. I was able to do it because I was always fit enough – keep moving, you're upsetting him. He'd like you to stand next to him, in front of him, but keep moving, even if some days you're knackered – keep moving.

Tricks

I don't know if you'd call it a trick, but what I liked doing when I won possession was running at an opponent, let him get close to you, then sidestep him, a swerve – I could jink off either foot, strike off either side, which is a big advantage. I worked very hard on that, always had it, even when I was going to school. Another one you might chance, if you were caught behind your man and a low ball coming in, just flick up his hurley, let the ball through. It's a free, but sometimes you'd get away with it if you did it discreetly enough, and I did. You might tap a ball over a fella's head as well, pick it up on the other side, but you wouldn't get away with that too often! You paid a price for it, the corner-back didn't like being made a fool of!

There was one where I'd go as if I was going to belt the ball into one corner, send the keeper the wrong way, then tap it into the other corner.

Did you place the ball or power the ball?

It all depended, but mostly power, low and for the corner. Trying to place the ball, you can be too clever, and I've seen that, but when you're so close I think you're nearly always better off to go for power, if you can.

Primary advice to a promising youngster, above all else, to master the corner-forward position

If he's a good hurler, if he has the touch you need in there, if he has the patience, I'd tell him to work on his fitness, his sharpness, his first touch. I'd also be telling him, any ball in around the square, first-time it; don't delay – be alert, pounce, take your knocks because if you get that goal, it's all worth it.

So many times it's been said that if there was a transfer system in the GAA, this guy would probably have set the record many years ago. Flagged early, he starred for Tipp U-21s at seventeen, was on the senior team at eighteen and has been there since.

EOIN KELLY
(b. 1982, Mullinahone and Tipperary, 2000–present)

AWARDS & MEDALS WON
2 All-Ireland senior (one as captain, 2010)
6 All-Star awards
2 Young Hurler of the Year awards
2 National Hurling League
1 Railway Cup
1 Tipperary county senior
Top all-time championship scorer for Tipperary, and still going strong

First position
My first game, I was eight years of age, playing U-12. I started at right-half-forward, but I played a lot in goal at underage. I was always that two or three years younger than the age, so that's where I was put. At U-12 I played all my hurling out the field, but when I was about ten I was in goals for the U-14 team; at twelve I was in goals for the U-16s; at fourteen in goals for the minors and U-21s; at fifteen I was sub-keeper for the senior team. I liked it there too, I was probably too young to be out the field anyway so it was great to be getting a game. I was big enough for my age, I was probably as big at twelve as I am now, and I had the hairy legs at fourteen, always had that strength.

Were you a good keeper?
Well, I played in goal at fifteen with the Tipp minors in 1997 against Waterford. I remember my first puck-out – bang, landed it out over the stand in Fermoy! Bad start. Next ball that came in, it landed on the ground in front of me but instead of getting the hurley under it to rise it, I picked it straight off the ground, gave away a penalty – brutal start! But I made a good save in the second half which redeemed me a small

bit. We then beat Limerick in the semi-final and I ended up at corner-forward for the final, against Clare, won that – Donal Shelley got two goals with the last two pucks of the game to win it. I was called into the U-21s then when I was seventeen as sub-keeper, but ended up out the field. That was 1999, the famous evening down in Ennis against Clare. That was pretty hostile! I played four years at minor, five at U-21.

On the day I finished my Leaving Cert in 2000 – Construction Studies – I got the call, my first night training with the Tipp seniors, 25 June. I was nervous, so nervous that I split Noel Morris; a high ball dropping down and I pulled with pure fear, split him. I was in goal, out the field – wherever they needed someone to fill in the numbers. We came to the championship, against Galway, I was wearing the sub-keeper's jersey, number sixteen, felt safe as houses. Brendan Cummins in goal, no fear I was going to see any action here anyway. And then he went down, injured. I got an awful shock, I was thinking, 'There's no way I'm going in here!' I remember turning to Paddy O'Brien [another sub] in the dugout – 'If they ask me to go on, where do I run to?' I was only delighted to be on the panel, but there was no way I wanted to go into goals. Brendan Cummins got up anyway, saved my bacon.

About fifteen minutes to go in the game, Nicky English [Tipp manager] shouted to Hotpoint [John 'Hotpoint' Hayes, long-serving Tipperary kitman who works for that company] to get the outfield number sixteen jersey. I had no idea what was happening, no one had told me anything. The previous night Declan Ryan had been fitness-tested and Nicky had called me out to fetch the balls in the ditch. They had about a dozen sliotars and Declan was to run onto them, put them over the bar and I'd run after them like a little dog, dig them out of the ditch, throw them back to Declan. I thought that was my job; only eighteen, whatever was to be done, I'd do it. And now I was being called onto the field. I don't know where they pulled that outfield number sixteen from – you couldn't have a lad going in with a keeper's jersey – but looking back now it was all for the best. I had no time to think about it, no time to get nervous. I went in full-forward on Brian Feeney, a hardy boy – all the Athenry boys were fierce tough. I was still minor then, around July. With the club, however, I'd have been corner-forward all the way up along.

You were very young to be playing senior hurling. In 2002, against Tipperary in Páirc Uí Chaoimh, you were bounced around between Ollie Baker and Seánie McMahon, like the ball in a pinball machine – did that hurt?

No it didn't – the adrenalin I suppose. To get hit by lads like Seánie and Ollie – these lads were stars in my eyes, still are – but you got a buzz off it. If you were hit by a lad from Feakle that you never heard tell of, that meant nothing, but you'd nearly relish getting a hit from the bigger players. They had that aura about them. I remember a day when it did hurt though, but I wasn't the one who was hit. In 2002, after winning the All-Ireland the year before, we played Wexford in Wexford Park in the league, a bit of a grudge match after beating them in the All-Ireland semi-final of 2001, after a replay. We were after coming back from holidays, had already lost our first league game, were not in great shape. John O'Brien – with whom I'd be very friendly – I can still see his hand going down to catch a low breaking ball and Liam Dunne [hardy Wexford centre-back] came in, let fly. A cold, miserable, wet day, but the ball was there, no complaints, and we got the free. As I bent down to pick up the ball, I looked at Johnno, nursing his hand. 'Phew,' I said to him, 'That must have hurt!' and then Liam Dunne looked at him, with a bit of a smile: 'I just can't keep away from those yellow cards!'

What was your favourite position?

I'm so used to corner-forward now, I have my own techniques, so I enjoy that. I like centre-forward also, I find you're in the thick of the game out there, you're on the ball a lot more, whereas in the corner you're out of the play a lot.

The qualities needed to be a top corner-forward

You have to be able to read the game, get onto the breaks. My dad would always have said to me – and he probably read it somewhere, probably something Christy Ring said at some stage – that you'll end up getting more scores from the other corner than you will from your own. If Christy Ring said it, we should all be paying attention. My dad would tell me, 'It's pointless going up to Thurles and training in November, December, January, February, March, April, May,

'I had the hairy legs at fourteen, always had that strength ...' Eoin Kelly drives past Antrim's Ciaran Herron during All-Ireland quarter-final match at Croke Park, Dublin.

seven months of the year, then going into corner-forward and standing beside the corner-back. Why did you bother going to Thurles all those months? For that?'

It makes perfect sense, doesn't it? Wouldn't the corner-back love you to stand beside him all day? When you're there he's comfortable, but if you're moving, popping onto the breaks here and there, he's under pressure. I know this, the days I don't work, the days I'm not moving around, I'm not as effective. After games like that my dad often says to me, 'You stayed in your corner, you stayed in your box.' That's why I'm saying you have to be reading the game, you have to be moving all the time, and moving into position. You never have it perfected. I'm always listening out for tips on how to do better in this position, for advice. I think even when you're finished you still won't have learned it all. And you're not just moving for the sake of moving – always move with purpose, know what you're doing.

Patience is big in the corner, definitely, which is one of the reasons why a move to centre-forward every now and then is like a new lease of life, you're on the ball more often. Knowing the fellas outside you, that's important; sometimes a little word in a fella's ear before the game can be beneficial, just to let him know the kind of ball you like, or just as important, the kind of ball you don't like. I know it sounds great, but this diagonal ball to the corner – I hate it. Your back is to the goal, you're outside the back, you're moving away from goal, so that number one, you have to win it; number two, you have to try to beat your man, to get back inside; number three, you have to try and score. The ball should be sent in between yourself and the goal. I'd always have a word with the number seven, with the midfielder who's on the opposite side of the field to me, with the twelve and with the eleven, those are the guys who are crucial to you at thirteen, they are the ones who will be giving you most of your supply of ball. The diagonal ball between you and the posts, you can have it in your hand and turned, gone the extra step before the back is turned, but that diagonal ball into the corner – no thanks. That's one thing I'm always preaching to the lads.

D. J. reckons that with a two-man full-forward line, the forwards should stay tight, draw the third man, then try to pounce on the breaks?

He's right; I remember that happened to us in a club game, we had a man sent off, bad weather, two-man full-forward line on three backs and I remember saying to the other corner-forward – let's bunch into the middle here and see what happens. My idea was to get in on the ball, get rooting, then get onto the break and you have a good chance of breaking through, or of winning a free. If it's wide and open, two can't cover three.

Where to stand in relation to your opponent

I'd agree with Charlie McCarthy, you never stand.

Tricks

I have that shot that I hit over my shoulder, almost impossible to block down. I think that shot came from going to the local GAA pitch with your mates, basically ghouling around, trying different shots – shots from the sideline, shots from the corner flag, shots with your back to the goal. At this stage it's automatic with me, I can calculate without thinking where the goals are. The best one I heard – I think it was Jimmy Doyle said it, and I've always carried this with me – the goalposts never move. It makes sense, and if you get that ball you could hit it with your eyes closed and you know where the posts are, it will go over. But it's never anything I plan, it just happens in games.

Tricks seen
Declan Ryan did this one very well, and Neil Ronan does it now – power into your man with the shoulder, he goes backwards a step, you bounce the other way but you're after making that yard of space to get off the shot.

Primary advice to a promising youngster, above all else, to master the corner-forward position
Assuming he has all the tools, the one thing I'd work on is his mentality. Attack the ball, no fear, don't be afraid to make mistakes – don't give two damns, basically. I'd have him attacking every ball at a hundred miles an hour, and if one went through his legs I'd run into him – 'Don't worry about it, well done, get the next one!' I'd nearly be hugging him, lift him – attack the ball, go crazy for the ball.

Full-Forward
The Rock-Breaker

Ray Cummins (Cork)
Joe McKenna (Offaly and Limerick)
Liam Fennelly (Kilkenny)
Olcan McFetridge (Antrim)
D. J. Carey (Kilkenny)

There are those who defined their positions, then there are those who re-defined their positions. Ray Cummins is generally acknowledged as being among the latter. He came on the Cork senior team in 1969 and was almost the antithesis of what would have been seen at the time as the ideal full-forward. Tall, gangly, non-confrontational, he should have been eaten alive by the flesh-eaters who guarded the edge of the square in those days. And yet he thrived, blossomed, to such an extent that even at club level team managers began to look at the position anew.

Brothers Ray and Brendan Cummins enjoy a Willie Murphy (Wexford) sandwich with Jimmy Barry Murphy in the background in the All-Ireland final on 5 September 1976.

RAY CUMMINS
(b. 1948, Blackrock and Cork, 1968–82)

AWARDS & MEDALS WON
5 All-Ireland senior (4 hurling, 1 football)
5 All-Star awards (3 hurling, 2 football)
3 National Hurling League
4 Railway Cup (3 hurling, 1 football, two in one year)
3 All-Ireland club hurling
12 Munster senior (a record; 9 hurling, 3 football)
6 Cork county senior (4 Blackrock, 1 UCC hurling, 1 UCC football)

First position
I started off in the backs, which is something that helped me an awful lot when I went to full-forward. I started in the half-back-line – a very moderate half-back I must admit, but what it taught me was the kind of thing that was difficult for a back to handle. I used that to my advantage afterwards, trying to do what I knew the back didn't like. When I'm coaching kids now and we're playing backs and forwards, I would often change them around, put the backs playing forwards, the forwards playing backs. That gives you a great insight into what your opponent doesn't want you to do, and a lot of hurling is just mind-games.

The transition
It happened in the College first, actually. I wasn't good enough for the half-back-line. I think it was a challenge game we were playing one evening and they put me into full-forward. I'd say it was because I was playing full-forward in football, so they probably felt I could do the same job in hurling. That's how it happened, pure luck.
Did you take to it straight away?
Well, the fact that I was playing full-forward in football was a definite advantage. Another advantage was that when I was training for the football, the College full-back at the time was Moss Keane, the rugby player, and he gave me a bit of an education. When Moss started to run, the first thing to start moving were his arms, pushing backwards. That was in the era when the square area was still very much Hell's Kitchen and Moss gave me a good introduction to that, in football training. I

wasn't big enough or strong enough to throw my weight around against fellas like him. I found that the only way to get away from that was to move out, move around. I also knew that this was something the full-back didn't like, so you could say a whole number of things combined to give me my style, if you'd like to call it that.

Was the football a help to the hurling?

I found it a break more than anything else. You can get stale from playing just the one sport all the time.

Did you play the same style in both?

More or less, yes. Physically I wasn't strong enough to mix it so you then had to become smarter.

And the distribution element?

As far as I'm concerned it's a team sport and you have to be a team player. There isn't much point in any one player playing very well if the team is beaten. It never bothered me who was doing the scoring as long as we were winning. That was the only important thing – the end result. As a full-forward anyway you're generally winning the ball on the way out from goal, meeting a couple of teammates on the way in, in better position to take a score, so it makes sense to give them the ball. One thing you can't be at full-forward is selfish.

Were you conscious of the fact that you were starting a revolution in that position?

No, all I was doing was playing to my own strengths, trying to complement my weaknesses, if you like.

Did you come to enjoy it?

I did, it's a position where you can really influence things. It's obviously the area where the ball is always headed, the funnel, right in front of goal, so you're probably going to get a lot of possession. You could be corner-back and never see a ball, you could be midfield and the ball could be going over your head – that wouldn't suit me. I liked to be in the thick of the action as much as I could, as often as I could. Does that sound selfish?

The qualities needed to be a top full-forward

First of all you need to know your own strengths and weaknesses. Then you need to know the strengths and weaknesses of your teammates, and finally you needed to know the strengths and weaknesses of your opponents. You can deliver a ball to Player A that mightn't suit Player B; likewise you might have a teammate who has a strength one day that might be a weakness the next, depending on who he was on. All these things have to go into the mix every day, because every game is different, and every individual is different. Awareness of where everyone is is important also, where they tend to roam – peripheral vision, I suppose you'd call it. Awareness of habits is important, what fellas tend to do in common situations. You can't really plan a game of hurling. The Cork team of the last few years has made a good stab at it, a plan they play to, but I'm not sure that can survive in the long term. Hurling is so fast, so unpredictable – a break of the ball and it can go anywhere.

Were you two-sided?

Not really – I had lots of failings, probably more weaknesses than strengths! You try to develop both sides as much as you can, but I don't think there was ever a hurler – apart maybe from Ring – who was as strong off one side as he was off the other.

Were you strong on ground hurling?

I'd say I was reasonable in all areas, but I wasn't top of the pile in any.

Fast?

Fast enough over the first ten yards, but anticipation was very important. I always tried to be gone before my opponent, whether that meant breaking early and taking a risk or standing on the side where I anticipated the ball would come. I wasn't a speed merchant but I wasn't slow.

You had a good hand

Not bad I suppose. We played what we called 'handball' in the local park as kids, two sets of goals, hurling rules, homemade ball from paper, tied with string – hurling without the hurley. That was very effective for developing the handpass, and for the dummy handpass.

Did you ship a lot of punishment?

I suppose that's a major thing at full-forward, you have to be prepared to take a lot of punishment simply because of the nature of the position. Full-backs aren't dirty players, but this is a place where you are going to get belts, whether you like it or not. The ball is in close proximity to you, close proximity to the goals – you're going to get hammered. Sometimes you can get hammered even before the ball is thrown in. Before one of the three-in-a-row All-Ireland finals, Seánie O'Leary got a belt across the nose in the puck-around, went into the dressing room and Con Murphy [long-serving Cork team doctor] went into him; Christy Ring [then a selector] followed, to see what was going on. Con told him Seánie had broken his nose. 'To hell with it,' says Ring. 'You don't play hurling with your nose – get out there!'

But even today you look at Brian Lohan, Diarmuid O'Sullivan, Noel Hickey, Stephen Lucey – full-backs are mean, not just tough?
They are, but I wouldn't say dirty. You meet guys like Pat Hartigan, who was as honourable a player as you could come across, yet he was tough, strong, and most certainly he wasn't soft. I rated him very highly as a full-back. I think though that hurlers have respect for each other, as hurlers. A hurley is also a weapon and no matter how good or bad you are, you can end a fella's career with one swing. There's a restraint there, a discipline, that you mightn't get in other games, but it has to be there. At club level it was slightly different, and I remember also playing inter-firm, which was a different story again! You're meeting the fella for whom it would be a great boast that he held such-and-such scoreless.

The worst experience I had was when I was starting off, eighteen or nineteen, playing junior, meeting fellas of forty who had grown up in the 1950s and whose primary aim was to slow you down by any means possible! That was the worst experience I had, but generally I had no serious injuries. I wore a helmet anyway, probably one of the first to do so, because you are going to get bangs on the head in there, a full-back who's camouflaging his stroke. From that point of view I was protected.

Where to stand in relation to your opponent

I hope I never stood and that was something I learned early, from my days as a half-back. You keep moving, keep him guessing as to where you are, where you're going to turn up next. Try and cause confusion, basically. Seánie, Charlie [O'Leary and McCarthy] and myself tended to keep on the move. You can develop a very effective defensive system if you know where your man is all the time, it makes it very easy for the defence – create a line and defend it; but if the forwards keep moving, the backs can't ever get comfortable. As much as possible I'd try to be behind the full-back, not let him know which way I was going to go.

Tricks

I didn't have any really.

Fan [Larkin, Kilkenny defender with whom he had some memorable tussles] had a few

It's a bit late to be telling me now! Mind games rather than anything physical, that was my game, trying to outwit my opponent.

Were you aware of Fan's little tricks?

I was, but there was nothing you could do about it, and the umpires weren't going to intervene. I think it was backs more than forwards who had the little tricks, the forward wouldn't get away with it. The dummy handpass, that was it really, but my focus was on winning possession, then trying to use it.

Primary advice to a promising youngster, above all else, to master the full-forward position

It would have to be his stick-work first of all, then his quickness off the mark, then anticipation of the break – go to a ball alley and learn the angles. I practised off the side of my house, the wall outside on the road, pebble dash, a rubber ball.

Ray Cummins on the rampage, Jim O'Brien (Limerick) giving chase in the Munster Senior Hurling final at Thurles on 8 July 1979.

He was a contemporary of Ray Cummins, built more in the traditional full-forward mould, yet Joe McKenna too became one of the new breed. Pacy, skilful, intelligent, he created and scored many a memorable goal for Limerick.

JOE MCKENNA
(b. 1951, Shinrone and Offaly 1971–72, South Liberties and Limerick, 1973–85)

AWARDS & MEDALS WON
1 All-Ireland senior
6 All-Star awards (4 at full-forward)
1 National Hurling League
4 Railway Cup (1 as captain)
4 Limerick county senior
1 Offaly junior (Shinrone)

First position
I went to Dunkerrin NS where Séamus Ó Riain, the former President of the GAA, was my teacher. Seven miles there, seven miles back, every day on the bike, hail, rain or snow. We had a very good school team and there was a good schools competition locally then, Roscrea was very strong. I actually started out playing corner-back, we got to the semi-final one year against Roscrea, that's where I was, then moved out to around midfield for the final. I was small enough 'til about my second year in secondary school, then I sprung up very quickly.

The transition
With Limerick I started corner-forward, 1973, the first match against Clare, Munster semi-final. I was dropped then for the Munster final, was sick for the All-Ireland semi-final, wasn't even there, and was back at corner-forward for the All-Ireland final. I started on Fan Larkin, though I actually played most of that game at centre-forward. The following year then, 1974, I was at wing-forward, won an All-Star there, was at centre-forward the next year, won an All-Star there. In 1975, I was in centre-field, played against Cork in a Munster final. It was in

1978 that I was put in full-forward, and I more or less stayed there then.

What was it like on Fan in the 1973 final?

Well, he said 'Hello' to me with a dig in the ribs! But it was the size of him – it was the first time I'd ever met him and he was a lot smaller than I'd thought. I was only on him for about fifteen minutes, thank God! I went out on Pat Henderson then for the rest of the game – I had marked Pat once or twice with Offaly, with whom I'd played for a year before I joined Limerick.

Being so much bigger, would you have fancied yourself on a fella as small as Fan?

Probably, but left-corner-forward was not my position, in fact I'd go so far as to say that of all the positions on the field, left-corner-forward was the one most unsuited to me. Right-corner alright, because I was left-handed, or full-forward, or anywhere on the half-forward-line, but not in the left corner. Still, I was just delighted to get my place anywhere on the team for that game. I was actually taking Eamonn Cregan's place, he went back to centre-back, I was brought into the corner. That game is pretty much a blur for me, really; my first All-Ireland final, only twenty-one, and we won – I was just delighted to be there.

What was your favourite position?

I'd say, as it turned out, full-forward was my favourite position. I had actually played Harty there with Flannan's in my last year and I always felt very comfortable there. The thing was to get a supply of the ball – high or low, it didn't matter, as long as I got enough of it.

You were mobile for a big man?

Yeah, I was lucky enough to have been blessed with a bit of speed, always. Up to 50 or 100 yards I was good, but after that I was in trouble. Don't ask me to go 500 yards, stamina wasn't my strong point! But centre-forward or midfield, I had no problem there.

The qualities needed to be a top full-forward

I think you have to be very quick there, which might surprise a few people. You have to be very mobile, a strong athletic-type player. You've got to be able to turn fast, that's critical. You get very little time on the ball in there, so you've got to be able to win the ball, turn and strike, all in a single motion. That's quite difficult to do; you're on or near the edge of the square, everyone is around you, you have very little room in which to work. One of the first things I did when I went to full-forward was I got a shorter hurley. I also threw up the ball differently to almost everyone else – I threw it up outside the hurley, where most people threw it up inside. I don't know why, I just always did. I was right hand top, but throwing up the ball like that enabled me to move forward as I was striking [he was striking off his left]. I developed that trick, half-turning towards the goal as I made the catch, which gave you a great advantage over the full-back. I didn't practise it, it just developed. It's not that easy to do, but if you get away with it you're in great position, a few yards ahead, gone, and he won't catch you. I was primarily left-handed, could strike off my right but not with any great power. I found though that that didn't really matter; when you were that close to goal it didn't really matter what side you struck with, there was very little time, so it was a case of making sure you got the shot in, just make sure of making good contact. I worked very hard on my left. I suppose most fellas would have worked hard to improve their weaker side, but I just practised on my left, left, left. I knew then that if I got enough of the ball I'd score.

Where to stand in relation to your opponent

It varied. I had a great understanding with Eamonn Cregan before he retired; if I was in around the square he'd move out, and if he moved in I'd move out – that became almost automatic. I always preferred to have a bit of space though, I'd often move out to the 14-yard line or even beyond. Then you might win the ball if it broke in behind the full-back, and I did have a bit of pace. Under long frees, I'd be in around the edge of the square, but then so would everyone else! In that situation you'd be hoping to double on the ball, get a deflection on it.

Tricks

One I got away with for years was getting in behind the full-back for the high ball, going up to make the catch, and just tipping his hurley out of the way. A lot of fellas stand too far back and get caught, but you made it look like you were just protecting your hand, tussling, going in over the shoulder of a player and tipping his hurley. When you made the catch then you were in great position to score, inside the full-back and already facing towards goal. You needed a bit of height to do that – I

Bainisteoirí *side by side* – *Limerick's Joe McKenna (right) and Tipperary's Ken Hogan, time running out in the Guinness Munster Senior Hurling Championship game in Thurles on 15 May 2005.*

was 6 foot 4 inches, which helped. And I was light on my feet. A lot of full-forwards didn't like the high ball – I loved it, and the higher the better. We had very good players that time, Liam O'Donoghue, Brian Carroll, Seán Foley – they were great men to deliver a ball, just get it and hit.

Tricks seen

You'd hear of several, the usual one about tipping a guy's helmet over his eyes, or talking to a fella, to put him off. I didn't do that, ever, and I think it's gone too far now in some cases.

Talking just to break a fella's concentration, while keeping your own, that's okay?

Yeah, that's fine. You can upset your own fellas too – Liam Devanney was moved into full-forward for Tipp one day, but the ball was coming in too high for him; after getting three or four like that anyway, he started shouting out to them: 'Hit it in higher, hit it in higher!'

Primary advice to a promising youngster, above all else, to master the full-forward position

I don't like to see youngsters pigeon-holed too early in their careers. You don't really know 'til a player develops what he's going to be like, where he would be most suited – I never thought I'd end up as a full-forward, for example. I'd prefer to wait, see how a youngster develops. At full-forward, winning control quickly is important, being able to turn quickly after you've won possession is important, so quick control, turn, and every chance you get make it pay, because you're not going to get a lot of opportunities at full-forward. Don't mess around, go for the score. But I wouldn't put any pressure on young players, just let them play, let them enjoy themselves, and they'll develop better.

The man with a unique record, a record that can never be broken – as Kilkenny captain in 1983, Liam Fennelly hoisted the old McCarthy Cup, the original McCarthy Cup; in 1993, he was again the Kilkenny captain, and this time he became the first man to hoist the new McCarthy Cup. The old, the first of the new, the only to have done both. One of seven outstanding hurling brothers, Liam was a worthy man to do it too, as wily a player as ever picked up a stick.

LIAM FENNELLY
(b. 1958, Ballyhale Shamrocks and Kilkenny, 1980–92)

AWARDS & MEDALS WON
3 All-Ireland senior
4 All-Star awards
4 National Hurling League
1 Oireachtas
3 All-Ireland senior club
9 Kilkenny county senior

First position
I started off at corner-forward, number fifteen, but probably did most of my hurling at full-forward.

The qualities needed to be a top full-forward
I'd say first touch; if you don't win the ball first time at full-forward it's gone, especially nowadays – gone. After that I'd say vision, use of the ball. You're not going to get a huge amount of ball in there, so you have to make use of what you get.

Where to stand in relation to your opponent
I'd be a divil for standing behind, beside, in front; most full-forwards stand where the full-back wants them to stand, out in front, which is stupid. As I got older, I started standing behind – win the ball from there and you were in perfect position. I love watching the corner-back/corner-forward battle in football – the corner-back isn't even watching the ball, he's just sticking to the corner-forward. Hurling is going to go like that.

Brian has it. Liam wants it. *Brian Corcoran (Cork) going past Kilkenny captain Liam Fennelly in the All-Ireland final of 1992. Liam was the one who ended up with the newly-minted McCarthy Cup and because he captained Kilkenny in 1983 as well, he created history as the only man to have lifted both cups.*

Tricks

I used to use my foot a lot to rise the ball, the flick up with the hurl – fellas couldn't understand why the full-back wasn't breaking your leg! I did it one day at corner-forward against Muckalee and Jim Moran was full-back, he let a roar at the corner-back: 'Break his f***ing leg!'

'I'm trying, I'm trying!' your man shouted back at him. I had the ball gone and he was still pulling, but it didn't matter anymore.

I used to come up behind a guy on my toes, silently, catch him off guard; I did that to wing-backs especially, when they had dropped back behind the wing-forward to win the ball. They think they have all day, aren't aware of you coming, which gave you a chance to hook them, take the ball off them.

I occasionally went as if to throw the ball – not even the dummy handpass – and that worked. In Croke Park one day, against Galway, the last year I was playing, I won the ball in tight, a couple of Galway fellas coming for me, and I just stopped dead, hid the ball. They didn't know what to do, didn't know where the ball was gone. I waited a couple of seconds, passed to D. J. and he put it over the bar. But the reaction of the two [Galway] boys was amazing.

Tricks seen

Fan had a lot of tricks and I asked him one time, where did you learn all that? 'From me father,' he said. 'Who did you expect?' I was standing beside him one day, Kilkenny were playing Cork in Gowran, and Philly [Fan's son] was under a dropping ball. The next thing I got an elbow in the jaw from Fan. He was following the flight of the ball, but he was doing what he felt Philly should have been doing, he was hurling with him!

I saw him one day, a corner-forward coming through, and he went as if to brain him, brought the hurley down straight over his head like an axe, then stopped it at the last second – the corner-forward dropped the ball. All he was doing was testing and if the fella was yella, he'd flinch. He was probably blown a few times for it but he wouldn't actually make contact.

You were held all the time, you got the elbow in the face, the helmet pushed down over the eyes. But it's amazing the number of fellas who had no tricks at all, who didn't think about it, just played the game as it was.

Primary advice to a promising youngster, above all else, to master the full-forward position

How to break to the ball, how not to let the full-back get position in front of you.

In 1989, Antrim reached only their second ever All-Ireland final. This wee man was one of the main reasons they did and he won an All-Star that year at wing-forward. His favourite forward position, however? Full-forward, further proof that a good hurler can play anywhere, regardless of size.

OLCAN MCFETRIDGE
(b. 1963, Glen Rovers Armoy and Antrim, 1988–93)

AWARDS & MEDALS WON
1 All-Star award
1 National Hurling League (Division 2)
2 replacement All-Star awards
3 Antrim county intermediate

First position
I started off midfield with my club, played there for years. I then moved to centre half-forward after seven or eight years, and from there to full-forward.

The qualities needed to be a top full-forward
The first thing I'd say here is that any full-forward is only as good as the ball he's getting. Around the time I was playing you had Pat Fox and Nicky English as the two corner-forwards for Tipp. They seemed to get every ball perfectly, every time.

You need to be able to score, obviously, you need an eye in your head, but you also need to be able to defend, you need to keep the full-back quiet. You need to know a bit about everything really. Know where to be, where to go – a lot of it is just using your head.

Did size matter?
I don't think so, not to me anyway. Obviously I preferred the ball in low, but a small player can out-jump a bigger man if he gets his timing right and I've often seen that. I was 5 foot 7, not the biggest! The funny thing was, I found it tougher being on a small full-back. But just as full-forward is a unique place, so is full-back, not many people can play those positions. As for corner-forward, that's absolutely unique.

Corner-forwards are born, you can't make a corner-forward of anyone, it has to be in you from the start.

Because of your size, I'd have seen you as more a corner-forward than full

I hated corner-forward, always. Nowadays they seem to play the ball the game differently, they use every player on the pitch, try to pick out the corner-forward with good ball, but back then it was just pumped down the middle. Tipp picked out their corner-forwards, but we didn't have it. Everything came down the middle, so if you were in the corner you were just living off scraps.

Did you score more goals or points?

Oh goals, always. And I'd try to place the ball; often you'd go straight down the centre, the keeper is expecting it to one side or the other and often he's already moving – down the middle.

Where to stand in relation to your opponent

I wouldn't be standing, I'd be looking at the play out the park all the time and I'd be planning where I should be, always moving. If a high ball was coming in I'd try to get behind the full-back, I'd take his position, play the full-back's role. For me, it's easier to catch the ball from behind than from the front and if you manage that, you're in on goal. For the low ball, certainly be out in front.

How would you manage to get in behind, surely the keeper would be alerting the full-back?

He would, but you wait for your opportunity, you don't go too early. Win that ball and you then have only one player to beat, the keeper.

Tricks

I didn't really have any, to be honest, you didn't have time for tricks in there!

Primary advice to a promising youngster, above all else, to master the full-forward position

Be alert, and never, ever retaliate. If you're a forward and a defender is at you all day long, he's making a statement, he's telling you that you're too good for him, he can't out-hurl you, so he has to do this. He's telling you he has a problem with you, don't make it easy for him by retaliating – just get on with it.

The best advice you were ever given

Just play the game, don't get involved in anything else; an old teacher of mine, Seamus Hegarty, told me that and it worked. I played hurling for twenty-eight years and I never even got a booking. I'm now forty-five, I played my last game recently, a charity game, and it nearly killed me! I told the people who organised it, any more ideas like that and I'll just give you a donation!

***Out on his own** – Antrim's Olcan McFetridge with his eye firmly on the prize, the only prize – the ball.*

D. J. – if you're ever in hurling company that's all it takes, D.J, and everyone will know who you're talking about. And when people are talking about best ever, he's mentioned, always, up there in the most august company, with Mackey, Ring, Rackard, Keher. In a word, a word that was often used to describe his play – genius.

D. J. CAREY
(b. 1970, Young Irelands and Kilkenny, 1988–2005)

AWARDS & MEDALS WON
2 Hurler of the Year (1993 and 2000)
5 All-Ireland senior
9 All-Star awards
1 All-Ireland U-21
1 All-Ireland minor
4 National Hurling League
2 Railway Cup
2 Oireachtas
2 Kilkenny county senior
1 Kilkenny county intermediate

First position
I started at left-half-forward, but I played in every position in the forwards. I never started at centre-forward, though obviously I'd have ended up there a few times, but I started in every other position in All-Ireland finals. I also won an All-Star in every position except centre-forward – I think! [Didn't win one at right-corner-forward either.]

What was your favourite position?
I'd say midfield, but I didn't play there very often. After that, full-forward, because in the corner you can be very much out of the game. Corner-forward is a very difficult position to play; even the odd scrappy ball that does come in, you might be under pressure to win it – it could take ages to get into the game. At least at full-forward you were more or less guaranteed to be in the game a lot, the ball was either going to come straight to you or break either side of you. Corner-forward wasn't really a place I ever enjoyed.

The qualities needed to be a top full-forward

Cleverness, you need a good head. You need to know when to go, when to stay, when to goal, when to take the easier option, when to give a pass. The guy who has a good burst also has an advantage, that first ten yards, and good first touch is crucial. The first thing though is the head, cleverness – how many options have you in your game? Just turn and go – that's not enough.

How many gears did you have?

That was just something I had naturally. When I was in school I did the 100 yards in eleven seconds, which was pretty fast at the time, especially when I didn't have any specialist training in sprinting. I was playing handball, hurling, Gaelic football, so I didn't have time for anything else. To get to the next level of sprinting, I'd have needed to bulk up a lot but it was never in my psyche to be an athlete. I was decent enough at long distance also, but I was never into that either, it never interested me. Ball games yes, athletics no.

When I was playing, the aim was to take as direct a line as possible for the goals. I never really focused too much on scoring points, that didn't interest me an awful lot. I always felt that if you get the ball, if there's even a half-chance there for the goal, go for it. Whether I got it myself or someone else got it didn't matter – get the goal. I also liked full-forward because once you got around your man you were gone, no one else between you and the goals. Even the corner-back closing in had to be mindful that he was leaving someone behind him who could end up getting the score, so they had to hold back a bit.

Full-forward really suited me – go for the jugular, that was my attitude, and that's what I'd be coaching teams. Have someone like Eddie Brennan or Aidan Fogarty at full-forward, someone with that attitude. He needs to be strong in the air, but he doesn't have to be 6 foot 3 or 6 foot 4 – the likes of Martin Comerford and Henry Shefflin, even though they can play almost anywhere, I'd see them as more corner-forwards than full. From the corner they can be drifting in, using their height, taking the full-back – who is static – out of it. For me, whenever the ball landed around the full-forward area, whether it came in high or not didn't matter, but when it hit the ground, you had a chance of a goal. Every chance you get around the full-forward area, because you're only about twenty yards out, should be a goal chance.

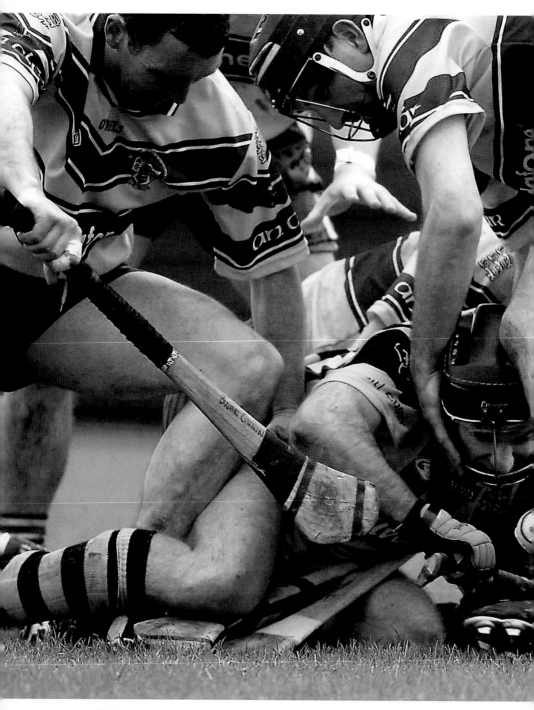

Grind them into the ground ... *D. J. Carey is gang-tackled by four Clare defenders, Brian Quinn and Sean McMahon to the fore in Ennis, County Clare, on 21 March 2004. And this was only the League!*

It cost Cork in the last few years, taking the easy option of a point when the goal was on and they missed a lot of opportunities to put teams away?

That's right – Kilkenny don't do that. If you look at Kilkenny's scoring stats it's a headliner when they don't score a goal. In over 100 years of Leinster finals, rarely have they failed to get a goal. A goal is worth three points, but when certain guys score it's worth even more. When Eddie Keher scored a goal, when Jimmy Doyle scored a goal, when Christy Ring scored a goal, when Henry scores a goal, when the Gooch Cooper gets a goal, it's worth more. Towards the end of my own career it was the same thing. It's the guy the opposition are looking at, thinking – 'We must hold him.' When he scores a goal their heads go down, so it's worth far more than just the goal itself.

Assists are a major measurement of a player in ice-hockey, but it's not used in GAA. That was a major element of Ray Cummins' game. Was it also a major part of yours?

I think if people were to look at the qualities of Brian Cody as a manager, outside of the four or five All-Irelands that he won himself as a player, he deserves every plaudit that's going. He has a philosophy that there are forty or fifty guys in Kilkenny who can put the ball over the bar, who can put the ball in the back of the net, but there aren't that many who can win the ball themselves to do that, there are not that many who can lay off the ball. That's why he has so many guys who can win their own ball, guys who are team players. That was a big part of my game, that's why it never bothered me if I didn't score an awful lot.

There are those who say D. J. was held in x number of finals, didn't score, while ignoring the assists, the frees won. Anthony Daly gives the flip side, people praising a defender for holding his man score-less while ignoring the pointed frees conceded

Yes, that's right. People would talk about me after a game, how much I scored or how little I scored, but they don't see what actually went on. It's only real hurling people who take notice of running off the ball – you can't even see it properly on television. One of the greatest guys to get into position in the modern game was Johnny Dooley. You'd see Johnny all on his own, 30 or 40 yards out from goal, waiting for the pass, and he did that so often – he had lost his man. Henry [Shefflin] is the same; he has every quality in the game, but he has that ability above all, the ability to get lost, to lose his man. Watch him, how he slips his man, appears then in a scoring position. That was something I don't think I ever had; I felt I was good at leaving a man for dead, I never felt I was good at being a ghost – that's what Henry is, a ghost, but I think Johnny Dooley was even better at that.

Where to stand in relation to your opponent

For the most part if I could stand behind him I loved it, particularly in the early days. I wouldn't have been rated too highly in the sky then, the impression was that I was small and that was why I was able to catch a lot of ball, I wasn't rated. More often than not though you hadn't a choice in the full-forward line, you were kept out in front.

Where does this impression come from about players being small? Eoin Kelly isn't small, neither is Tommy Walsh, neither were you, but the impression was out there?

Yeah; I'd be 5 foot 11, 12½ stone – not small – and I was that since 1992, but some people get the impression that a guy is small and it seems to stick.

Did you ever do weights?

No, could never get into them. I made an attempt when Kilkenny went to weights in my latter years, but I did it for the sake of it, I could never motivate myself to do them. I might have to start doing it now though, to keep in shape. I bought a little multi-gym, but couldn't set it up. It's still sitting there!

Tricks

I had none, and I never worked on tricks. It was just get the ball, put the head down and go. The one thing I always felt I had was awareness of what was all around me, I always felt I knew where the other guys were, that I could handpass to. If I had carte blanche on youngsters starting off in hurling, nine or ten years of age, I'd advise them to do four things: skip, ballet, Irish dancing and handball. Get your footwork right and you'll be a much better hurler. Get the ball in your hand as quickly as possible, that's another. This business of tipping it and bouncing it, no good. Get it in your hand and you have control, you're the boss. If people could get out of their heads the image that ballet and Irish dancing has – and I have it myself – it would be a great advantage. It teaches you such balance, controlled balance. So many young fellas today are lost because of poor footwork, and I don't mean lost to hurling, I mean lost to a higher level of hurling.

Did you play on your toes?

That was a major part of my game, I took off on my toes. Don't plant your feet unless you have to.

The handball pass, able to pick out the player left or right, pass off left or right, that was a feature of your game

The guys who played with me knew they were likely to get that pass, so they made the effort. They made sure they were in position to take that pass where, with a lot of other fellas, they'd stop running because they knew they weren't going to get the pass. The fellas I played with knew they were going to get that pass, unless my mind was made up to go for goals myself, if that opportunity arose. I never felt I was being unselfish, this was just the way I played the game. It's lovely to have your name up in lights but it never bothered me if I wasn't scoring, as long as the team was scoring.

Making his point after scoring yet another point, or was it a goal? *D. J. Carey in exultant mood in the All-Ireland final in Croke Park, Dublin, in 2003.*

The additional aspect of it was that the defender never knew what I was going to do, where with another fella he might know he's definitely not going to pass. The 2002 All-Ireland semi-final against Tipperary, when I was coming through, I didn't know myself right 'til the last second whether I was going to handpass to Charlie [Carter] or Jimmy Coogan. Those two options were there [he choose Coogan, who buried it]. That was one of my strengths, something I was happy to play to.

That was a killer goal

It was, but goals are. Cork put a huge amount of effort into creating a point-scoring opportunity from 30 yards in front of goal, when a point could have been scored much earlier. An awful lot of extra effort, for what?

The dummy handpass made your regular handpass an even more lethal weapon

Yeah, though guys got wise to that too.

Primary advice to a promising youngster, above all else, to master the full-forward position

You probably need to be lucky to be blessed with speed, but I go back to the head; if you're going out with the impression that you have to score, then forget about it.

Can you work on vision?

I believe you can, but I also believe that when the guys you play with know your game, they're going to be in the right position to take the pass. A lot of the time I didn't even see who I was passing to, I just knew there would be someone there. I can remember an incident in a league final a few years ago, against Clare. I knew Henry [Shefflin] was gone inside when the ball came to me, all I had to do was run out and pull. As it turned out, when I pulled on the ball it went in at just the right height, onto Henry's hurl, he controlled it with one touch, bang, back of the net. Looked spectacular, and it was, but that pass would have been just as effective if I'd just pulled on the ball and let it through along the ground. Whatever ability I had, and I'm not sure what it was, I could see that black-and-amber shirt out of the corner of my eye. I wouldn't always know who it was but I knew someone was there.

Sure, who needs fourteen clubs? *The putter, that's all I need... Two lethal finishers, Pat Fox (left) of Tipperary and Limerick's Eamonn Cregan tearing up the course at Fota Golf Club in 2001.*

Left-Corner-Forward
The Fall-Guy

Eamonn Cregan (Limerick)
Nicky English (Tipperary)
Ben O'Connor (Cork)

How often have you seen it happen – the team is playing badly, something needs to be done, the wise men go into caucus, and minutes later the poor corner-forward, who probably hasn't seen a decent ball all game, is trooping to the sideline, head down, hurley trailing behind him. It's a terrible position on any team, but on a team that's struggling – forget it. One man, however, who never had to make that sad walk to the sideline, was this man.

EAMONN CREGAN
(b. 1945, Claughaun and Limerick, 1964–83)

AWARDS & MEDALS WON
1 All-Ireland senior
3 All-Star awards
1 National Hurling League
5 Railway Cup
1 Oireachtas
3 Limerick county senior

First position

All through underage, midfield was my primary position. I played my first senior championship match there in 1965, against Tipp, down in the Athletic Grounds in Cork, on Larry Guinan – couldn't have met a tougher man! Then some genius decided I should go to left-half-forward.

The transition

Later in my career, I suppose when I was slowing up, another genius decided I should go to the corner. That was around 1971 and that's where I finished up. I was playing there in 1973 when we had a challenge match against Waterford. Pat Hartigan had cried off for that game and I thought they'd move Eamonn [Ned] Rea to full-back from corner-back, but they brought him to full-forward. In those days you needed a player at full-forward who would have a certain amount of skill, obviously, but he'd also need a bit of size, to break up the play. In that sense Ned suited Frankie Nolan [the other corner-forward] and myself perfectly. He did the hard work, we benefited from it.

What was your favourite position?

Centre-field, but centre-back was a position I always enjoyed. I played there with my own club. It's a demanding position, but a commanding role [Eamonn starred there in the All-Ireland final of 1973, won by Limerick].

The qualities needed to be a top corner-forward

You have to have skill, that's a must; you have to have anticipation, you have to have courage, and you have to have patience. You could say speed as well, but I'd say anticipation makes up for that. Watch Jimmy Barry Murphy, he was fast, but it was his anticipation that really made space for him.

It's the most God-awful place to play; you're depending on the guys outside to give you the right ball and if you don't get that, you're in trouble. You needed fast low ball; the slower it came in, the more it suited the back.

You had to be able to read your half-forwards, and I'll give you an example of that. Kieran Brennan [star Kilkenny forward] was in the army, stationed in Limerick, came up to Claughaun to train with us. We played a match, I was corner-forward, and when he got the ball at half-forward I took off. All I had to do then was stick out my hand and the ball was there. I played corner-forward at hurling and football, for club and county, but often when you'd move like that nothing happened, the ball was hit instead to where you had just left, and you got the abuse. We were playing Clare one day, I was on Jackie O'Gorman, the ball was coming down the left and I moved, expecting the pass; the ball was hit straight to Jackie, he cleared it 90 yards and there was a great roar – at me! I was made look like an eejit.

You needed patience; a ball mightn't come to your corner for five minutes but when it did you had to be ready, and when you got it you had to score, or make a score. You've got to take the stick that comes with the position – fellas digging you in the back, in the ribs, fellas kneeing you in the thigh, fellas whispering in your ear, terrible abuse. And you never got the break from the referee – retaliate and the free was against you, try doing the same thing to the back and the free was against you, and probably a warning as well. The back always got the call. It was very frustrating and eventually I got tired of it. It was even worse in the 1960s, when I started. Jim Hogan, the former Limerick goalie, tells this story.

J. J. Bresnihan played full-back on the minor team in 1968. The opening of the Dromcollogher field in 1969, Cork against Limerick, J. J. was brought into full-back, a raw nineteen-year-old; Ring was at full-forward. In those days the forwards lined up at centre-field and they then made a dash back to their positions after the throw-in. J. J. was there, 6 foot 4 tall, leaning on his hurley, Ring comes back, looks up at him, his cap covering the bald head: 'Are you a new boy?'

'I'll soon let you know whether I'm a new boy or not!'

Hogan is inside, listening to all this, thinking to himself, oh-oh – at that time Ring would kill you. First ball came into the square anyway and this missile flew past Jim, into the back of the net. He goes back to retrieve it and he's thinking, 'That's his first, anyway,' bent down to pick up the ball to puck it out – it was Ring's cap! Bresnihan had pulled with the ball, taken the cap clean off Ring's head – he was tough as nails, but nineteen, do that to Ring?

There was a man in Claughaun, Jack Molyneaux, who had Molyneaux's pub. We were playing the Glen [Ring's club], Patsy Harte centre-forward, they were beating the shite out of us; a Claughaun ball went wide, well wide, and Jack shouted on the sideline – point, point! Ring came roaring over to him, grabbed him by the throat: 'What do you mean a point? It was wide, well wide!' Poor Jack – the Glen were winning by about sixteen points, only a tournament, but that was Ring, had Jack up against the wire anyway. But all the Glen fellas were fierce competitive. Eamonn Goulding, the youngest man to play in an All-Ireland final, they were playing indoor soccer in Kilkenny, winning 6-0, John Kyle got the ball in front of goal, just stroked it and Eamonn came up to him: 'Don't ever do that again! Finish it off!' That was why the Glen won so much.

Would you think of taking your own score first when you won possession?

At times, yes, but you also had to be prepared to give the pass, you couldn't be too selfish.

Where to stand in relation to your opponent

Always on the outside, generally on the end line. I was always trying to anticipate so I'd prefer to be a fraction in front. Too far in front and if the ball comes high you're trying to fight your way back. But you have to get to the ball first.

In the 1960s it was the back's job to protect the keeper, stop the forward from going into the square. There was a great photo in the *Evening Press,* All-Ireland final, Kilkenny against Tipperary, Ollie catching the ball and all the Tipp forwards – McLoughlin, McKenna, Nealon – were nailed to the ground, couldn't get within an ass' roar of the ball, or of Ollie.

Tricks

One that worked for me in a Harty Cup semi-final against Chríost Rí, in 1964; I got a ball in my hand, there was a fella coming at me, and I did a dummy throw, which held him. I did the same thing in 1980, against Conor Hayes. It gives you the split second that allows you to turn, get off the shot.

Another one – one we were allowed do in the old days until the referees made a bags of them – the touch on the hurley to let the ball through, if the corner-back was outside you. Some fellas are still getting away with it – Kilkenny are expert at it, getting the catch under the high ball, little flick across the hurley first. But you have to be good at playing the referee too, and some are better than others at that.

Tricks seen

Tomás Mulcahy, catch the ball three times [the Cork forward got away with it in a Munster championship game against Limerick]!

Primary advice to a promising youngster, above all else, to master the corner-forward position

He must have the ability to control the ball with one touch. You're not going to get many opportunities, you must control the ball with one touch or you're lost. Fail and the back has the advantage, so first touch is vital, as is striking with left and right.

As player, as manager, this guy has done it all, one of hurling's marquee names.

NICKY ENGLISH
(b. 1962, Latin-Cullen and Tipperary, 1981–96)

AWARDS & MEDALS WON
1 Hurler of the Year (1989)
2 All-Ireland senior hurling
6 All-Star awards
1 All-Ireland U-21
1 All-Ireland minor
2 National Hurling League
2 Railway Cup
1 Oireachtas
1 Tipperary county intermediate hurling
1 Tipperary county junior hurling
1 Tipperary county intermediate football

First position
We had no underage club hurling, it was mainly a football club, but I started at midfield/wing-back with the school. I started with Tipp at number ten, played there on the U-21s of 1981, then senior there for the next four years.

The transition
In 1987, after Babs [Keating, manager] came in, he said he wanted me nearer the goals, in the corner. I didn't take to it straight away, I felt confined in there, didn't like it, but the more I played there the more I got used to it, and the more I liked it. It's a dangerous position, if you like to score goals it's a lot easier to do it from fifteen than from ten. But the corner-forwards – no more than the corner-backs, let it be said – are at the mercy of the type of the ball being sent in by the half-back-line. Good ball in front of the corner-forward from the half-back-line is gift-wrapped, a good corner-forward should be almost unmarkable in that situation. They're getting good primary possession, should be able to

score more often than not. If your half-back-line is on the back foot, being pushed backwards by the opposition half-forward-line, invariably then their clearances aren't directed. They're probably up in the air, not travelling as far, hanging in the air which gives the back plenty of time to settle under it. That's a much more difficult ball to win or get a score from.

The qualities needed to be a top corner-forward

One of the great traits of a good corner-forward is patience. Things mightn't be going well for you, you're tempted to drift out further and further into the play, you're squeezing out to the half-forward-line. That's what happened to us in the 1988 All-Ireland final [lost against Galway], our full-forward line pushed out to the half-forward-line, we were all competing then for our own puck-out. The corner-forward must be patient, he must be content with secondary ball from the puck-out. Even if there's a huge wind I'd be advising the goalie not to be trying to find the full-forward line with the extra-long puck-out, I'd be advising the full-forward line not to be trying to contest that ball. It's in the air too long, all the defenders are settled under it. Even if you do win it you're in traffic immediately. Patience is key, in this position. You want to be involved, but wait; even if the ball isn't coming in, have patience. Having played for so long on the wing, involved in so much of the play, I found that aspect of it very difficult in the beginning, in the corner. You really are at the mercy of the ball coming in. At number fifteen the ideal ball is the one coming diagonally from the number five, hopping in front of you. You want to take that on the hop, sweep onto what should be your good side, over the bar. But that's a rare ball, you have to wait for it, and be ready for it.

The ability to win the ball is huge at corner-forward. You'd love to have the ideal ball all the time but you're not going to get it. The most dangerous fifteen is the one who is good in the air, who can field the high ball, turn and go, head straight for goal, go in rather than come out; a bit of pace then to get away and any defence is in trouble. A ball-winner, one who doesn't mind heading into heavy traffic, taking the hits.

I don't know if you have to be born there, you could play anywhere in the forward line really. I played at full-forward for a while also, found that even more difficult. Because my physique wasn't really suited to

'I saw it first!' Tipp corner-forwards Nicky English and Pat Fox go after the same ball in the All-Ireland semi-final against Antrim in 1988. The unfinished Hill 16 of Croke Park is in the background.

full-forward I was even more dependent on the ball coming in being the right kind of ball, where in the corner at least you can play off someone else, and you have a little bit more space.

Did you score more goals or points?

The situation would dictate that, whether the goal was on or not, whether your team needed a goal or not; but certainly a goal was always more on in there than out the wing. The half-forward is depending, to a large extent, on ball coming back out; the corner-forward has to be able to win his own ball, turn his man and go. If you have pace then, the goal chances will come fairly regularly.

Did you place the ball or go for power?

When I started you could still handpass the ball to the net, which was a huge advantage for a forward. All you had to do was run as far as you could with the ball, carry it to the edge of the square, handpass – you couldn't be hooked, you couldn't miss, he had no chance. I know John Commins made a famous save from a Liam Fennelly handpass in the All-Ireland final of 1987, but that was the exception. Kicking was also an option, and I had that advantage from playing football, that I could place it with the foot. Power is always an option in there but if you have the presence of mind, I think it's best to place it.

Where to stand in relation to your opponent

As far from him as possible! You're always trying to move, to drift, anticipate the ball. Keep yourself between him and the ball, and as far away from him as possible.

Tricks

I saw Eamonn Cregan score a great point in the All-Ireland final of 1980 against Conor Hayes of Galway: he showed him the ball on one side then flashed it over with the other. My feet were good, if I could get on the ball I could get away from people playing football. I was also quite good at pulling the ball back into myself with the stick, the dummy shot if I was under pressure, but to me, the simpler I could keep it the better.

Primary advice to a promising youngster, above all else, to master the corner-forward position

Be patient, number one; then, when you do get a chance, make sure you win the ball, don't have it hit before you have it won, before you have the ball under control. You don't score it before you get it – make sure you have control, the score will follow.

He's a flyer, this guy, an absolute flyer – 'Ben the Bullet' was the name put on him by Wexford centre-back Liam Dunne. Often a good hurler can be wasted in the corner, but with Ben O'Connor the position was nominal – usually, and with his club especially, he was off roaming the prairies, looking for work, looking to be where he could do most damage to the opposition.

BEN O'CONNOR
(b. 1979, Newtownshandrum and Cork, 1999–present)

AWARDS & MEDALS WON
3 All-Ireland senior
4 All-Star Awards (2 GPA, 2 Vodafone)
1 All-Ireland senior club
4 Cork county senior
3 Munster senior club
1 Cork intermediate
1 Railway Cup
3 All-Ireland Vocational (2 county, 1 college)

First position
My first real match was against Ballyhea in Charleville and I was half-forward, but for most of my underage career I was centre-back/half-back. It wasn't 'til I was sixteen that I was really moved to the forward line and after that it was anywhere in there.

On the wing your touch doesn't have to be spot on, you can run onto a break and if you don't get the ball up first time you can tip it ahead, run onto it again – you can run yourself into a game.

I think the most difficult place to play in hurling is the full-forward line. Your touch has to be spot on. Miss the ball in there, fail to control it the first time and it's probably gone – the goalie has it behind you, the corner-back is in. The other thing, you're totally dependent on those out the field. You can be anticipating a certain type of ball, running out to meet it, and next thing it's gone in over your head to the corner-back, the guy you've just lost with your run. The next time you might decide to stay back, the corner-back goes, and the ball is rolled into your corner, straight to the corner-back, out in front of you.

Like Charlie McCarthy, getting abused no matter what?
Yes, you can't win in there! With the club I never really played at wing-forward until maybe a couple of years ago. It happened with Cork, really. A lot of my senior hurling with Newtown was at left-corner-forward.

But did you ever stay in the corner?
No, I was allowed move around the place. But I could never go right-corner-forward. I hated that position.

What's the difference?
I don't know why it is but a lot more ball goes into the left corner than the right. Myself and Fraggie [Kieran Murphy from Sars] have been talking about this for ages – you go into the right corner, you're lucky to get two or three balls in the hour, whereas if you're in the left you get a lot more ball. Maybe it's because most fellas are right-handed hurlers and have a natural tendency to clear the ball diagonally down the left, I don't know, but people say, 'Corner-forward, it makes no difference which side,' but I hated the right.

Because you're coming onto your right side, your strong side, from the left corner?
Not really. In training I prefer to have a shot at Cusack [Donal Óg] coming in off the right side and striking with my left, I can get more power and more accuracy off my left. When I'm in the left corner, if I get the ball into my hand and if I'm forced out, down the wing, it doesn't bother me to have to shoot off my left, put it over the bar. The big thing is the supply of the ball, you get more in the left corner.

So the corner does matter?
You can be sure it does, and every fella has his preference. If you get it into your head at all that you don't like some place, it makes it an awful lot harder to play well there.

What was your favourite position?
Left-corner-forward.

Would you say you know more about that position than right-half-forward?
No, I've played out on the wing for so long now I think I understand that position as well. If I had my choice I'd be left-corner-forward always, but if it was to be a choice between right-corner-forward and right-half-forward, I'd take right-half. Out there you can really play yourself into a game.

When people think of Ben O'Connor, the classic Ben score is the ball on the stick down the right sideline, the strike from about 40 yards, over the bar.

Maybe, yes, and with Cork I don't mind playing on the right wing, I actually enjoy it. You don't have to stay there, you're given licence to roam out the field to pick up breaks in your own half-back-line, across the line.

Under the puck-out?

I wouldn't be the best at it; everyone has their strengths and weaknesses and that wouldn't be one of my strong points, I'm not very good under the dropping ball, but I'd tussle away, I'd be in there trying my best. Out of ten balls if I win four, I'd be happy enough, but the big thing is to make sure the wing-back doesn't win clean ball – as long as it's breaking, you have a chance.

Do you have a signal system with Donal Óg?

Everyone would have their own signals and obviously we have ours, but they change from game to game. It was either last year or the year before that our signals were copped after one game – he [Donal Óg] tried them again the next day and they were onto it, we had to change them around again at half-time. But that's just an indicator of how closely fellas are examining teams now. I'd say fellas are going to matches, standing in the terrace so they're seeing the field the same way as the goalkeeper, and they analyse the puck-outs from there.

The qualities needed to be a top forward

The main thing for a half-forward now is mobility – no point winning a ball if you can't get away from your man. You have to use your brain. A lot of fellas you see now, they get the ball, turn and just hit it, anywhere at all, or they take off and they run and run and run, up a blind alley. Next thing there are three fellas around him, bottling him up, nowhere to go, no room to pass the ball. A half-forward has to first win the ball, then know when he should drop back and find a fella, or go and take on his man. If you draw a man, part early with the ball, don't wait too long. All a fella needs is half a step and he's gone. Most important, if there's someone open and in better position than you, give it on to him; you see fellas shooting from impossible angles, they might score one from five, maybe from out near the corner. I hate that, I hate when fellas are greedy.

'Still' photography, how are you? *You can almost feel the page rustle as Ben O'Connor whizzes by.*

I prefer to see a fella holding onto the ball, throwing it around, maybe two or three passes to get the handy point, rather than holding onto four or five balls, losing them or shooting from impossible angles. One of those goes over and you're walking out afterwards, listening to fellas – 'Wasn't that a great score by your man!' They don't talk at all about the other three or four bad balls.

With Newtown we don't care who's doing the scoring, we throw the ball around for fun. One fella might have eight or nine points today, he mightn't get a score the next day but he'll be involved in scores.

At corner-forward, definitely touch and concentration are needed. You might go for twenty minutes without seeing a ball, but when it comes you must be ready. You must control with one touch and you must then use your body to turn. There's nothing better than having the ball coming in flying, the corner-back coming out with you to meet it, but just at the right moment you plant your leg and give him a touch of the hip, send him flying away from the goal, and you're straight in. Patience – it's a different game in there, you have to be far cuter.

Preparation is very important. The first time Setanta [Ó hAilpín] came on the team we were playing in Wexford, so we were staying overnight. I was rooming with Setanta, we were watching *Match of the Day* on television, then out with the lights. About half an hour later I could hear all this tearing over at the bags; eventually I turned on the light and there was Setanta, fully togged out, all the gear – togs, socks, boots, the whole lot, and he stretching mad.

'What are you doing?' I said to him.

'I just wanted to try everything on, make sure it fits, that it isn't too tight!' And he kept on stretching.

'Jaysus,' I said to myself, 'What have we here!' But he was making sure, that was all, he was checking everything – half an hour, that was it, back into bed, satisfied.

A pity he isn't still playing?

Yeah, imagine if he came back hurling now, and the size of him. And Tomás O'Leary [Munster rugby scrum-half, All-Ireland minor winner with Cork] as well.

Where to stand in relation to your opponent

At wing-forward, I'd always stand on the outside, nearer the sideline, that's where I think most of the balls will go. I have a tendency to turn onto my left; the ball comes, the wing-back comes to you, a touch of the elbow and throw him back, you're inside him straight away and gone, whereas if I'm on the inside I'm turning into him.

At corner-forward, Charlie Mac says never stand?

He has a point, I'd be moving a lot of the time as well, but when I did stand, it was side by side with the corner-back, always keep him on my left side, goal-side, so that when the ball came down the wing I was closer to it.

Most corner-backs are happy to stay goal-side anyway?

Yeah, isn't that the first thing they're taught, stay goal-side of the corner-forward? I was happy enough with that.

Tricks

None really; a few dummies and things like that, that's really all it is. Draw a fella in as if you're going to hit, then tap it over his head and go. **How many times would you do that to the same fella in one match?** If you get away with it once that's fine, but if you can do it a second time that fella shouldn't be there at all! Normally if it's something fancy though, you'll only get away with it once.

Ever try them in training, as John Fenton did, the ball flip trick? I wouldn't be trying that anyway, I'd break my own legs! Ah you'd do a bit of messing alright at the field, sidelines from your knees, taking 20-metre frees from the sideline, maybe even closer to the corner-flag. 'Time up lads, drawn game, one chance to win it with this free ...', that sort of thing.

Tricks seen

John McCarthy [captained Newtownshandrum to the All-Ireland club title in 2004] was a different breed, he was all tricks. The older McCarthy got, the longer his hurley got. He ended up with a 39-inch hurley! [Ben, along with his father Bernie, makes those hurleys in his native Newtownshandrum]. You look at the size of him [compact], he reckoned he needed that extra few inches to get in with the flick, the high ball. His party piece was when he got the ball on the ground, then he'd play soccer with it. Left foot, right foot, didn't matter, he'd get it out of the danger area, sometimes tapping it from one foot to the other – he was unbelievable at it. He was so good with his feet, and he was so good on his feet, great balance. You'd be on him in training, think you were in the clear, getting ready to take the shot, and the hurley would come in, flick the ball away. I marked him a lot in training in 1996 and '97 when he was really going well, and he was as good a back as you'd ever see, very unlucky not to have got a run with Cork. He had a fantastic year in 1996 when we won the intermediate county and Avondhu won the senior. People talk about tight backs – I'd hate to have been on him. He was deadly for the little flicks, the hook, the touch, perfect timing just as you were about to get off your shot, and the ball would be gone then, cleared straight away, so you didn't get a second chance. He played full-back for Newtown for years, out of position – corner-back was his best position – but he was still outstanding there.

Primary advice to a promising youngster, above all else, to master the corner-forward position

At wing-forward, ball-work and fitness; if you have the two of those you're flying it. At corner-forward, touch, first touch, you must be able to win the ball with one touch. You can play corner-forward without being fully fit, if you have that touch.

What did yourself and Jerry do to perfect the touch?

People can go on all they like about different things, but there's absolutely nothing better than the ball and a wall. In the alley we'd use a tennis ball, we'd play the same rules as handball but with the hurleys instead of the hands. At home, I'd always use a sliotar, the tennis ball would get away from you to easy out here. In training though it's different. You go up to a crowd of young fellas at the field, all they want to do is play a match. They don't want to learn the basics, they don't want to learn how to hook and block, but if they were to come up to see us training one evening, that's what we're doing every night of the week, hooking and blocking, and we're supposed to be one of the best senior teams in the county.

   You try to tell people you're doing that for Cork as well and they won't believe you, they think you're off the wall. You see these young fellas up at the field belting the ball all over the place, but it's the young fella that's practising his hooking and blocking, the fella that's at home hitting the ball off the wall, he's the fella who has real interest in improving himself.

What about first-time pulling?

I know you still have fellas who pull first-time, and you'll see the odd score coming from that, but an awful lot of time when that happens you have no idea where the ball is going. The surest option is to take the ball up into your hands, take the score.

But there are so many times, even at inter-county level, when the situation is crying out for the forward to just whip

I'd agree with you, but only at times. You see there's so much that can go wrong when you're pulling first-time on a moving ball.

But what if you practised that, as Charlie McCarthy did, as so many others did back then, what if you perfected it?

I suppose, yes, but you see these All-Ireland Gold programmes on TG4, where they show All-Ireland finals from back in the 1960s and '70s, you see backs coming out and letting fly on balls where they had plenty of time to rise the ball and really clear it, fellas just flaking away on the ground for the sake of it – what sense did that make?

You were the nearest thing to the team of 1966, the '99 kids – six U-21s, brought success back to Cork hurling?

Before the All-Ireland semi-final that year, 1999, very few of us had been in Croke Park before. We went up on the Saturday anyway, out on the field, walked around, looking at this, looking at that. Cusack was the goalkeeper, went to the Hill 16 end, walked to one side of the goal, put his hand up, and touched the cross-bar; walked across to the other side, put his hand up – a gap of nearly a foot! That will tell you how much of a difference there was in the old pitch in Croke Park.

Was it easier then, nineteen, twenty, carefree?

I'd say it was. There's no pressure, you just go out and play, whereas the older you get the more you realise how big this is, what's at stake, and the pressure comes on. All we did that year was go out and hurl; even the build-up, you weren't aware of it, I can't remember any of that now, took no notice of it at all, we just had the craic. Loughnane was the main man in hurling that time, with Clare. That day in Croke Park, Fergal Ryan was one of the senior fellas on our team, about twenty-five I think; he went into the dressing room, came back out, and he was wearing white sneakers, tracksuit bottom tucked into his socks – Loughnane. And he started taking him off, going up and down the line, across the pitch, behind the goals, shouting, roaring, telling us what to do – the craic we had that day! But that was Fergal Ryan, a great character.

You talk about corner-backs, when we played the Rockies you had a choice – you could be on Fergal, or you could be on Wayne [Sherlock]! Either one of them, you didn't want to know, brilliant corner-backs. You talk about defence being an art in Kilkenny – you couldn't hit the ball with either of those, Fergal especially, he was like John McCarthy.

Sherlock was more out in front of you, pacy, deadly control – into the hand and gone. Even the high ball with Sherlock, all he'd do is hand down, across you, and by God you weren't going to get your hand up to get that ball. He's still good enough to play at the top level.

What about all the controversy over the Newtown game? What do you say to those who believe hurling is too spontaneous for tactics?

No, that's wrong. A lot of people think hurling is totally off the cuff, just go out and play, but that day is long gone. Even club teams now have tactics, different plans for different situations. The game is changing all the time, whether we like it or not. In twenty years time, when kids are looking back at our games, do you think it will still look as fast? I don't think so.

FREE-TAKING

They can be the difference between winning and losing, they can be the making or breaking of a team; the free-taker, the poor ould free-taker. It comes as a double-edged sword, the free-taking duty. Score and your name is up in lights, your confidence is riding high, you're feeling good about yourself; miss, miss the crucial one especially, and it's a very lonely feeling. This is not an attempt to break down the art into easy-to-learn form; that requires a different medium – the video, the DVD, or best of all, the one-on-one. Hopefully, however, there are one or two tips here worth taking on board.

John Horgan, long-range free-taker

I used to go to Rochestown pitch on the morning of a big match, early, bring seven or eight sliotars, practise from distance; I'd score four or five of the ones I wanted to get, then I'd miss one, miss another, miss another. When I'd miss three in a row I'd quit. On the law of averages I was due the next one, and that would be in the match itself!

Richie Bennis

A fella who wasn't able to hurl at all called me aside one time. 'C'm 'ere Rich – how do you rise the ball?' I showed him, he wasn't impressed. 'Put it down like this and rise it with the grain of the ridge – don't roll it across the grain!' And he was right, that's how I placed the ball from then on and I never looked back. I liked to roll it, keep my balance, rather than stepping in for a jab lift. I learned something else that day too though – always listen, to anyone, because you never know what you'll learn, or from who.

John Fenton

I'd aim for a point halfway between the crossbar and the top of the posts and drive the ball at that; I'd also aim for a target well behind the goals, drive the ball through the goals. Have your target and drill it. For a penalty I'd jab-lift, step into it, get a few extra yards before striking, and I'd do the same for a long free where I was unlikely to get it all the way, I'd use the jab-lift, build up a bit of momentum into the ball. Over the years though, the more frees I took, the more I went to the roll-lift. But you had to be proficient in both. My feet I'd line up with the posts – I'd liken it to a golfer taking his shot, he'll usually line up his feet with the target.

Jimmy Doyle

Free-taking was something I practised over and over. When you came to the end of the year, for some reason your accuracy would be going. Even with the club there was something happening with your accuracy, it was like you were getting cheesed off, everything was just starting to tail off. I wouldn't know what it was, whether it was the hands, the follow-through, but it would just start going wrong. You'd have to work then to get that accuracy back, to get your confidence back, and I'd do that on the field. I was a shoe-repairer and my father would say to me, about four o'clock of an afternoon, 'Why don't you take the rest of the day off, go up to the field and practise your frees. You might get back your accuracy.' I would keep at it and at it and at it 'til the ball was travelling straight again.

Johnny Dooley

I adopted a basic enough style when I was about seventeen. I practised and practised and practised, jab lift similar to Eoin Kelly and Henry Shefflin. I wonder could I claim that they copied my style? I'd square my shoulders with the post, the same with my feet, have the ball in the centre of the stance and always, get down low. There's nothing worse than seeing young fellas trying to jab lift in an upright position – get under the ball, bend the knees, bend the back, then one step forward and drill it. Don't float it, that's a lottery. I didn't pick a target behind the goals, just split the posts.

It's all about confidence and you get that by practising. I'd go up to the pitch on my own, bring about fifteen balls, and start my routine;

Old rivals: *Former Cork players and teammates Tom Mulcahy and Willie John Daly with Tipperary great Jimmy Doyle (centre) at the launch of Tim Horgan's new book,* Christy Ring – Hurling's Greatest, *at the Kingsley Hotel on 7 November 2007.*

centre of the field to begin with, about 30 yards out, then work your way to the side, building your confidence all the time. If you want to get your percentage up, that's how you do it. It won't always work, but the more practice you do, the more consistent you'll become. I remember in many a county final, I'd have no fear no matter what the distance, and if one goes wide, you'd know you have a good chance of getting the next one, you wouldn't be going into it with all this negativity in your head. We were playing O'Toole's of Dublin in a Leinster championship game in Portlaoise, we got a last-minutes free to level it, about 80 yards out, on the right sideline. I struck it beautifully, between the posts, delighted with myself, when the ref came up to me. 'I didn't blow my whistle,' he said, 'You may go back and take that again!' And I did, and I scored it again. A county final in Birr, against Rynagh's in 1998, the first day, we got a 65 and the ref told me, you have to score direct. I slotted it over, full of confidence, no fear – you have to have that attitude.

Eddie Keher

If we needed a goal and the free was in front of goals, I'd go for it. Mentally it was almost defined – a penalty you went for a goal, and I nearly always did that. I practised it all the time. The jab lift, but there's a fallacy around that; a lot of people say I gained about ten yards with the jab lift and follow-through, but I didn't. Throw it too far ahead of you and you wouldn't get behind it with full power, and that was the idea behind that style – get the momentum going forward, bring the full weight of your body to bear in the stoke, get a full swing at it.

I'd aim for the left if the goalie held his hurl to the right, but I'd always make my mind up early. The best one was just under the crossbar. If it came up right from the jab lift and if you struck it properly, no one could get up to that to block it, and even if they did, it would still go in off the hurl, either for a goal or a point. I used to put a bit of spin on the ball also, left to right spin, inside out.

Eoin Kelly

I used to stand with my feet kind of crossed, and someone said to me one day, after I missed a free like that – I think it was Nicky English – 'I knew you were going to miss.' He got me to line up my feet with the goals, line up my shoulders also. Now I line up my feet and my shoulders towards the goal, like taking a golf shot. And I jab lift, with the nose of the hurley, I always did that.

The best bit of advice I ever got, and I'd pass it on to anyone; it was 2001, my first game against Clare, roasting hot day. In the warm-up in Douglas Nicky came up to me, and I'll always remember what he said – 'You'll be taking the frees, I want you to get a good strike on the ball every time. I don't care where it goes after that, but get a good strike on it.' He didn't tell me I had to score every one, he didn't tell me I had to score a certain percentage – just get a good strike on the ball. Don't be tentative, don't try to lob it – drive it. We won, fifteen points to fourteen [Eoin scored seven points, six from frees, not a single wide].

I'm always looking for tips like that. I remember the 2004 All-Ireland U-21 final in Nowlan Park, I went with a few lads from home and I was sitting in the stand. Who happened to be sitting alongside me only Eddie Keher. I was delighted with myself, sitting so close to one of the all-time greats. But I noticed something – every time Kilkenny went on the attack he started getting jumpy – he was playing the game with them. A lad would be about to hang it up in the back of the net and his elbow was going, his leg was hitting into my leg. And that was with Kilkenny hammering us! At half-time, I introduced myself, told him I was delighted to meet him and asked if he had any tips for free-taking. 'The only advice I have,' he said, 'is to take your time; don't worry about anyone else, you're the one taking the free. Take your time, don't strike 'til you're comfortable.' And that's what I do now. Some people might think I take too long at times but that's where that came from, Eddie Keher, Tipp/Kilkenny U-21 All-Ireland final, Nowlan Park.

When I step up to a penalty my aim is for just below crossbar height, and I'd go for power. When you hit a penalty, they have only a split-second to react, and when you go just under the crossbar the least you'll get from it is a point, because if they do manage to get a hurley up to it, nine times out of ten it will deflect over the bar. But the penalty all depends on the lift of the ball.

Caught for position but not for possession – not yet anyway! *Note how Liam Fennelly is already 'trapping' Eamonn Cleary's hurley as they battle for the ball in the Leinster semi-final in Croke Park, Dublin, on 18 June 1989.*

THE HURLEY

To some it was merely an implement, a tool, to others it was a work of art – perfect, individual. In Munster they call it the hurley. In Leinster, Connacht and elsewhere around the country, it is the hurl. Over the decades, even as the sport itself has changed, the hurley has itself been adapted. Once upon a time, in the days when the game was almost entirely ground-based, the stick was long, narrow, sharply-curved, heavy-heeled, which made hitting off the sod that little bit easier; as the game took to the air, however, the stick flattened out, the base – or bas – became broader, more suitable for the solo run, for aerial control.

Nowadays, in fact, they've almost developed to the point where the outfield hurley isn't much smaller than the keeper's stick, something that doesn't please former Cork star John Fenton, for one: 'The bas at the moment is way too big,' says John; 'I compared a modern hurley to one of my own from about twenty years ago and I'd say there's at least another third again of timber in the new one, which means it's heavier to carry, it's slowing down the swing, it's easier to block down and to hook. The big thing in striking is eye-ball coordination; look at a baseball player, smaller ball than a sliotar, smaller striking area – and round at that – and the ball coming at him faster than in hurling, yet he's able to make contact. You don't need a big hurley for striking.'

Perhaps not, argues Clare's Anthony Daly, but it's no hindrance either. 'Did you ever see anyone winning Wimbledon with a squash racquet?' is Anthony's argument, with which current Cork star Ben O'Connor – a hurley-maker by trade – concurs. 'Obviously there's a limit, you can't go so big that it slows down your swing. But look at the size of hurleys fellas had ten years ago – it was like a wooden spoon! Now they're all into the big bas, because it makes more sense – it definitely helps. Anthony Daly is dead right!

'If you look down the handle of our hurleys, it goes down the middle of the bas, which gives it a better balance,' Ben explains. 'You mess around with different shapes 'til you find the one that works best.' Balanced lengthways, balanced crossways, and, in the vast majority of those interviewed, it was that balance more than anything else that they felt was most critical, in the feel of a hurley. There are other elements of course, so let's look at those.

Length

39-inch: Only one entrant here, Newtown's own John McCarthy – see Ben O'Connor in chapter 15.

38-inch: Eamonn Cregan reckoned Pat Hartigan didn't have a hurley at all, he carried a battle-axe. Pat confirmed that. 'I liked a big hurley, at least 37 inches, maybe even 38. The funny thing is, I don't have long arms, so I compensated by having a longer hurley. And I liked a heavy hurley, I had no trouble handling any hurley with one hand. Going back to the weight-lifting, we did a lot of curls which was great for building up the wrist strength. I used to practise hitting a ball with one hand, the old heavy sliotars, and I could hit a ball over the bar from 70 yards with one hand.' Diarmuid O'Sullivan also recalls a teammate, Mossie Cahill, using a 38-inch.

37-inch: Diarmuid O'Sullivan himself uses a 37-inch. 'Early on I had a heavier hurley, you wanted to hit the ball as hard and as long as possible; nowadays it's lighter, almost as light as the normal 36-inch or 35-inch even though some fellas would still find it heavy. In comparison to what I used to use though it's quite light.' Pat Henderson and John Horgan, another two big men, also used 37-inch, but oddly enough, so did Len Gaynor, who used a different logic. 'I'm not the biggest man so the extra few inches under the high ball helped, and you could always shorten the stick for the clearance, to avoid being hooked or blocked down.' Dan Shanahan, Hurler of the Year 2007, uses 37-inch, as does his predecessor Henry Shefflin, as did Joe Cooney before them again, but with a little twist. 'I would hold it about 2 inches off the top. If I needed the extra couple of inches then, I had it. Probably a 35-inch or 36-inch would have done me if I'd got used to it, but I always had the 37-inch. If you were using a 37-inch for sidelines, as I was, you could never get used to taking them with a shorter hurl, you'd be topping the ball. I'd give it the full length for a sideline ball, the same for a free.'

36-inch: Most of those interviewed used the 36-inch or slightly shorter. 'I've used 35.5 inches for the last seven or eight years,' Michael Kavanagh explained; 'Before that it was 36 inches but maybe my growth was stunted over the years, all those big lads I was on!'

35-inch: Though they disagreed on bas size, both John Fenton and Anthony Daly used 35-inch hurleys, as did several others, including Patjoe Whelahan and Joe McKenna, after he moved to full-forward – for better control, he reckoned. D. J. Carey used a slightly longer stick, between 35 and 36, Liam Fennelly's was shorter, between 34 and 35, again, as is Eoin Kelly's of Tipperary, for the extra control it gave them. Stephen Lucey gets his handmade by craftsman and philosopher Jimmy Ryan in Newport to the same length, 34.5 inches.

34-inch: Only one of those interviewed was on this size – Ben O'Connor. '34-inch, 24 ounces, with a good pole. Most fellas now use much lighter hurleys, 18 or 19 ounces, but because mine was heavier I had a good pole in it, about an inch, for taking sidelines. Maybe you don't need that, but I just had it in my head, and I think it does make a difference.' And then, Ben threw a bit of a curveball. 'And no spring in the hurley,' he added. 'Absolutely none, couldn't use a hurley like that at all. I think the spring affects your hurley when you're striking.' But from time immemorial, after checking the grain, the weight, the length, testing a prospective new hurley for spring was pivotal to the final decision. Ben disagrees 'Not for me; I'd use any hurley – shape, weight, anything – as long as it was 34 inches, no spring and heavy. When I'm striking the ball I like to know it's going where I'm hitting it, that the hurley won't bend with the swing and change the direction. And that does happen.'

It's a view repeated by D. J. Carey: 'I preferred a stiff hurl, which gave you a truer strike. It's the same in golf, I don't like a whippy shaft.'

Honing the hurley, sharpening the blade – *Tommy Dunne in the family shed, sharing hurley space with brothers Benny, Terence and Kenny. Spaces for Barry and sister Triona's slot are hidden from view by the kit bags.*

Weight

Ben O'Connor and Brian Whelahan were the only players who knew the exact preferred weight of their hurley (24-ounce and 18-ounce, respectively), but that's not to say weight isn't a factor for most players – it is, very much so.

There were exceptions, as told by Fan Larkin. 'Chunky [O'Brien, famous Kilkenny midfielder] could pick out any hurl at all and play with it – the handle of a shovel even!'

Most players liked a medium-weight hurley, but a significant few expressed a preference for a light stick. Why is that significant? Well, their position, mostly, but their scoring record might have something to do with it. Michael Kavanagh, Ollie Canning, Liam Dunne (who went from heavy to light over the course of his career) and Len Gaynor were the only defenders who went for light hurleys (in Len's case, 'light' is comparative, given he used a 37-inch!). In midfield, Pat Critchley and John Fenton also favoured the lighter blade. It was up front, however, that the difference becomes clear. Jimmy Doyle, Eddie Keher, Charlie McCarthy, Eoin Kelly (like Liam Dunne, coming down the scale), Ray Cummins and Joe McKenna, all expressed a preference for the lighter stick. D. J. Carey was even more emphatic – 'I'd be most specific about weight. I could use a 36-inch, I could use a 35, but I couldn't use a heavy hurl.'

For Jimmy Doyle, the argument that you needed a heavier hurl for power and distance didn't hold water. 'I'm not sure of the exact size of my hurley, but it was short and it was light. A lot of people say you can't drive a ball with a light stick but I could drive a ball 90 or 100 yards, no bother; if you gave me a heavy one I couldn't drive it 60 – why, I don't know. But you have a lot more control with a short, light hurley.' There were those, however, and there still are, who like a heavy stick.

Christy Ring was one and there are no shortage of stories about his strength, physique and hurley – described by Ned Wheeler as 'a half-hewn ash-tree'. Denis Coughlan, who played with Ring in the Glen, recalls showing him his own hurley before the 1972 Munster final against Clare. 'He asked for a look at it, I gave it to him, he took it in his hands – massive hands – and whatever he did with it, it broke in two, in his hands. He got an awful fright, so did I, and I also got very upset. The first thing he said to me was, "Don't tell anyone." I told him I wouldn't. He took me over to his own car, took out a hurley and it was the one he had used in the three-in-a-row, 1952/'53/'54. "Is that any good to you?" he asked. I took it, but there was no way. It was too heavy.'

Pete Finnerty was another who liked a hurley of tree-trunk dimensions, as did Pat McGrath, Pat Henderson and Martin Storey, with Dan Shanahan the only one of the modern players interviewed who still goes for weight. One or two players, like Johnny Dooley, went between one and the other, heavier for the league games, lighter in summer, while Eddie Keher had a variation on that theme: 'If I got a penalty I'd often change the hurl. I had a special hurl for that, heavier. I'd have a lad in behind the goals would come out, bring me the hurl.'

Number of Hurleys

About a half dozen seems to be the modern norm, but there are a couple of telling tales going back to earlier years.

Len Gaynor: 'The first real hurley I ever got, my brother arrived home one day from the local hurley-maker with a hurley for himself and a little small hurley for me – I'll never forget that day. Up to then you'd be using bits of hurleys, bits of stick, but this was the real McCoy. It was a local man made them, Phillip Heenan, he only did it part-time, a horsey man – he had that great stallion Clover Hill. He made the hurleys with a little hatchet and a spoke-shave, that was it; he didn't do it for a living or anything, just a skill he had, and a passion, made them for the local lads. Local ash, we'd whip it where we could find it, brought it down to him.'

Pat McGrath: 'In the early 1970s you might have two and if you broke one, Jack Byrne would fix it out of nothing. Your hurley could be in bits and he'd have a certain stuff, sawdust, glue, and he'd put it all together – a great man with a hurley. In the beginning you'd be trying to save your hurleys, you couldn't afford to buy a new one, you'd be looking after it, trying to make it last as long as possible. Towards the end I might have three, but there was nothing worse than breaking your good hurley during a tap-around, the mind wouldn't be right after that.'

There's a tale in that also. A common enough tactic back in those days was to deliberately try to break an opponent's hurley, in the fairly certain knowledge that it would be his number one, and that he would not be at all as happy with number two! 'Those days are gone,' says Diarmuid O'Sullivan. 'You have to have every hurley almost identical now. You need to have the confidence in the hurley to know that if you have to pass the ball 30 or 40 yards, you can do so. You look at the fellas playing snooker or darts, they have their own cue, their own darts, and the weight, the balance, is critical to them. Hurling is no different, you don't want to suddenly find yourself with a hurley that's totally alien to what you've been using.'

Ned Wheeler: 'I had two and I was well off for the times [1950s/'60s] with those – now they have bundles.' And such bundles! Eamonn Cregan probably thought he was well off too with his collection of fourteen or so, a count matched by Tommy Dunne. Really, though, they were only in the ha'penny place. 'I hope you asked Michael Kavanagh this question,' said Henry Shefflin, 'He's a disgrace – he'd open his car boot during the summer and it's packed with hurls, crazy!'

'I'd say Brian Cody thinks I'm supplying the club, I go to him for so many dockets,' says Kavanagh. 'I would have anything between thirty and fifty at any one time. I'd be very fussy as regards the hurl I'd use, even in training; I'd try out a lot of different hurls during the year, but I always end up with the same few for matches, the tried and trusted. You just get a feel for the ones you like. I bring about four with the county, but I don't break many, maybe five or six in the year, nor do I give them out easily either.'

Eoin Kelly of Tipp is another man with a large collection. 'I'd be embarrassed to tell you. I'd have between thirty and forty hurleys in my garage at home at any one time, maybe even up to fifty. And it's amazing, you know, but in about forty championship games, I don't think I've broken more than three hurleys. But still I'd have five or six hurleys going to every championship game, all identical.'

Look what we brought home with us! *Martin Coleman and Charlie McCarthy holding up the McCarthy Cup after defeating Kilkenny in the All-Ireland final in 1978.*

PICKING A TEAM

You're the team manager, you have your squad of twenty-five, they've been in training now for several months, championship is approaching – how do you line them out? Where do you start, which is the most important position, where do you go from there? It was a question which, like several others that didn't make it to the final cut, was thrown in as a filler, but it was a question that really exercised the mind of everyone interviewed. So, where do you start?

Down the middle, said practically every single interviewee, though it was a toss-up as to whether you went goalkeeper/centre-back or centre-back/goalkeeper. 'Goalkeeper!' said Noel Skehan, 'The best player is always in goal!' Noel wasn't alone in that observation, however; many, including Séamus Durack, Pat Henderson, D. J. Carey, Eoin Kelly and Tony Considine, were in agreement.

Goalkeeper, centre-back, centre-forward, full-back, full-forward, that was the majority opinion. A good free-taker/scoring forward was high up on a lot of lists, might even have made it ahead of the full-forward; after that, form the cross – fill in the half-back-line, universally accepted as being the most important line in the field, then go to midfield (one holder, one runner). Many then went for the full-back-line to be filled in, arguing that a good defence will keep you in any game, but many also went for filling in the half-forward-line, choosing guys who could win their own ball, who could take on the opposition half-forward-line. In almost every instance, the last positions filled were the corner-forwards.

There was one, however, who stood apart from nearly everyone else in the order in which he would line out his team, a guy who has helped build a few successful teams in his time, at both club and county level. Tony Considine had very much his own take on things. Tony is now well known as an **Irish Examiner** *hurling columnist, his views, previews and match analysis are hugely respected across a wide audience. As a player, he lined out with his native Cratloe in Clare for many years, won an county intermediate championship with them; he also won three championships in London, two in hurling and one in football, but not under the name of Tony Considine – enough said!*

It's as a coach and selector, however, that Tony really made his name. In 1993, in tandem with current Clare senior coach, Mike McNamara, he was coach to the Clare team that won the junior All-Ireland title, a huge achievement then for a county long in the hurling doldrums; two years later, along with current Clare manager Mike McNamara, he was one of the famous management triumvirate under manager Ger Loughnane that guided Clare to the senior All-Ireland breakthrough, a feat they repeated in 1997. On the club scene Tony has also been successful, four county titles won with various teams, the most recent of which was in 2006 when he guided Garryspillane to their first senior title in Limerick. In two years with them they won thirteen of fourteen championship matches, their only loss coming in the 2005 county final, to a late and controversial injury-time free. Immersed in hurling all his life, recently Tony has been involved with Tipperary intermediate club Burgess, and again he has worked the oracle, taking them further than they've been in over sixty years.

Picking a Team

Going back to my youth we were always told, put your best player in goal, so I'd start with keeper, and with Clare in the '90s Davy Fitz was exceptional, as good as was around during those years. I think even he would admit though, he had outstanding men in front of him; they gave him great protection, and anything they couldn't handle he was able to tidy up.

Could Davy have played outfield?
Without a shadow of a doubt. Davy Fitz could have made an inter-

county corner-forward, his skill level was that good. Lookit, Seamus Durack was a great goalkeeper for Clare but he was also an outstanding forward.

The number one quality a goalkeeper needs, he needs a fierce will to win, greater even than any of the outfield players. He's in a madman's position, he has to be a dictator. He has to be able to read the game, he's the only player who has a full view of the whole pitch at all times. He has got to be minding the house; if he's not able to control his backs, tell them where to go, what to do – without going overboard, and it can be a fine line – he's wasting his time.

A keeper is selfish, has got to be selfish; he's on his own back there, can't afford to make a single mistake or he's in trouble. Anywhere else on the field they might get away with it, the keeper won't.

He has to be mad, but he also has to have the perfect temperament, and that's not a contradiction. If backs see the goalkeeper getting excited that's detrimental. The keeper has to be cool.

Building a team is all about building a defence, if you don't have a good defence it doesn't matter how good your forwards are; you'll win an All-Ireland with poor forwards but you won't win with a poor defence. Clare won All-Irelands – we didn't win many of them – but we won two without any of our forwards really playing well on the day. Our backline was outstanding, all six, but they would never have been as good but for the midfield we had. Colin Lynch and Ollie Baker were brilliant, both of them.

After the goalkeeper I'd go to centre-back, and here I'd be looking for someone who reads the play, who strikes the ball well left and right, and has a commanding presence. I'd like a good fielder, someone who can catch the ball.

Next I'd have the wing-backs, 5 and 7, two good attacking wing-backs who also know how to defend. This is my main line, the main line in any team.

After that I'd take a different tack to most people – I'd go for the corner-forwards, then the wing-forwards. I know you can get an exceptional centre-forward, and that's where most fellas would start building their forward line, but nine times out of ten the centre-forward is there to do just one thing – disrupt the centre-back, let the ball through. Usually the centre-back is the best player on the opposing team – if you have a very good forward, why waste him in that position when you can put a mullacker in there who can be just as effective, maybe even more so because he's not going to try to hurl with the centre-back? There are exceptions, centre-forwards who had it all, but they're very rare. So, 1, 6, 5, 7, 13, 15 – two good scoring corner-forwards – then 10 and 12.

On the wing you need athletes, of the Ben O'Connor style; Jamsie [O'Connor] had it, up and down that line, come back to the half-back-line when needed, in around midfield. You want your wing forwards to be moving back up the field, make room for your inside forwards; you want them to be able to chase back, win the ball, deliver it quickly to the corner-forwards, then chase up after it, with pace, and be in position to take the pass coming through. My policy would be to play the ball up the lines, keep it away from the centre-back altogether, take him out of the game that way.

After the wing forwards I'd go to midfield. Midfield is absolutely crucial to the modern game, much more so than the older game – I'm talking about from the mid '60s on. A lot of people say that midfield is now being bypassed – it is if you're standing there, looking at the ball going over your head all day. What I look for in a modern midfielder is someone who can run all day. Everyone talks now about a fella having a great engine – that's what you want. How many times did you see our two midfielders on one 21 one minute, on the other 21 the next?

Full-forward, I'd be looking for someone who can bring those around him into play, an intelligent player, possibly the most intelligent player on the team. A good hand would be a decided asset here also.

I'd then go back to the full-back-line and there, I'm looking for spoilers. Their number one job is to stop scores, stop scorers. If they can't do that they have no business there. I think of the full-back-line as a unit, I'd look for three guys who really balance each other, who get on, who work together. I don't look for any kind of flamboyancy in my full-back, I'm not looking for the big clearance, the big hit, and the fact that Brian Lohan brought that with him was pure coincidence, a bonus. Just give me the basics around the edge of the square, protect the goal area, prevent the scores. At corner-back I'm looking for the little man who'll stick to his man, stop him scoring, that's the number one job for anyone in the full-back-line, far more so than in the half-back-line.

Finally I'd go to the centre-forward, and again I'd be looking for a spoiler, someone to break the centre-back. I know he's last on my list, but he'd have to be an exceptional character. He has to be prepared to sacrifice his own game completely, take the belts, bulldoze his way forward if necessary. I'm thinking of the likes of Donie O'Connell of Tipperary, Mick Malone of Cork, Niall McCarthy today – they're not finesse players, but they do a very important job. There are exceptions of course, fellas who could do all that and hurl as well, but they're a rare breed. So, to finish, 1, 6, 5, 7, 13, 15, 10, 12, 8, 9, 14, 2, 3, 4, 11.

How did you come up with the Lohan brothers?
Frank didn't start against Cork in '95, he came on as a sub. A great athlete, I think it was harder to get scores off Frank than it was off Brian! But Brian was superb, no question, and that whole full-back-line combined very well. In '95 we had Michael O'Halloran in the right corner and he was like a third Lohan brother; they grew up together in Shannon, were great friends, had played with each other since childhood. They had it off to a T themselves, inside there; we worked hard on them to make sure that someone would always be minding the house [the square area], but they were brilliant at that, they had a great understanding there.

There are certain players who lift people – Brian Lohan was one of those, in the same way that Diarmuid O'Sullivan is for Cork still. The sight of that red helmet bursting out with the ball, belting it down the field – that was always a huge lift for Clare. The other two boys could do the very same thing but it wouldn't have nearly the same impact. Pat Hartigan of Limerick was the same, the crowd loved to see him coming out with the ball, and he was outstanding at that. How many All-Stars in a row did he win – five? That says a lot. Leonard Enright was a great full-back as well, as good as most.

Jamsie was a really good player for us, but he lacked consistency. In '95, in the All-Ireland semi-final against Galway, he was absolutely outstanding, the same in '97 against Kilkenny in the semi-final – in fact I think that was his best ever game for Clare – but he didn't bring that form into the All-Ireland final, in either year. It was only in the last twenty minutes he came good in '97, scored the winning point. A brilliant player, but just lacked that bit of consistency.

That was a problem generally with our forwards in those years; on certain days certain fellas would play well but we couldn't get any consistency, which meant we had to do a lot of juggling. I always thought Stephen Mac[Namara] had the potential to be a really great forward. He had the cunning, he could get goals, he was lethally fast. He suffered a lot of injuries though and he was one of those fellas who, if he was injured, he was injured – he didn't work as hard as maybe he should have. But he'd put the ball through the eye of a needle for you, his accuracy was fantastic, and he got some outstanding scores for us. The penalty we won against Limerick in '95, it was Stephen Mac made it, the run he made. Of course he was a nephew of Ger Power, the great Kerry footballer, a grandson of Jackie Power, so the breeding was there! I think he was the best finisher we had – Sparrow [Ger O'Loughlin] was good but Mac was better, and if he gave it the same effort as Sparrow did, he'd have been absolutely brilliant. Anyway, those were our two corner-forwards, Mac and Sparrow, and they were the best we had. They were good too, and think of the '95 semi-final against Galway – Stephen Mac, a goal; Sparrow, two goals.

On the other wing to Jamsie we had Fergie Touhy, another fine player; he sometimes changed with P. J. O'Connell at centre-forward. Fergie was a frustrating player; you knew he had the talent but there were days he was as likely to blow the ball 100 feet wide as put it over the black spot. That was our biggest problem in the whole forward line, a lack of consistency; we didn't have anyone like a Shefflin or an Eoin Kelly or a Joe Deane where people said, 'You have to really watch this fella today.' And you know, maybe we were as well off; Jamsie would get an ould score, Touhy, P. J., Sparrow would get a goal, Mac – they all chipped in on different days. But you had no huge star of the calibre of Shefflin and those.

I think P. J. O'Connell, at centre-forward, made a lot of the players around him. A great man to catch a ball, he had really fast hands – P. J. would have pulled three times while another man was thinking about the first. He could take a score, had massive pace as well. And strong – he was like an elastic man, you couldn't break him. PJ made a lot of the Clare scores for a couple of years, made the other lads look good; himself and Conor Clancy at full-forward broke up a lot of the play.

How did you come up Baker and Lynch?

I had had Colin at U-16 level and he was brilliant, absolutely brilliant, went on to play minor for Clare. But a lot of people forget, Colin wasn't on the '95 team – Fergal Hegarty was there, alternating with Jamsie at wing-forward. Colin had got a dose of glandular fever, but maybe he wasn't putting in the full commitment at that stage either. He trained hard in '96 though, but didn't make the team; to this day I wonder if we didn't make a mistake in not bringing him on against Limerick. He was playing well but he wasn't established at that time.

Baker was a project. The first night he came into training I remember thinking – this fella is going to do himself an injury if someone doesn't take that hurley off him! The work that went into him! He had hurling but it was very innocent – you could hook him from the next county. But he had savage commitment, savage strength, savage fitness – there was no end to him. We worked and worked and worked on him, he worked and worked and worked, and it started coming good, he started hitting the ball well, started hitting people in midfield, started making a real nuisance of himself. And he started scoring, points and goals – we wouldn't have beaten Cork in '95 if he hadn't been around the square in those last few minutes. Like the three half-backs, he had the temperament for the big day as well; he'd stroll in there, a Munster final, not a care in the world. People think it's all about pure hurling ability but temperament is hugely important. Mental strength, mental ability, a ruthless streak – you need all that.

The famous half-back-line?

We went for Seánie at centre-back because he has perfect temperament for the big day. He wasn't the fastest centre-back around by a long shot but his reading of the game was superb, his striking was superb, and above all, his temperament was perfect, his nerve was brilliant, his character was right. On the big day you always knew McMahon was going to perform. One problem though, he found it hard to get fit, you wouldn't have been picking him out in league games, which led to another reason to pick him at centre-back – he wasn't fast enough for anywhere else, not even at wing-back. Centre-back was the only position Seánie McMahon was going to make the grade at inter-county level. He was moved to the wing against Limerick in the '94 Munster final and he was brutal, Mike Galligan went to town on him. I don't blame Seánie for that, I blame those who put him there. He had the hurling but he just didn't have the pace. As a matter of fact even at centre-back, when he was up against a centre-forward with pace, one who took him on, he was in trouble. The man who stood shoulder to shoulder with him, that was the man that suited him, because Seán had the hurling.

The two wing-backs? Liam Doyle?

I picked Liam Doyle as a corner-back on the junior team that won the All-Ireland in 1993 but I said at the time, Liam was one of those players you could have played anywhere, including in goals, because he played there for the Clare minors. He could certainly have played in any of the back positions, he was that good. One quality he had that many of our backs hadn't, he could catch the high ball, he was the best of the backs at that, by a long shot. Liam Doyle had the best skill levels of all the Clare backs, and make no mistake about that, his skills were superb – Liam Doyle would hurl in a saucer for you, beautiful stroke. A lot of people thought he was a hatchet-man but that's wrong; if you wanted to mix it with him he could do that too, you took him on at your peril, but his biggest asset was his skill level. We could have played him at corner-back, and he was superb there in '94, superb also in '93 in the juniors, but we moved him to the wing in '95 and he never looked back, formed a superb understanding with McMahon and Daly. His best day, I thought, was against Tipperary in the All-Ireland final in '97, when he came out after the interval and scored a brilliant point – that point was worth three or four points to Clare, because of the man who scored it.

What did you say at half-time in that game? Did it get a bit hot in the dressing room?

We didn't have to say anything, they knew themselves they hadn't done themselves justice in the first half. They knew also that if they didn't improve after the break they risked being taken off. But there was no roaring and shouting – there never was, in that Clare dressing room, and never is in any dressing room in which I'm involved. What's the good in that? You have to analyse, break down where things are going wrong, put them right for the second half – what does shouting achieve? Stay cool, don't lose the head. Psychologically anyway we were in better shape than Tipperary. They should have been much further ahead, the game should have been over; in fact if hadn't been for our two midfielders, Baker and Lynch, and Brian Lohan at full-back, the game would have been over – Tipp knew that and we knew that. Our half-back-line was absolutely cleaned, Declan Ryan was destroying Seánie, John Leahy was scoring points off Liam Doyle. Tipp would have been saying to themselves, 'We have them now,'; we'd have been saying, 'Ye have f***-all!' We knew there was much more in us than we'd showed; we knew also that if we could score the first three points of the second half we were back in the game. In fact we'd have gained the upper hand, psychologically. And that's what happened. The doubt started creeping into Tipp, our confidence was growing.

The captain, Anthony Daly?

I've always maintained the captain should be around that area, half-back/midfield/half-forward. We inherited Daly as team captain, Len Gaynor has to get the credit for that move. We kept him there because it was obvious he was the man for the job. The big thing he had, he was a guy who was never fazed by anything. He was also completely in tune with the players, would always say the right thing at the right time; and maybe he knew what to say to the fellas he was marking as well, and the time to say it! He has this great sense of humour, a great wit, a great way about him when relating to the players. For all the joking, however, he knew what was happening; an ideal captain should always be a step ahead of the rest and Daly was that, he was in tune with the other players, knew their problems, knew their needs. I'd often meet him on the Thursday night before a game and he'd let me know what was happening; it would be a general conversation but he'd keep me informed of any concerns. And in that sense, we always got on very well.

You could rely on him to take the instructions out on the field, you could rely on him to do the right thing, and you could rely on him to take responsibility for what was happening on the field. The best proof of that was the 65 in the dying minutes of the '95 final, against Offaly, with the game tied. Seánie had been taking the long-range frees that day but Anthony stepped up, took over. He could have missed that 65, and the repercussions – on him and on us, for letting it happen – would have been huge. But he didn't miss, and he was never going to miss. He was an excellent captain.

Were you tempted to overrule him?
No, never. I know we'd have been called right clowns if he'd missed and if Offaly had gone on to win the game, and maybe people would have been right, but those kind of long-range frees were between the two of them. They were playing long enough to know what to do without instruction from anyone; Daly felt good about it, stepped up and got the point.

He played full-back in '93, got an All-Star at corner-back in '94, so he too was a very versatile player. At wing-back, however, he was out-standing for those few years. Mind you, if you look back at the tapes of those years, you see the protection Baker gave Daly. Ollie always played on that side of midfield and he always covered for Anthony Daly – how many times did you see Ollie Baker chasing down Daly's man? But Anthony then had the guile to stay back in Ollie's position, make himself available for the ball coming out.

All three of those half-backs were great to read the game; none of them were fast but they could read the game, knew where to be. I would maintain, however, that as good as they were, they were made even better by the two midfielders we had. I often said to those two – 'Cover, cover, cover.' And they did for those three or four years, before they finally ran out of steam.

I'll say this, though, and I know it's not going to make me too popular in a lot of quarters; when Clare and Wexford and Offaly were winning those All-Irelands from 1994 to 1998, the big three were weak. The great Cork team of 1986–90 was gone; the Kilkenny team of 1992/'93 was gone, the Tipp team of 1987–91 was gone. From '94 to '98 those teams were gone and we made hay, as did Limerick in Munster, Offaly and Wexford in Leinster. Cork, Tipp and Kilkenny were poor during those years, and that's a fact. They got their act together, however, in '99, and they've been there since, Kilkenny and Cork especially. They're going to take some shifting again now.

Tony Considine's ideal all-time fifteen

Goalkeeper: Ollie Walsh. I saw a lot of great goalkeepers, but Ollie played in a time when the rules were different, when the forwards could come in on top of the keeper, bury him in the back of the net, and often did. I think Ollie would still be outstanding in today's game. Noel Skehan is another who would play in any era, but I'm not sure some of today's keepers would have been as good back then. I was only a young lad when Ollie was playing, but he was the first GAA poster-boy – the shock of blond hair, the flamboyance in his play – people went out to kill him but he just side-stepped everything. Ah, he was brilliant.

Right-corner-back: I picked a man here that a lot of people overlook, and that's Denis Mulcahy of Cork. Big, strong, fast, tough, very competitive, he won only one All-Star but he was worth a lot more. I never remember him being cleaned, by anyone.

Full-back: Brian Lohan. This man was never beaten, never defeated, never bowed the head. I don't think any full-forward ever looked forward to spending seventy minutes in Brian's company.

Left-corner-back: I struggled here, a lot of outstanding number 4s, but I went for Brian Murphy of Cork, the first Brian Murphy, a man who played in both corners. The fact that he was so effective for so long decided it for me. He was a pure corner-back; you hardly knew he was around but he didn't concede scores, to anyone.

Right-half-back: Brian Whelahan, you couldn't go past this man. Brilliant hurler, fantastic man to read the game.

Centre-back: Mick Roche – another early pin-up boy, with the long curly hair, the hairnet. Some of the displays he gave – 1964, '68 against Wexford. And he stood strong as well. Seánie McMahon and Brian Corcoran were in contention here, along with Ken McGrath, but I went with Roche.

Left-half-back: Another problem position, a lot of great players, but I went with the small man from Kilkenny, Tommy Walsh, as good a piece of stuff as I've ever seen. Reminds me of another small man from Kilkenny, Joe Hennessey, and it was between the two of them.

Midfield: Frank Cummins, an automatic, and then, someone a lot of people would overlook again, John Connolly of Galway. John was on a bad Galway team for years, but carried them almost on his own. Great athlete, big and strong, but superb stick-man, he was midfield for all those years then finally won his All-Ireland at full-forward. That takes a good man, to adapt to that. John Fenton is very unlucky to lose out here, was well in the reckoning; Jerry O'Connor and Tom Kenny from the modern era are outstanding, but they still have a few years to go to catch up on Cummins and Connolly.

Right-half-forward: Only one man for this spot, the magical Jimmy Doyle. I didn't see Christy Ring play, so he's not in contention for any of the forward spots, but no one would dislodge this man from this position.

Centre-forward: This was between two men, Declan Ryan and Henry Shefflin, and I went with Henry. Declan was outstanding, seemed to have it all for a centre-forward, but Shefflin has brought a new dimension to this position. I would put Joe Cooney, John Power, a step below these. Cooney never impressed me as a stylist – I wouldn't pay to see him, but I'd pay to see Henry, and I'd have paid to see Ryan.

Left-half-forward: Again an automatic, Eddie Keher. Mr Consistency, good for about ten points a game, every game, maybe more if it was an All-Ireland final – sign of greatness.

Right-corner-forward: Eoin Kelly, another from the modern era who has already done enough to win this position. Phenomenal player, he seems to have been around for years yet he's still a few years short of thirty. Another player I'd pay to watch. Ben O'Connor is unlucky here, as is Johnny Dooley of Offaly on the right wing – two great players. Seánie O'Leary, another great poacher, but this is Eoin's position.

Full-forward: Ray Cummins. Every modern full-forward should say a prayer to Ray Cummins, because he was the man who single-handedly changed this position. Cummins put an end to the crossbar-breaker, the fellas who hustled and bustled, went in and gave the crossbar a belt when the ball was going over the bar to try and intimidate the goalkeeper. Cummins was a hurler and he made this a position for hurlers. He was the first intelligent full-forward I saw, and maybe I'm being insulting to all the others in that. Cummins brought a new dimension to forward play, he was a proper genius; we were used to seeing big, rough, tough full-forwards, bursting everything in their way, tussling and wrestling – he brought an intelligence to that position, an elegance. He never got involved in dirty play, ever, but he was never bullied either, never lost his focus. A brilliant player, he was the best I saw, but Joe McKenna was a man who also impressed hugely in this position.

Left-corner-forward: Only one man for this position – D. J. Carey. Lethal, outstanding speed, great man to make or take a score.

Those are my fifteen, and I know you could pick a different team, a completely different team that might look just as impressive, but I'd put that team up against anyone. In fact, I'd love to see them playing backs and forwards – that would be a sight!

QUALITIES NEEDED
WEB SURVEY

Survey conducted on website www.diarmuidoflynn.com, on the qualities needed for the various hurling positions. Top five qualities (plus ties) as follows:

1 – Goalkeeper	Concentration, confidence, courage, reflexes, tie between hurley size (bas only), mental strength, leadership.
2 & 4 – Corner-backs	Man-marker, speed in the turn, tackler, speed off the mark, tie between stopper, courage, ball control and hardness.
3 – Full-back	Man-marker, ability under the high ball, courage, strength, speed off the mark.
5 & 7 – Wing-backs	Ability under the high ball, reading the game, ball-striking, intelligence, tie between ball control, hardness and strength.
6 – Centre-back	Ability under the high ball, ball control, leadership, size, tie between reading the game and team player.

8 & 9 – Midfield	Team player, reading the game, stamina, intelligence, tie between speed, leadership and overhead striking.
10 & 12 – Wing-forwards	Ball control, accuracy, ball-striking, coolness under pressure, ability under the high ball.
11 – Centre-forward	Team player, reading the game, stamina, intelligence, leadership.
13 & 15 – Corner-forwards	Ball control, speed off the mark, speed in the turn, accuracy, tie between coolness under pressure, courage and ability on the ground ball.
14 – Full-forward	Ability under the high ball, courage, leadership, size, tie between strength and overhead striking.

Index

Page numbers in bold indicate pictures.